MATH SENSE

Skills, Problem Solving, Tools, and Applications

Decimals, Fractions, Ratios, and Percents

Ellen Carley Frechette

New Readers Press

Acknowledgments

Advisers

Connie Eichhorn
Supervisor of Transitional Services
Omaha Public Schools
Omaha, NE

Lois Kasper
Instructional Facilitator
Board of Education of the City of New York
New York, NY

Jan Phillips
Assistant Professor
William Rainey Harper College
Palatine, IL

Mary B. Puleo
Assistant Director
Sarasota County Adult and
Community Education
Sarasota, FL

Margaret Rogers
Coordinator
San Juan Unified Adult Education
Sacramento, CA

Consultant/Field-Test Adviser

Ernest Kettenring
Teacher, Teacher-Advisor, and Learning Center Coordinator
Wilson-Lincoln Community Adult School
Los Angeles Unified School District
Instructor
Pasadena City College Community
Skills Center

Math Sense®: Decimals, Fractions, Ratios, and Percents
ISBN 1-56420-388-3
Copyright © 2003, 1995 New Readers Press
New Readers Press
Division of ProLiteracy Worldwide
1320 Jamesville Avenue, Syracuse, New York 13210
www.newreaderspress.com

Printed in the United States of America
9 8 7 6 5 4 3 2

All proceeds from the sale of New Readers Press materials
support literacy programs in the United States and worldwide.

Developer: Learning Unlimited, Oak Park, IL
Content Editing: Sybil M. Sosin Publishing Services
Photo Illustrations: Mary McConnell
Series Editor: Judi Lauber
Production Director: Heather Witt
Illustrations: Linda Tiff, James P. Wallace
Production Specialist: Jeffrey R. Smith
Cover Design: Kimbrly Koennecke

Casio fx-260 image courtesy of Casio, Inc.

Contents

5   **Introduction**

6   **Skill Preview**

12 Unit 1: Numbers Smaller Than 1

14   Understanding Decimals

16   Reading Decimals

18   Writing Decimals

20   Comparing Decimals

22   Reading Digital Measurements   Application

24   Using Your Calculator   Tools

26   Writing Expressions   Tools

28   Solving Word Problems   Problem Solver

30   Understanding Fractions

32   The Size of Fractions

34   Forms of Fractions

36   Equivalent Fractions

38   Filling in a Grid   Tools

40   Reading Fraction Measurements   Application

42   Understanding Percent

44   Solving Multistep Problems   Problem Solver

46   Unit 1 Review

48 Unit 2: Decimals

50   Rounding and Estimating Decimals   Tools

52   Understanding the Question   Problem Solver

54   Adding Decimals

56   Subtracting Decimals

58   Addition and Subtraction Equations   Tools

60   Solving Addition and Subtraction Equations

62   Balancing a Checkbook   Application

64   Multiplying Decimals

66   Gridding in Decimal Answers   Tools

68   Mixed Review

70   Dividing a Decimal by a Whole Number

72   Dividing by a Decimal

74   Metric Measurement   Application

76   Estimating with Friendly Numbers   Tools

78   Order of Operations   Problem Solver

80   Calculators and Decimal Answers   Tools

82   Mileage and Miles per Gallon   Application

84   Unit 2 Review

86 Unit 3: Fractions

88   Estimating the Size of Fractions

90   Adding and Subtracting Like Fractions

92   Choosing Necessary Information   Problem Solver

94   Writing Equivalent Fractions

96   Adding Unlike Fractions

98   Subtracting Unlike Fractions

100   Adding Mixed Numbers

102   Subtracting Mixed Numbers

104   Working with Distances   Application

106   Mixed Review

108   Multiplying Whole Numbers and Fractions

110   Multiplying Fractions

112   Multiplying Whole and Mixed Numbers

114	Drawing a Picture	Problem Solver
116	Dividing Fractions	
118	Dividing with Mixed Numbers	
120	Multiply or Divide?	Problem Solver
122	Multiplication and Division Equations	Tools
124	Solving Multiplication and Division Equations	
126	Fractions and Your Calculator	Tools
128	Fractions and Money	Application
130	Gridding in Fraction Answers	Tools
132	Unit 3 Review	

134 Unit 4: Ratio and Proportion

136	Fractions and Ratios	
138	Writing a Ratio	
140	Ratios and Patterns	
142	Unit Rates	Application
144	Understanding Proportion	
146	Making a Table	Problem Solver
148	Solving Problems with Proportions	
150	Gridding in Ratio and Proportion Answers	Tools
152	Calculators and Proportion Problems	Tools
154	Scale Drawings and Maps	Application
156	Unit 4 Review	

158 Unit 5: Percents

160	Understanding Percents	
162	Estimating the Size of Percents	
164	Changing Decimals and Percents	
166	Changing Fractions and Percents	
168	The Percent Statement	
170	Does the Answer Make Sense?	Problem Solver
172	The Percent Equation	
174	Solving a Percent Equation	
176	Gridding in Percent Answers	Tools
178	Statistics and Percents	Application
180	Mixed Review	
182	Using a Calculator with Percents	Tools
184	Two-Step Percent Problems	
186	Discounts	Application
188	Percent of Increase/Decrease	
190	Unit 5 Review	

192	**Posttest**
200	**Answer Key**
231	**Glossary**
235	**Tool Kit**
The Five-Step Problem-Solving Plan
Fraction Chart
Decimal, Fraction, and Percent Equivalencies
Measurement Tools
Calculator Basics

Introduction

Math skills play an increasingly vital role in today's world. Everyone needs to work confidently with numbers to solve problems on the job and in other areas of daily life.

This book and the others in the *Math Sense* series can help you meet your everyday math needs. Each unit is organized around four key areas that will build your competence and self-confidence:

- **Skills** pages present instruction and practice with both computation and word problems.

- **Tools** pages provide insight into how to use mathematical devices (such as rulers) and to apply key ideas (such as estimation) to solve math problems. Throughout the book, these pages focus on applying **calculator skills** and filling in **answer grids** similar to the ones used on many standardized tests.

- **Problem Solver** pages provide key strategies to help you become a successful problem solver.

- **Application** pages are real-life topics that require mathematics.

Key Features

Skill Preview: You can use the Skill Preview to determine what skills you already have and what you need to concentrate on.

Talk About It: At the beginning of each unit, you will have a topic to discuss with classmates. Talking about mathematics is key to building your understanding.

Key Concepts: Throughout the book, you will see this symbol ▶, which indicates key math concepts and rules.

Making Connections: Throughout each unit, you will work with topics that connect math ideas to various interest areas and to other math concepts.

Special Problems: These problems require an in-depth exploration of math ideas. You may be asked to explain or draw or to do something else that demonstrates your math skills.

Working Together: At the end of each unit, you will work with a partner or small group to apply your math skills.

Mixed and Unit Reviews: Periodic checkups will help you see how well you understand the material and can apply what you have learned.

Posttest: At the end of the book, you will find a test that combines all of the book's topics. You can use this final review to judge how well you have mastered the book's skills and strategies.

Glossary: Use this list of terms to learn or review key math words and ideas.

Tool Kit: You can refer to these resource pages as you work through the book.

Skill Preview

This survey of math skills will help you and your teacher decide what you need to study to get the most out of this book. It will show you how much you already know and what you need to learn in the areas of decimals, fractions, ratios, and percents.

Do as much as you can in each section below. If you can't do all of the problems in a section, go ahead to the next section and do all of the problems that you can.

Part 1: Numbers Smaller Than 1

Write the following values in decimal form.

1. seven hundredths _____

3. two hundred twenty thousandths _____

2. five tenths _____

4. one hundred forty-five thousandths _____

Put each fraction in lowest terms if possible. If the fraction is already in lowest terms, just rewrite the fraction.

5. $\frac{6}{8}$ = _____

8. $\frac{2}{3}$ = _____

11. $\frac{4}{32}$ = _____

6. $\frac{2}{4}$ = _____

9. $\frac{12}{18}$ = _____

12. $\frac{3}{8}$ = _____

7. $\frac{11}{17}$ = _____

10. $\frac{5}{100}$ = _____

Write the correct fraction and decimal form of each percent. Simplify fractions where possible.

13. 25% = $\underset{\text{fraction}}{\underline{\hspace{1cm}}}$ = $\underset{\text{decimal}}{\underline{.25}}$

15. 50% = $\underset{\text{fraction}}{\underline{\hspace{1cm}}}$ = $\underset{\text{decimal}}{\underline{\hspace{1cm}}}$

14. 90% = $\underset{\text{fraction}}{\underline{\frac{9}{10}}}$ = $\underset{\text{decimal}}{\underline{.9}}$

16. 6% = $\underset{\text{fraction}}{\underline{\hspace{1cm}}}$ = $\underset{\text{decimal}}{\underline{\hspace{1cm}}}$

Choose the number with the larger value in each pair.

17. $1\frac{1}{2}$ or $\frac{9}{10}$

20. $\frac{2}{3}$ or $\frac{3}{8}$

23. 1   or $\frac{4}{3}$

18. .086   or   .1

21. 3.4   or   2.93

24. $\frac{1}{10}$ or $\frac{3}{100}$

19. 125%   or   12.5%

22. $\frac{3}{5}$ or $\frac{7}{10}$

Part 2: Decimals

25. $7.65 + .01$

26. $145.9 + 100.1$

27. $58.05 + 32.001$

28. $10.5 - 3.2$

29. $89.2 - 14.9$

30. $100 - 10.7$

31. $\begin{array}{r} 2.5 \\ \times\ .8 \\ \hline \end{array}$

32. $9.24 \times .02$

33. 3.5×4.25

34. $3\overline{)1.5}$

35. $.9\overline{)81.9}$

36. $24.5 \div .07$

Solve the following problems.

37. Sonja poured 31.5 quarts of solution into beakers that each hold 1.75 quarts. How many beakers did she fill?

38. If a train travels 4.5 hours at 110 miles per hour, how many total miles will it travel?

39. Nicolai deposited a $200.50 refund check and his $476.89 paycheck into his bank account. His new balance is $1,240.90. What total amount did Nicolai deposit?

40. A sculptor used 15.75 pounds of clay, 18.9 pounds of steel, and 8.5 pounds of scrap wood. What total amount of materials did he use?

Problems 41 and 42 refer to the following information.

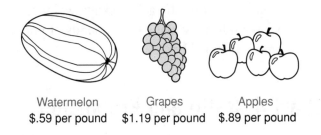

| Watermelon | Grapes | Apples |
| $.59 per pound | $1.19 per pound | $.89 per pound |

41. A customer bought 2 pounds of grapes and 2 pounds of apples. What total amount did he pay?

42. A cashier receives a $10 bill in payment for a 5-pound watermelon. How much change should she give the customer?

Part 3: Fractions

43. $\frac{1}{2} + \frac{1}{2}$

44. $\frac{2}{5} + \frac{3}{4}$

45. $4\frac{6}{7} + 2\frac{1}{6}$

46. $\frac{3}{4} - \frac{1}{2}$

47. $\frac{7}{8} - \frac{1}{5}$

48. $3\frac{3}{8} - 1\frac{3}{4}$

49. $\frac{1}{2} \times \frac{1}{8}$

50. $\frac{3}{4} \times \frac{1}{9}$

51. $9 \times 4\frac{1}{2}$

52. $\frac{3}{4} \div \frac{1}{8}$

53. $\frac{9}{10} \div \frac{1}{2}$

54. $10\frac{1}{2} \div 1\frac{1}{4}$

Go on to next page.

Solve the following problems.

55. Yolanda finished $\frac{3}{4}$ of a $10\frac{1}{2}$-mile race. How many miles did she complete?

56. A shipping clerk packed the following weights onto the outbound pallet: $4\frac{3}{5}$ pounds, $2\frac{1}{2}$ pounds, $15\frac{1}{10}$ pounds, and $12\frac{1}{2}$ pounds. What total weight did she put on the pallet?

57. Mr. Wu cut 2 pieces of lumber, each $8\frac{1}{4}$ inches long, from a 2-foot board. How many inches of lumber did he have left over?

58. A mother poured 10 packages of mixed nuts into a bowl. If each package weighed $1\frac{3}{4}$ pounds, how many total pounds of nuts are in the bowl?

Problems 59 and 60 refer to the following drawing.

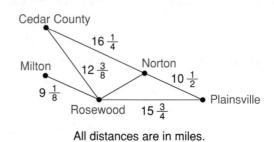

All distances are in miles.

59. How many more miles is it from Plainsville to Rosewood than it is from Plainsville to Norton?

60. A delivery truck started in Norton and made stops in Cedar County, Rosewood, and Milton. How many total miles did the truck travel on this route from Norton to Milton?

Part 4: Ratio and Proportion

Write a ratio that shows the relationship being described. Use labels, and simplify when necessary.

61. In a class of 25 people, there are 17 non-English-speaking students. What is the ratio of students who don't speak English to total students?

62. Of the 100 people surveyed, 65 said they skipped breakfast regularly. What is the ratio of breakfast-skippers to total surveyed?

63. Renate planted 70 tulip bulbs and 35 daffodils. What is the ratio of tulips to daffodils?

64. Out of 470 computer keyboards assembled in a factory last week, 10 did not pass quality control checks. What is the ratio of keyboards that *did pass* to those that *did not pass?*

Fill in the missing values in the pattern shown below.

65.

Employees on shift	2		6			12	
Number of offices cleaned	3	6				18	

Solve the following proportion problems.

66. $\dfrac{7}{12} = \dfrac{\blacksquare}{60}$

67. $\dfrac{2}{3} = \dfrac{8}{\blacksquare}$

68. $\dfrac{1}{8} = \dfrac{\blacksquare}{160}$

69. $\dfrac{\blacksquare}{15} = \dfrac{110}{165}$

70. $\dfrac{4}{\blacksquare} = \dfrac{52}{39}$

71. $\dfrac{3}{4} = \dfrac{\blacksquare}{80}$

Part 5: Percents

72. What is 15% of 60?

73. 40 is 80% of what number?

74. 75 is what percent of 150?

75. What is 25% of 220?

76. 12 is what percent of 6?

77. 120 is 75% of what number?

Solve the following problems.

78. Nancy bought a shirt at a 25%-off sale. If the shirt was originally priced at $32, how much did she save?

79. Carlos completed 90% of his exam. If he completed 117 questions, how many questions in total were on the exam?

80. While Max was driving the 26-mile distance to his mother's house, his car broke down. He had gone 24.7 miles. What percent of the distance had he traveled before the car broke down?

Problems 81 and 82 refer to the following chart.

Unemployment Rates by County

County	Rate
Eastham County	6.5%
Shore County	5%
Handson County	7%
Ford County	8%

81. If there are 4,000 employable people in Shore County, how many are unemployed?

82. There are 750 unemployed people in Ford County. How many employable people are there?

1. 0.07
2. 0.5
3. 0.220
4. 0.145
5. $\frac{3}{4}$
6. $\frac{1}{2}$
7. $\frac{11}{17}$
8. $\frac{2}{3}$
9. $\frac{2}{3}$
10. $\frac{1}{20}$
11. $\frac{1}{8}$
12. $\frac{3}{8}$
13. $25\% = \frac{1}{4} = .25$
14. $90\% = \frac{9}{10} = .9$
15. $50\% = \frac{1}{2} = .5$
16. $6\% = \frac{3}{50} = .06$
17. $1\frac{1}{2}$
18. .1

19. 125%
20. $\frac{2}{3}$
21. 3.4
22. $\frac{7}{10}$
23. $\frac{4}{3}$
24. $\frac{1}{10}$
25. 7.66
26. $246.0 = 246$
27. 90.051
28. 7.3
29. 74.3
30. 89.3
31. 2
32. 0.1848
33. 14.875
34. 0.5
35. 91
36. 350

37. **18 beakers**
$31.5 \div 1.75 = 18$

38. **495 miles**
$4.5 \times 110 = 495$

39. **\$677.39**
$\$200.50 + \$476.89 = \$677.39$

40. **43.15 pounds**
$15.75 + 18.9 + 8.5 = 43.15$

41. **\$4.16**
$(2 \times \$1.19) + (2 \times \$.89) =$
$\$2.38 + \$1.78 = \$4.16$

42. **\$7.05**
$5 \times \$.59 = \$2.95$
$\$10.00 - \$2.95 = \$7.05$

43. 1
44. $1\frac{3}{20}$
45. $7\frac{1}{42}$
46. $\frac{1}{4}$
47. $\frac{27}{40}$

48. $1\frac{5}{8}$
49. $\frac{1}{16}$
50. $\frac{1}{12}$
51. $40\frac{1}{2}$
52. 6

53. $1\frac{4}{5}$
54. $8\frac{2}{5}$
55. **$7\frac{7}{8}$ miles**
$\frac{3}{4} \times 10\frac{1}{2} = 7\frac{7}{8}$
56. **$34\frac{7}{10}$ pounds**
$4\frac{3}{5} + 2\frac{1}{2} + 15\frac{1}{10} + 12\frac{1}{2} = 34\frac{7}{10}$
57. **$7\frac{1}{2}$ inches**
$2 \times 8\frac{1}{4} = 16\frac{1}{2}$ inches cut off
24 inches (2 feet) $- 16\frac{1}{2}$ inches $= 7\frac{1}{2}$ inches
58. **$17\frac{1}{2}$ pounds**
$10 \times 1\frac{3}{4} = 17\frac{1}{2}$
59. **$5\frac{1}{4}$ miles**
$15\frac{3}{4} - 10\frac{1}{2} = 5\frac{1}{4}$
60. **$37\frac{3}{4}$ miles**
$16\frac{1}{4} + 12\frac{3}{8} + 9\frac{1}{8} = 37\frac{3}{4}$
61. $\frac{17 \text{ non-English speakers}}{25 \text{ total}}$ or 17:25 or 17 to 25
62. $\frac{13 \text{ skippers}}{20 \text{ total}}$ or 13:20 or 13 to 20
63. $\frac{2 \text{ tulips}}{1 \text{ daffodil}}$ or 2:1 or 2 to 1
64. $\frac{2 \text{ tulips}}{1 \text{ daffodil}}$ or 2:1 or 2 to 1
$470 - 10 = 460$
$\frac{460 \text{ did pass}}{10 \text{ did not pass}} = \frac{46}{1}$

65.

Employees on shift	2	4	6	8	10	12	14
Number of offices cleaned	3	6	9	12	15	18	21

66. 35
67. 12
68. 20
69. 10
70. 3
71. 60

72. 9
73. 50
74. 50%
75. 55
76. 200%
77. 160

78. **\$8.00**
$\$32 \times .25 = \$8$
79. **130 questions**
$.90 \times w = 117$
$w = 117 \div .90$
$w = 130$
80. **95%**
$n \times 26 = 24.7$
$n = 24.7 \div 26$
$n = .95$ or 95%

81. **200 people**
$.05 \times 4,000 = p$
$200 = p$
82. **9,375 people**
$.08 \times w = 750$
$w = 750 \div .08$
$w = 9,375$

Skill Preview Diagnostic Chart

Make note of any problems that you answered incorrectly. Notice the skill area for each problem you missed. As you work through this book, be sure to focus on these skill areas.

Problem Number	Skill Area	Unit
1, 2, 3, 4	Writing decimals	1
5, 6, 7, 8, 9, 10, 11, 12	Writing equivalent fractions	1
13, 14, 15, 16	Relating fractions, decimals, and percents	1
17, 18, 19, 20, 21, 22, 23, 24	Comparing fractions, decimals, and percents	1
25, 26, 27, 39*, 40*, 41**	Adding decimals	2
28, 29, 30, 42**	Subtracting decimals	2
31, 32, 33, 38*	Multiplying decimals	2
34, 35, 36, 37*	Dividing decimals	2
43, 44, 45, 56*, 60*	Adding fractions and mixed numbers	3
46, 47, 48, 59*	Subtracting fractions and mixed numbers	3
49, 50, 51, 55*, 57**, 58*	Multiplying fractions and mixed numbers	3
52, 53, 54	Dividing fractions and mixed numbers	3
61*, 62*, 63*, 64*	Writing a ratio	3
65	Ratios and patterns	3
66, 67, 68, 69, 70, 71	Solving proportions	4
72, 73, 74, 75, 76, 77	Solving percent equations	5
78*, 79*, 80*, 81*, 82*	Solving percent problems	5

*one-step word problems
**multistep word problems

Numbers Smaller Than 1

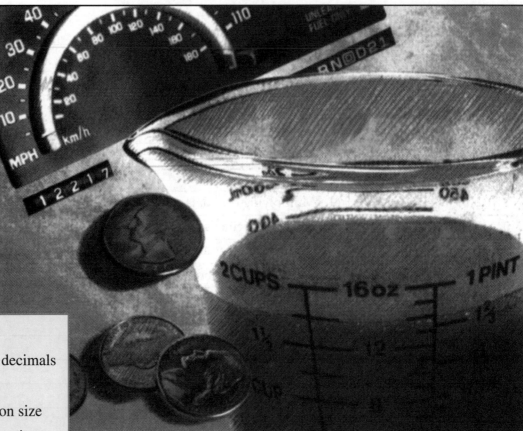

Skills

Reading and writing decimals

Comparing decimals

Understanding fraction size

Finding equivalent fractions

Understanding percents

Relating decimals, fractions, and percents

Tools

Calculator

Writing expressions

Problem Solvers

Solving word problems

Solving multistep problems

Applications

Digital measurements

Fraction measurements

Numbers smaller than 1 are a part of everyday life. For example, each of the following number values is less than 1:

- a half $\left(\frac{1}{2}\right)$ of a cup of coffee
- eight-tenths (0.8) of a mile
- forty percent (40%) off the original price

Each of these numbers represents a **part of a whole.** The **fraction** $\left(\frac{1}{2}\right)$ represents *part* of a cup of coffee. The **decimal** (0.8) is a part of one mile. The **percent** (40%) represents a part of the whole original price.

In this unit, you will learn to read, write, and understand numbers smaller than 1. You will also see the connections between decimals, fractions, and percents.

When Do I Use Numbers Smaller Than 1?

Each of the following situations involves a number smaller than 1.
Check off any experiences you've had:

- ☐ following a recipe
- ☐ figuring out mileage
- ☐ determining a sale price
- ☐ using a measurement tool such as a ruler or tape measure
- ☐ reading percents in newspaper headlines and articles
- ☐ paying for something with coins
- ☐ using the metric system for measurement

If you've done any of the things above, you've probably used numbers smaller than 1. Answer the questions below.

1. Describe the last time you used fractions when measuring something. For instance, you may have measured water for a recipe or used a ruler to measure the length or height of an object.

    _____

    _____

2. Where have you seen the word *percent* or the symbol %? Perhaps you've seen it in a sale advertisement or in a newspaper headline or article. Write the percent and what it was describing.

    _____

    _____

3. When is the last time you used digital measurement? For instance, you may have used a digital scale at the grocery or hardware store. You may have weighed yourself on a digital scale. Or you may have used a car odometer or a digital thermometer. Describe what you used.

    _____

    _____

Talk About It

You use money every day. Have you ever thought of money as decimals? For example, $.01 is a penny, and $.10 is a dime.

With a partner or a group, list other places that you see decimals. Use a newspaper, interview classmates, and ask your teacher for ideas.

Understanding Decimals

Each time you use money, you are working with decimals. In money systems that use dollars, a **decimal point** separates dollars from cents. Numbers after the decimal point represent a value *less than one dollar.*

Similarly, our number system uses the decimal point to separate **whole numbers** from numbers with a value *less than 1.*

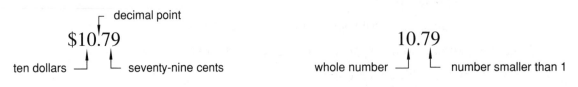

The number of digits following the decimal point tells you how small the decimal value is. Look at the **place value chart** below.

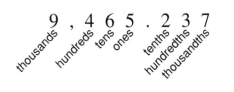

Tip

Numbers *after* the decimal point end in *ths:* tenths, hundredths, thousandths, and so on.

What place is the 5 in? _____   What place is the 3 in? _____

You're correct if you said that the 5 is in the *ones* place and the 3 is in the *hundredths* place.

Decimal values can go much further than the thousandths place. In this book and in most of everyday life, however, you will not need to use values less than a thousandth.

Understanding the Value of a Decimal

Example: What is the value of **0.7?** Of **0.07?**

Step 1
Look at the place value of the *last* digit in the decimal.

$$0.7$$

The place value is tenths.

$$0.07$$

The place value is hundredths.

Step 2
Think of a box divided into that many parts.

The box is in tenths.

The box is in hundredths.

Step 3
Visualize the decimal as a part of that box.

7 tenths (.7)

7 hundredths (.07)

A. Use the place value chart on page 14 to fill in the blanks below.

1. To write the number *forty-three and eight hundred seventy-five thousandths,* put a

   - 4 in the tens place
   - 3 in the ones place
   - 8 in the tenths place
   - 7 in the hundredths place
   - 5 in the thousandths place

   _____ _____ . _____ _____ _____

2. In the number 7,890.254, what digit is in the

   a. tens place? _____

   b. tenths place? _____

   c. hundredths place? _____

   d. ones place? _____

3. In the number 4,056.29, what digit is in the

   a. tens place? _____

   b. tenths place? _____

   c. hundredths place? _____

   d. ones place? _____

B. Match each picture with the decimal value given.

_____ **4.** .6

_____ **5.** .06

_____ **6.** .006

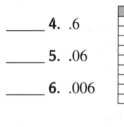 

a b c

Making Connections: Decimals and Money

In money systems that use dollars, two digits are written after the decimal point, for instance, $1.99. The numbers after the decimal point tell us what *part* of a dollar we have. Since there are 100 pennies in a dollar, 1 penny is *one hundredth* of a dollar and 99 cents is *99 hundredths* of a dollar.

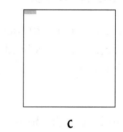

Write how many wholes (dollars) and how many parts (hundredths) are represented.

1. $100.09   _____ wholes   _____ hundredths

2. $100.90   _____ wholes   _____ hundredths

3. $21.50   _____ wholes   _____ hundredths

4. $21.05   _____ wholes   _____ hundredths

Reading Decimals

To read a decimal number, use your knowledge of place values.

Reading a Decimal

Example: How would you read the number **.985?**

Step 1
Read the number just as you would read a whole number.

Nine hundred eighty-five

Step 2
Read the place value of the *last* digit on the right.

The last digit in the number is a 5. It is in the *thousandths* place.

The number is read as **"nine hundred eighty-five thousandths."**

Zero as a Placeholder

How do you read the decimal number **4.05?** In this number, the zero means that there are *no tenths*. The zero is a placeholder. It holds the 5 in the hundredths place. The number is read "four and five hundredths." Remember that 4.05 does *not* have the same value as 4.5.

4.05 is equal to 4 and 5 hundredths.   4.5 is equal to 4 and 5 tenths.

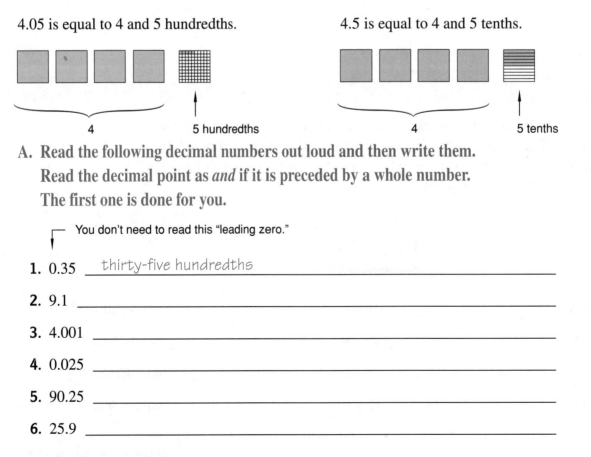

4   5 hundredths   4   5 tenths

A. **Read the following decimal numbers out loud and then write them. Read the decimal point as *and* if it is preceded by a whole number. The first one is done for you.**

You don't need to read this "leading zero."

1. 0.35   _thirty-five hundredths_ _____

2. 9.1 _____

3. 4.001 _____

4. 0.025 _____

5. 90.25 _____

6. 25.9 _____

B. Choose the correct answer for each problem below.

7. What is this number, written in words: 120.002?

   (1) one hundred twenty-two thousandths

   (2) one hundred twenty and two hundredths

   (3) one hundred twenty and two thousandths

8. Read this number aloud: .042.

   (1) forty-two thousand

   (2) forty-two thousandths

   (3) four and two tenths

9. Lorraine had thirty-three dollars and five cents in her purse. How much did she have?

   (1) $3.35

   (2) $33.05

   (3) $335.00

10. Jamal wrote a check for $250.50. What is that amount written in words?

   (1) Two hundred fifty dollars and fifty cents

   (2) Two hundred dollars and fifty cents

   (3) Two hundred fifty fifty

11. Read the following decimal aloud: 5.09.

   (1) five hundred nine

   (2) five and nine tenths

   (3) five and nine hundredths

12. **Multiple Answers** Which two answers represent twenty-five hundredths?

   (1) 0.25

   (2) .25

   (3) 25.00

C. Read the following information. Then answer the questions.

Car speed is usually measured in whole numbers. For example, the speed limit on many highways in the United States is 55 miles per hour. City drivers average about 20 miles per hour.

In the fast-paced world of car racing, however, speed is measured precisely—even to the *thousandths* place.

Indianapolis 500 Winning Speeds	
1913	75.933 mph
1925	101.13 mph
1991	176.457 mph
1993	157.207 mph

13. Write the winning speed for 1913 in words.

_____

14. In what year was the winning speed measured in hundredths of a mile? _____

15. In which year listed was the fastest speed recorded? _____

16. **Write** What is the advantage of measuring speed to the thousandths place? _____

_____

Writing Decimals

When writing a decimal, be sure that

- a decimal point separates the whole number from the decimal
- the correct number of places follow the decimal point

Writing a Decimal

Example: Write "four and twenty-five thousandths" in numbers.

Step 1
Write the whole number. Replace the word *and* with a decimal point.

Step 2
Decide how many places will follow the decimal point. Since this decimal value is *thousandths,* you need 3 places.

Step 3
If necessary, use zero as a placeholder. Since 25 has only 2 places, write 25 in the last 2 of your 3 decimal places. Put a zero in the tenths place.

4. ¬

Decimal point replaces *and*.

4. _____ _____ _____

three places for thousandths

4.025

holding zero

Four and twenty-five thousandths is **4.025.**

When there is no whole number, write a **leading zero** before the decimal point.

Example: *Nine hundredths*

leading zero ¬ ¬ holding zero

0.09

A. **Write the following decimal numbers in numbers. Replace *and* with a decimal point. Use holding zeros if necessary.**

1. seventeen hundredths __.__ __

2. two and three tenths __.__

3. one hundred forty and seven tenths

   __ __ __.__

4. twenty-nine and seventy thousandths

   __ __.__ __ __

5. two thousand and seventy-five hundredths

   __ , __ __ __.__ __

6. one and eighty hundredths __.__ __

7. forty thousandths __.__ __ __

8. forty and four thousandths

   __ __.__ __ __

9. seven hundred twenty-one and four tenths

   __ __ __.__

10. eight and eight hundredths __.__ __

B. Choose the correct answer for each problem below.

11. A grocer gave Antoine a dollar and 53 cents in change. Which of the following shows how much money Antoine received?

   (1) $.53

   (2) $1.53

   (3) $153

12. A machinist wrote down the width of a hole punch that measured eight tenths of a centimeter. What number did she write?

   (1) 8.10

   (2) 0.08

   (3) 0.8

13. A bank offered loan rates as low as six and twenty-five hundredths percent. What is this percentage in numbers?

   (1) 6.25%

   (2) 6.025%

   (3) 625%

14. Meg read "three and one hundred twenty-five thousandths of a gram." Which number was she reading?

   (1) 0.3125

   (2) 3.125

   (3) 3.0125

C. In your job in an industrial lab, your partner calls out the time for an experiment. You write it in the chart on the right. Replace *and* with a decimal point, and watch out for *th* endings. The first one is done for you.

15. "Two and three hundredths of a second"

16. "One hundred twenty-five thousandths of a second"

17. "One and twenty-five thousandths of a second"

18. "Two tenths of a second"

19. "Two and fifteen thousandths of a second"

20. "Two hundred fifty-five thousandths of a second"

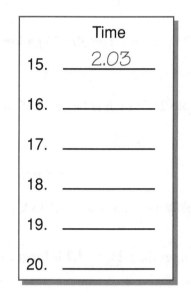

Time
15.   2.03
16. _____
17. _____
18. _____
19. _____
20. _____

Making Connections: Reading Decimals Out Loud

We often use the word *point* when reading decimals out loud. For example, we might read 1.025 as "one point zero-two-five" instead of "one and twenty-five thousandths." The word *point* stands for *and*. Dictating numbers in this way helps others know exactly what we mean.

Go back and read the decimals in Part C above, substituting the word *point* for *and* and reading the numbers as described above.

Comparing Decimals

Comparing decimals—deciding which is larger or which is smaller—is similar to comparing whole numbers. For example, you know that 7<u>3</u> is larger than 7<u>1</u>, because 3 is larger than 1.

Similarly, .73 (seventy-three hundredths) is larger than .71 (seventy-one hundredths) because 73 of *anything* is more than 71 of the same thing.

Comparing Decimals

Example 1: Which is larger, **.75** gallon of milk or **.5** gallon of milk?

Add zeros to the end of one number so that the decimals you are comparing have the same number of decimal places.

.75   .50 ⟵⎤

Add this zero so that you are now comparing hundredths.

Since 75 is larger than 50, **.75 gallon is larger than .5 gallon.**

Example 2: Which is larger, **4.25** or **4.9**?

4.25   4.90

added zero ⟶⎤

Since the whole numbers are equal, look at decimals next.

90 is larger than 25, so **4.9 is larger than 4.25.**

Example 3: Which is larger, **40.55** or **38.9**?

40.55   38.9

You know that 40 is greater than 38, so there is no need to compare decimals.

40.55 is greater than 38.9.

A. Choose the larger number in each pair below.

1. 9.55 or 9.05   **3.** 45.25 or 49.9   **5.** 5.6 or 5.55

2. 0.9 or 0.09   **4.** 10.75 or 10.009   **6.** 4.3 or 4.03

B. Arrange the numbers in each group below in order from *smallest to largest*. Use zeros as placeholders if necessary.

7. 5.75	**8.** 10.625	**9.** 20.4	**10.** 75.5
4.75	10.67	21.12	75.55
5.9	10.85	21.04	75.07
4.8	10.9	21.2	75.7

C. Solve the following word problems.

11. A machinist needs the thickest piece of sheet metal in his shop. Which should he use?

    (1) 0.125 millimeter

    (2) 1.1 millimeters

    (3) 1.02 millimeters

12. Which of the following is in the correct order, if the numbers are to be arranged from *smallest to largest?*

    (1) 2.12, 2.21, .221, .22

    (2) 2.21, 2.12, .22, .221

    (3) .22, .221, 2.12, 2.21

13. Each box below contains a lump of gold. The weight of the gold is written on the box. Which one would you choose?

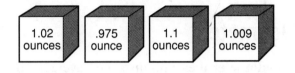

14. Arrange the numbers below in order from *largest to smallest.*

    2.625

    2.7

    2.009

    2.10

    2.01

Making Connections: Comparing Numbers

Comparing numbers—whether they are decimals, whole numbers, fractions, or percents—is a skill you'll use often.

For instance, which job would you prefer—one that pays $8.05 per hour or one that pays $8.50 per hour?

To answer this question, you *compared* 8.05 with 8.50 and found that $8.50 is a better hourly wage.

> ▶ **Comparison Symbols (Symbols Used for Comparing Numbers)**
>
> > means "is greater than"
>
> < means "is less than"
>
> = means "is equal to"

Use the symbols above to show the relationship between each pair of numbers below. Remember—the symbol points to the *smaller* number. (Example: 5.3 < 5.5) The first one is done for you.

1. $333.09 __<__ $333.90

2. 0.175 __>__ 0.157

3. 1.9 _____ 9.1

4. $900.50 _____ $899.90

5. 3.125 _____ 3.12

6. 5.5 _____ 5.15

7. 1,040 _____ 1,040.01

8. 3.005 _____ 3.05

9. $77.02 _____ $770.20

Reading Digital Measurements

Many measurement tools use decimals to express distance, temperature, weight, or size. **Digital measurement** uses whole numbers and decimals. In this lesson, you will become familiar with the odometer, the digital thermometer, and the digital scale.

Odometer

An **odometer** measures distance traveled. All motor vehicles have odometers to keep track of mileage.

The odometer at right shows that the car has traveled 73,451.2 miles (*73 thousand 451 and 2 tenths miles*).

Odometer

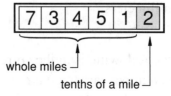

whole miles ⏐

tenths of a mile ⏐

Where distances are measured in miles, most odometers measure whole miles and tenths of a mile. Often, the whole numbers are shown in black and the tenths are in red or white.

A. Answer each question below.

1. Read aloud and write in words the mileage on each odometer.

   a. | 5 | 5 | 4 | 7 | 8 | 9 | _____ miles

   b. | 9 | 9 | 3 | 1 | 8 | 4 | _____ miles

   c. | 6 | 5 | 6 | 3 | 0 | 8 | _____ miles

2. Which cars have a mileage between 20,000 and 50,000 miles?

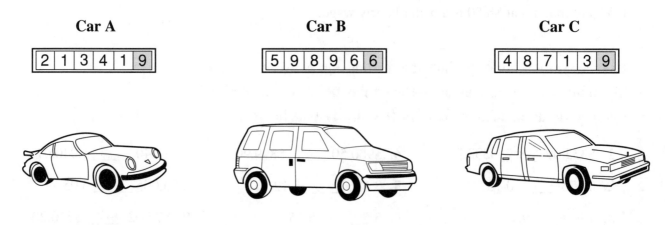

Car A | 2 | 1 | 3 | 4 | 1 | 9 |

Car B | 5 | 9 | 8 | 9 | 6 | 6 |

Car C | 4 | 8 | 7 | 1 | 3 | 9 |

Digital Thermometer

Digital thermometers display temperature as whole numbers and decimals.

A change in body temperature can indicate illness. The digital thermometer at right reads 98.6° (*ninety-eight and six tenths degrees*). This is a normal temperature: greater than 97°, but less than 99°.

Digital Thermometer

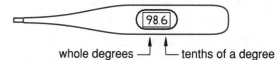

whole degrees ⌐ ⌐ tenths of a degree

Normal human body temperature ranges from 97° to 99° Fahrenheit. A temperature higher than 99° indicates a fever.

B. Answer the following questions.

3. At 2:00 A.M., a child has a temperature of 100.8°. Does she have a fever?

4. At 4:00 A.M., the child's temperature is 99.8°.

   a. Is it higher or lower than her 2:00 A.M. temperature?

   b. Does she still have a fever?

5. **Explain** The doctor recommends medicine for temperatures above 99.5°. Should the child receive medicine at 4:00 A.M.? Why or why not?

Digital Scale

Digital scales measure weight. They can measure weight to the tenths, hundredths, or thousandths place—or even more accurately.

A produce or deli scale like the one on the right measures weight to the hundredths place.

If you order two pounds of cheese, the salesperson puts cheese on the scale until the digital reading shows 2.00.

Digital Scale

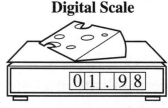

The cheese being weighed here is 1.98 pounds—almost 2 pounds.

C. Decide whether the scale shows the correct weight for each produce order.

6. "I want two and five tenths pounds of apples."

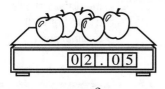

correct?

7. "I want twenty-five hundredths of a pound of pears."

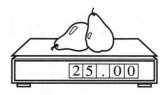

correct?

8. "I want four and twenty-five hundredths pounds of grapes."

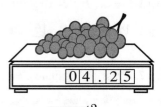

correct?

Using Your Calculator

A **calculator** can make working with numbers much easier. The calculator you use may look different from the one on the right. That's OK. As long as your calculator has the same **digit keys** and the four **operations keys** labeled, you'll be able to do all the exercises in this book.

The calculator shown here is a scientific calculator, but it has all basic calculator functions. Many classes and tests, including the GED, use a scientific calculator.

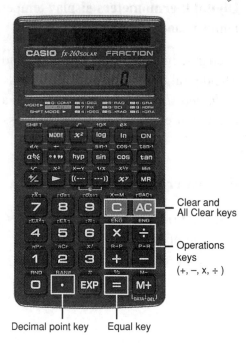

Clear and All Clear keys

Operations keys (+, −, ×, ÷)

Decimal point key   Equal key

The Calculator Display

Calculators have a digital display that shows values in whole numbers and decimals. Most displays can show up to eight digits at once. A calculator display can express decimals to many different place values.

When you turn your calculator on, the digital display reads **0.** Each digit you enter will also appear on the display.

Entering Digits on a Calculator

Example 1: How do you enter the number **95?**

Step 1. Turn your calculator on. Press the ⑨ key. Then press the ⑤ key.

Step 2. Press ⌷AC⌷ . This key clears the display.*

  *The Clear key on your calculator may be different.

Your display reads:

| 95. |

| 0. |

> **For another look** at the scientific calculator, see pages 239 and 240.

Example 2: Enter the number **.25.**

Step 1. Press · ② ⑤ . Be sure you press the decimal point key.

Step 2. Press ⌷AC⌷ again to clear the display.

| 0.25 |

If there is no whole number, the display shows a zero before the decimal point.

| 0. |

Now try some basic computing with your calculator.

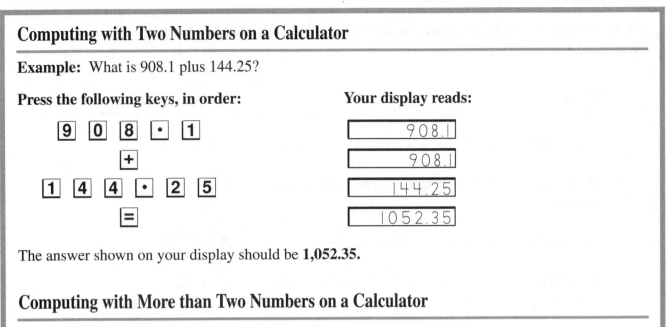

Computing with Two Numbers on a Calculator

Example: What is 908.1 plus 144.25?

Press the following keys, in order:

[9] [0] [8] [·] [1]

[+]

[1] [4] [4] [·] [2] [5]

[=]

Your display reads:

| 908.1 |
| 908.1 |
| 144.25 |
| 1052.35 |

The answer shown on your display should be **1,052.35**.

Computing with More than Two Numbers on a Calculator

Example: What is 13.5 and 2.8 subtracted from 194?

Press the following keys, in order:

[1] [9] [4]

[−]

[1] [3] [·] [5]

[−]

[2] [·] [8]

[=]

Your display reads:

| 194. |
| 194. |
| 13.5 |
| 180.5 |
| 2.8 |
| 177.7 |

The answer shown on your display should be **177.7**.

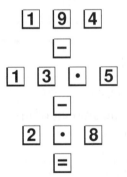 **Use a calculator to find the answer to each problem.**

1. 345.8 + 92   27 × 60   908 ÷ 1.5   9,076 − 321

2. 22.68 ÷ 4.2   43,908 − 886   314 × 4.25   2,184 + 31.1

3. 670 − 522 − 75   917 − 331 − 12   5,901 ÷ 10   195 + 4,200 + 407

4. Victor's crew needs to plant 150 trees in the city park. On Monday they planted 22. On Tuesday they planted 36. How many more trees do they have to plant?

5. Mina inherited $11,550 from her great-grandmother. She decided to share the money equally with her 2 children. How much money did each of the three receive?

Answers start on page 201.

Writing Expressions

When you write a math **expression,** you use math symbols to represent a situation. Look at the examples below.

Words	Symbols
• Anita had $17 in her wallet. She spent $12 on groceries.	$17 - 12$
• Mr. Vasquez divided the 12 tickets evenly among his 3 friends.	$12 \div 3$
• Cathy earned $8 per hour for 7.5 hours.	8×7.5
• A carpenter glued a $\frac{3}{4}$-inch-thick board to a frame that measured 2 inches thick.	$\frac{3}{4} + 2$

You can write an expression even when you do not know a number value. Simply use an **unknown** or a **variable** (a letter) in place of the number you do not know. Here are some examples.

Words	Picture	Symbols
Rodrigo's bank balance was $1,245.99. Then he deposited his paycheck into the account.	Balance $1,245.99	$\$1{,}245.99 + p$ (p = the amount of his paycheck)
A librarian removed 7 of the books from a shelf.	s	$s - 7$ (s = the number of books on the shelf before the librarian removed some)
Mrs. Mitsui divided the ground pork into $\frac{1}{4}$-pound patties.	x	$x \div \frac{1}{4}$ (x = the number of pounds of ground pork Mrs. Mitsui had in all)
Each box of cereal Tamika bought cost $3.40.	$3.40 b	$\$3.40 \times b$ (b = the number of boxes Tamika bought)

You may use whatever letter you'd like in an expression. However, be careful to show the correct operation: $+$, $-$, $\times$, or $\div$.

► The order in which you write a **subtraction** or **division** expression is important.

Example 1: You know that $10 - 5$ is *not* the same as $5 - 10$.
Thus, $r - 12$ is *not* the same as $12 - r$.

Example 2: You know that $8 \div 4$ is *not* the same as $4 \div 8$.
Thus, $t \div 3$ is *not* the same as $3 \div t$.

► You can use any order of numbers in **addition** and **multiplication.**

Example 3: Marcia had several dollars in her purse. Her husband gave her $20 more. Which *two* expressions show how much money Marcia has in all?

    (1) $b + \$20$

    (2) $b - \$20$

    (3) $\$20 + b$

Example 4: Fred bought 3 packages of hot dogs. Which *two* expressions represent the total number of hot dogs Fred bought?

    (1) $3 \times h$

    (2) $h + 3$

    (3) $h \times 3$

If you answered **(1)** and **(3)** for each example, then you understand how addition and multiplication expressions work.

Choose the correct expression for each problem below.

1. Mel divided the students into 5 groups. How many students were in each group?

    (1) $g \times 5$

    (2) $g \div 5$

    (3) $g - 5$

2. Arthur wrote a check against his bank balance of $912. Which expression shows his new balance?

    (1) $b + \$912$

    (2) $b - \$912$

    (3) $\$912 - b$

3. A clerk typed for several hours. How many *minutes* did he type?

    (1) $60 \times h$

    (2) $60 \div h$

    (3) $h \div 60$

4. Which expression represents the number of marbles in the picture below?

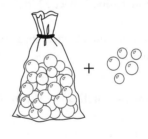

    (1) $s + 5$

    (2) $s - 5$

    (3) $s \times 5$

5. **Multiple Solutions** Dottie added 4 pounds of ground lamb to some ground beef. Write two expressions that represent the total pounds of meat Dottie has now.

Solving Word Problems

You have already done some word problems in this book. A **word problem** is a story with numbers that asks a question. To solve a word problem, you need to get a sense of the problem.

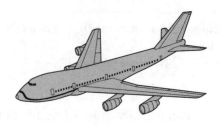

Instead of this:

$$207$$
$$- 105$$

You have this:

Northway Airline flight 45 had 207 passengers and 4 flight attendants aboard. In Baltimore, 105 passengers got off the plane. How many passengers remained on the plane?

To succeed with word problems, follow the plan below.

Step 1. Understand the question. What are you being asked to find? Put the question in your own words.	After 105 passengers got off the plane, how many of the original 207 were still on the plane?
Step 2. Decide what information is needed to solve the problem. Word problems may give you more numbers than you need or not enough numbers.	Needed: 207 original passengers 105 passengers who got off plane Not needed: 4 flight attendants
Step 3. Think about how you might solve the problem. • To combine, add. • To find a difference, subtract. • To find a total, multiply. • To find a part, divide.	207 original passengers − 105 passengers who got off passengers left
Step 4. Estimate an answer. About how large or small should the answer be? Round the numbers to make them easy to work with.	$207 \approx 200$ $\approx$ means "is approximately equal to" $105 \approx 100$ $200 - 100 = 100$
Step 5. Solve the problem. Check your answer. Do the computation. Then look at your answer. Does it make sense? Is it a reasonable solution to the question?	207 original passengers − 105 passengers who got off 102 passengers left on plane **102** is close to the estimate, and it is a reasonable answer.

Use the five-step problem-solving plan to answer the following questions.
Follow each step as shown.

1. Janelle's credit card balance was $346. She paid $150 cash for her son's music lessons. Then she charged a $52 dinner with a client to the credit card. What is Janelle's new credit card balance?

Step 1. Understand the question. What are you being asked to find?	**a.** After she charged $52, what is Janelle's new credit card balance?
Step 2. Decide what information is needed to solve the problem. What numbers do you need?	**b.**
Step 3. Think about how you might solve the problem. Choose the operation. Set up the problem.	**c.**
Step 4. Estimate an answer. Round the numbers.	**d.**
Step 5. Solve. Check your answer. Does the answer make sense?	**e.**

2. A chef needed 2 dozen eggs to make a breakfast casserole, 6 to make fried eggs, and 8 to make egg salad. How many eggs does she need in all?

   a. What is the question?
   b. What information is needed?
   c. What strategy should you use?
   d. Estimate an answer.
   e. What is the solution? Is it sensible?

3. Meg and Molly split their grocery bill of $122 evenly between the 2 of them. This bill was $50 more than what they usually spend. How much did each woman spend?

   a. What is the question?
   b. What information is needed?
   c. What strategy should you use?
   d. Estimate an answer.
   e. What is the solution? Is it sensible?

4. Tim spent $14 on 1 gallon of paint. He decided to buy 5 more gallons to finish the job. He bought 2 brushes for $4.99 each. How much did he spend on the 5 new gallons of paint?

   a. What is the question?
   b. What information is needed?
   c. What strategy should you use?
   d. Estimate an answer.
   e. What is the solution? Is it sensible?

For another look at the five-step problem-solving plan, turn to page 235.

Understanding Fractions

Decimals and fractions both express a part of a whole. Decimals represent a whole divided into 10, 100, or 1,000 parts. Fractions can represent a whole divided into *any number* of parts.

In a fraction, the bottom number (the **denominator**) tells you how many equal parts are in the whole. The top number (the **numerator**) tells how many of those parts you have. When the top number of a fraction is *smaller* than the bottom number, the fraction is *smaller than 1*.

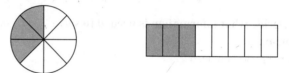

$\frac{3}{8}$ number of parts you have (numerator)
total number of parts in whole (denominator)

Both wholes are divided into 8 equal parts. In each whole, 3 parts are shaded. This represents $\frac{3}{8}$.

Writing Fractions

Example 1: What fraction of the whole is shaded in this figure?

Step 1. Count the total number of parts. Write this as the denominator.

$\overline{3}$ total number of parts

Step 2. Count the number of shaded parts. Write this as the numerator.

$\frac{1}{3}$ number of shaded parts

The shaded portion of the triangle represents $\frac{1}{3}$, which is less than 1.

Example 2: There are 5 children in the Taylor family. Three of the children are boys. What fraction of the Taylor children are boys?

$\overline{5}$ total number of children

$\frac{3}{5}$ number of boys

Three-fifths $\left(\frac{3}{5}\right)$ of the Taylor children are boys.

A. Write a fraction representing the shaded part of each figure below.

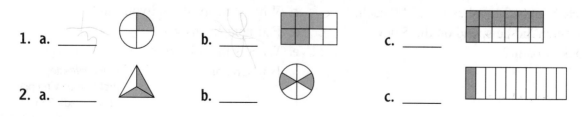

1. a. _____   b. _____   c. _____

2. a. _____   b. _____   c. _____

B. Write a fraction for each situation below.

3. There are 27 people on a bus. Twelve of them are women. What fraction of the people on the bus are women?

$$\frac{\blacksquare}{\blacksquare} \quad \frac{\text{number of women}}{\text{total number of people}}$$

4. A foot is equal to 12 inches. What fraction of a foot is 7 inches?

5. Natalia earns $212 a week cleaning houses. She spends $45 a week on food. What fraction of her earnings does she spend on food?

6. Of the 2,180 parts coming off an assembly line, 2,003 were of excellent quality. What fraction of the parts were excellent in quality?

7. David works 6 days a week. What fraction of a week does David work?

8. Carmine works an 8-hour day. He spends 1 hour on the telephone each day. What fraction of Carmine's workday is spent on the phone?

Making Connections: Fractions and Decimals

Fractions and decimals both show part of a whole. To write a decimal as a fraction, just put *part* over *whole*.

Example: What fraction of a dollar is 97¢, or $.97?

Look at the place value of the decimal. 0.97 is ninety-seven *hundredths*.

Therefore, $0.97 = \dfrac{97}{100} \quad \begin{array}{l}\text{parts}\\ \text{total parts}\end{array}$

Try writing these decimals as fractions: .7   .085   .03

Did you write $\frac{7}{10}$, $\frac{85}{1,000}$, and $\frac{3}{100}$? If so, then you've made the connection between decimals and fractions.

Write the following decimals as fractions. Remember—the decimal's place value is the fraction's denominator.

1. **a.** 0.275   0.32   .9   **b.** .1   .01   .001

Write these fractions as decimals. The fraction's denominator will be the decimal's place value.

2. **a.** $\frac{3}{10}$ $\frac{21}{100}$ $\frac{875}{1,000}$ **b.** $\frac{7}{1,000}$ $\frac{7}{100}$ $\frac{7}{10}$

The Size of Fractions

Which is larger—$\frac{1}{2}$ or $\frac{1}{3}$? Think of each fraction as part of a pound of gold.

The first pound of gold is divided into **2** parts, and you get 1 part.

$\frac{1}{2}$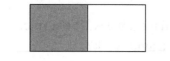

The second pound of gold is divided into **3** parts, and you get 1 part.

$\frac{1}{3}$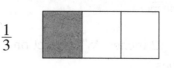

You can see that *one part out of two* $\left(\dfrac{1 \text{ part}}{2 \text{ parts}}\right)$ is larger than *one part out of three* $\left(\dfrac{1 \text{ part}}{3 \text{ parts}}\right)$.

▶ When fractions have the **same numerator,** the fraction gets *smaller* as the denominator gets *larger.*

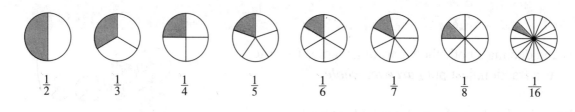

What happens when fractions have the same denominator but different numerators?

▶ When fractions have the **same denominator,** the fraction gets *larger* as the numerator gets *larger.*

> **For another look**
> at the size of fractions, turn to the Fraction Chart on page 236.

A. Divide and shade in the figures below. Then choose the larger fraction.

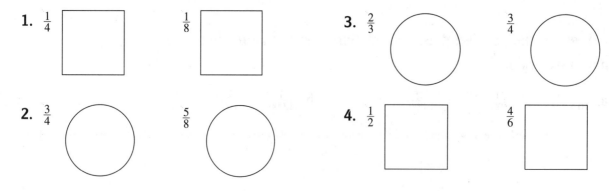

1. $\frac{1}{4}$ ☐ $\frac{1}{8}$ ☐

3. $\frac{2}{3}$ ◯ $\frac{3}{4}$ ◯

2. $\frac{3}{4}$ ◯ $\frac{5}{8}$ ◯

4. $\frac{1}{2}$ ☐ $\frac{4}{6}$ ☐

Comparing Fractions to $\frac{1}{2}$

A fraction is smaller than $\frac{1}{2}$ if its numerator is less than half its denominator.

$\frac{1}{3}$ 1 is less than half of 3.

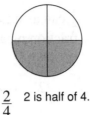

$\frac{2}{4}$ 2 is half of 4.

$\frac{3}{5}$ 3 is more than half of 5.

Since 1 is less than half of 3, $\frac{1}{3}$ is **smaller** than $\frac{1}{2}$.

Since 3 is more than half of 5, $\frac{3}{5}$ is **larger** than $\frac{1}{2}$.

B. Determine the size of each fraction. Draw a picture if you'd like.

5. $\frac{1}{4}$ Less than $\frac{1}{2}$?   Equal to $\frac{1}{2}$?   More than $\frac{1}{2}$?

6. $\frac{5}{8}$ Less than $\frac{1}{2}$?   Equal to $\frac{1}{2}$?   More than $\frac{1}{2}$?

7. $\frac{4}{7}$ Less than $\frac{1}{2}$?   Equal to $\frac{1}{2}$?   More than $\frac{1}{2}$?

8. $\frac{3}{6}$ Less than $\frac{1}{2}$?   Equal to $\frac{1}{2}$?   More than $\frac{1}{2}$?

9. $\frac{7}{8}$ Less than $\frac{1}{2}$?   Equal to $\frac{1}{2}$?   More than $\frac{1}{2}$?

10. $\frac{5}{10}$ Less than $\frac{1}{2}$?   Equal to $\frac{1}{2}$?   More than $\frac{1}{2}$?

C. Before taking inventory, you need to separate bags of dried fruit according to their weight. Sort the bags into the bins below.

11. $\frac{3}{8}$-pound bag goes in Bin _____.

12. $\frac{8}{16}$-pound bag goes in Bin _____.

13. $\frac{2}{3}$-pound bag goes in Bin _____.

14. $\frac{5}{8}$-pound bag goes in Bin _____.

15. $\frac{3}{4}$-pound bag goes in Bin _____.

16. $\frac{2}{4}$-pound bag goes in Bin _____.

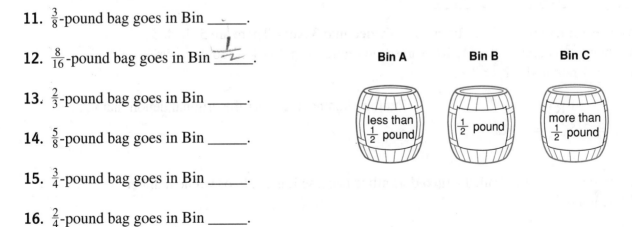

Bin A   Bin B   Bin C

less than $\frac{1}{2}$ pound $\frac{1}{2}$ pound   more than $\frac{1}{2}$ pound

Forms of Fractions

Fractions represent a part of a whole. They can also represent **division.**

The fraction $\frac{1}{2}$ can mean "1 out of 2 parts."

$\frac{1}{2}$ can also mean "1 divided by 2." The line in a fraction means "divided by."

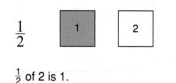

$\frac{1}{2}$

$\frac{1}{2}$ of 2 is 1.

$\frac{1}{2}$

1 divided by 2 , or $\frac{1}{2}$ of a whole

▶ When the numerator of a fraction is the **same** as the denominator, the fraction is **equal to 1.** $\frac{2}{2} = 1; \frac{90}{90} = 1$

Write a fraction to express this figure:

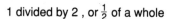 $\dfrac{\text{number of shaded parts}}{\text{number of total parts}}$

The correct fraction, $\frac{4}{4}$, is the same as **1.** In other words, the whole figure is shaded. To express the figure as a division problem, write 4 ÷ 4 = 1.

▶ When the numerator of a fraction is **larger** than the denominator, the fraction is **larger than 1.** $\frac{5}{4} > 1; \frac{20}{10} > 1$

Write a fraction to express the shaded portions of these figures:

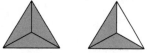

$\dfrac{\text{number of shaded parts}}{\text{number of parts each triangle is divided into}}$

The correct fraction is $\frac{5}{3}$. Each triangle is divided into 3 parts. There are 5 shaded parts shown. $\frac{5}{3}$ is greater than 1. To express the figures as a division problem, write 5 ÷ 3 = 1 remainder 2, or $1\frac{2}{3}$.

$$\frac{5}{3} = 3\overline{)5}^{\,1\,R2} = 1\ R2$$

Put the remainder, 2, over the original denominator, 3.

$$\frac{5}{3} = 1\frac{2}{3}$$

The number $1\frac{2}{3}$ is often called a **mixed number** because it is a mix of whole number and fraction.

A. Write each fraction as a whole number or as a mixed number.

1. $\frac{7}{3} = 7 \div 3 = 2\frac{1}{3}$ $\qquad$ $\frac{3}{2}$ $\qquad\qquad$ $\frac{9}{2}$ $\qquad\qquad$ $\frac{8}{3}$

2. $\frac{4}{3}$ $\qquad\qquad\qquad$ $\frac{7}{4}$ $\qquad\qquad$ $\frac{9}{7}$ $\qquad\qquad$ $\frac{9}{5}$

Changing Mixed Numbers to Fractions

To write a fraction as a mixed number, you divide. To write a mixed number as a fraction, you do the opposite—you multiply.

Writing a Mixed Number as a Fraction

Example: How do you write $3\frac{1}{2}$ as a fraction?

Step 1
Multiply the whole number by the denominator of the fraction. Write this product over the denominator.

$$3\frac{1}{2} = \frac{6}{2} \longleftarrow 3 \times 2 = 6$$

Step 2
Add the original numerator to the product of Step 1.

$$3\frac{1}{2} = \frac{6}{2} + \frac{1}{2} = \frac{7}{2}$$

$$3\frac{1}{2} = \frac{7}{2}$$

B. Change these mixed numbers into fractions.

3. $3\frac{1}{2}$ $\qquad\qquad$ $4\frac{1}{5}$ $\qquad\qquad$ $2\frac{1}{3}$ $\qquad\qquad$ $2\frac{1}{8}$

4. $4\frac{1}{2}$ $\qquad\qquad$ $3\frac{1}{4}$ $\qquad\qquad$ $1\frac{3}{5}$ $\qquad\qquad$ $1\frac{5}{8}$

Making Connections: Expressing Fractions as Decimals

At times you may need to work with decimals instead of fractions. To convert a fraction to a decimal, divide.

Example: ShipFast shipping requires the weight of all packages be written as decimals. Kareem needs to ship a box that weighs $\frac{3}{4}$ pound. How would he write this as a decimal?

$$\frac{3}{4} = 3 \div 4 \ \text{ or } \ 4\overline{)3.00} \quad \overset{.75}{\phantom{4\overline{)3.00}}} \longleftarrow \frac{3}{4} \text{ can be written as .75.}$$

Write the following fractions as decimals. Use a calculator if you'd like.

1. $\frac{4}{5}$ $\qquad$ 2. $\frac{1}{4}$ $\qquad$ 3. $\frac{1}{2}$ $\qquad$ 4. $\frac{3}{8}$ $\qquad$ 5. $\frac{2}{5}$ $\qquad$ 6. $\frac{5}{8}$

Equivalent Fractions

Write a fraction to express each figure.

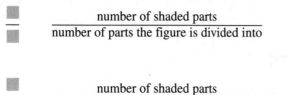
$$\frac{\blacksquare}{\blacksquare} = \frac{\text{number of shaded parts}}{\text{number of parts the figure is divided into}}$$

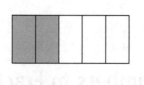

$$\frac{\blacksquare}{\blacksquare} \quad \frac{\text{number of shaded parts}}{\text{number of parts the figure is divided into}}$$

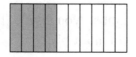

Compare the two shaded areas. What do you notice?

The shaded parts of the two bars above are the *same size*. $\frac{2}{5}$ and $\frac{4}{10}$ are called **equivalent fractions** because they are equal to each other. The shaded amounts represent equal values.

$$\frac{2}{5} = \frac{4}{10}$$

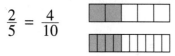

▶ To write an equal fraction, you can *multiply* both numerator and denominator by the *same* number. This is the same as multiplying by 1.

Example: $\frac{2}{3} \times \boxed{\frac{2}{2}} = \frac{4}{6}$

          means 2 ÷ 2 or 1

A number divided by itself equals 1. Since $\frac{2}{2} = 1$, you are not changing the value of $\frac{2}{3}$ when you multiply by $\frac{2}{2}$. You are only changing the *form* of the fraction.

▶ To write an equal fraction, you can also *divide* both numerator and denominator by the *same* number. This is the same as dividing by 1.

Example: $\frac{4}{8} \div \boxed{\frac{4}{4}} = \frac{1}{2}$

          means 4 ÷ 4 or 1

Since $\frac{4}{4} = 1$, you are not changing the value of $\frac{4}{8}$ when you divide by $\frac{4}{4}$. You are only simplifying the fraction, or changing its *form*.

▶ A fraction is in **lowest terms** when it is in the simplest form possible. For example, $\frac{9}{15}$ simplified to lowest terms is $\frac{3}{5}$.

Example: Is $\frac{5}{10}$ written in lowest terms?

$$\frac{5}{10} \div \boxed{\frac{5}{5}} = \frac{1}{2}$$

No. Both numerator and denominator can be evenly divided by 5. $\frac{5}{10}$ written in lowest terms is $\frac{1}{2}$.

A. Write equivalent fractions for each fraction below. Choose a fraction equal to 1 (such as $\frac{2}{2}$ or $\frac{4}{4}$) and multiply each fraction in row 1 by it. Multiply each fraction in row 2 by a different fraction equal to 1. The first one is done for you.

1. $\frac{2}{7} \times \boxed{\frac{4}{4}} = \frac{8}{28}$ $\frac{3}{5} \times \underline{\quad} = \underline{\quad}$ $\frac{1}{8} \times \underline{\quad} = \underline{\quad}$ $\frac{3}{4} \times \underline{\quad} = \underline{\quad}$

2. $\frac{3}{8} \times \underline{\quad} = \underline{\quad}$ $\frac{1}{4} \times \underline{\quad} = \underline{\quad}$ $\frac{2}{3} \times \underline{\quad} = \underline{\quad}$ $\frac{1}{5} \times \underline{\quad} = \underline{\quad}$

B. Write equivalent fractions by dividing each fraction in row 3 by $\frac{2}{2}$ and each fraction in row 4 by $\frac{3}{3}$. The first one is done for you.

3. $\frac{4}{6} \div \boxed{\frac{2}{2}} = \frac{2}{3}$ $\frac{6}{8} \div \underline{\quad} = \underline{\quad}$ $\frac{2}{6} \div \underline{\quad} = \underline{\quad}$ $\frac{6}{10} \div \underline{\quad} = \underline{\quad}$

4. $\frac{15}{21} \div \underline{\quad} = \underline{\quad}$ $\frac{3}{9} \div \underline{\quad} = \underline{\quad}$ $\frac{12}{15} \div \underline{\quad} = \underline{\quad}$ $\frac{3}{18} \div \underline{\quad} = \underline{\quad}$

C. Are these fractions in lowest terms? If so, write *yes*. If not, put the fraction in lowest terms.

5. $\frac{2}{5} = \underline{\quad}$ $\frac{6}{9} = \underline{\quad}$ $\frac{4}{7} = \underline{\quad}$ $\frac{2}{9} = \underline{\quad}$

6. $\frac{6}{18} = \underline{\quad}$ $\frac{7}{14} = \underline{\quad}$ $\frac{1}{6} = \underline{\quad}$ $\frac{4}{16} = \underline{\quad}$

Making Connections: Equivalent Fractions and Decimals

Adding zeros to the end of a decimal number does not change the number's value. For example, .1 = .10 = .100. Here's another way to see that same relationship:

Why does .1 = .10?

.1 = $\frac{1}{10}$ and .10 = $\frac{10}{100}$

$\frac{1}{10} \times \boxed{\frac{10}{10}} = \frac{10}{100}$

$\uparrow$ $\uparrow$
.1   .10

Why does .30 = .300?

.30 = $\frac{30}{100}$ and .300 = $\frac{300}{1,000}$

$\frac{30}{100} \times \boxed{\frac{10}{10}} = \frac{300}{1,000}$

$\uparrow$ $\uparrow$
.30   .300

Use fractions to show why the following pairs of decimals are equal in value. Use the example above as a model.

1. Show why .40 is equal to .4000.

2. Show why .9 is equal to .900.

3. Show why .800 is equal to .80.

4. Show why .50 is equal to .5.

Filling in a Grid

On some tests, you will be asked to record the answers to certain problems on special grids. These questions measure your ability to find a solution without the benefit of selecting from multiple-choice answers. Because tests are scored by machine, you must follow certain rules when entering answers on grids.

A sample grid is shown to the right. It has the following features:

- Five columns of numbers and symbols.
- A row of blank boxes at the top to record your answer.
- A row of slash marks (/) to record fractions.
- A row of decimal points (.) to record decimal numbers.
- Rows of numbers from 0 through 9.

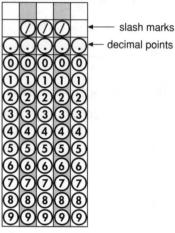

To use the answer grid, follow these steps:

1. Solve the problem.

2. Write the answer in the top row. Write only one number or symbol in each box. You may start in any column as long as your answer will fit.

3. Fill in the one correct circle in each column.

Filling in the Grid

Example: Last week, Nicole spent 10 hours setting up a new filing system at work. If she worked 40 hours last week, what fraction of her time did she spend on the new filing system? Write your answer as either a decimal or a fraction in lowest terms.

Step 1
Solve the problem. Nicole spent 10 out of 40 hours on the filing system. Write the fraction: $\frac{10}{40}$.

Express in lowest terms:
$\frac{10}{40} = \frac{10}{40} \div \frac{10}{10} = \frac{1}{4}$

Or, express as a decimal:
$10 \div 40 = 0.25$

Step 2
Write your answer in the top row of boxes. You can start in any column as long as your answer fits. Leave unneeded boxes blank.

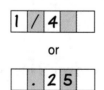

or

Step 3
Fill in the correct circles on the grid. Use the digits in the top row as a guide. Both examples are correct because they represent the same value.

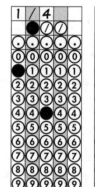

These answers would be scored as incorrect. Don't make these common mistakes.

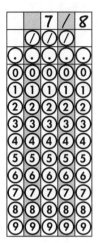 The answer is written on the top row, but the grid circles are blank.

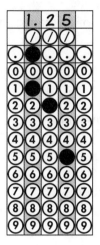 More than one circle in a column is filled in. Do not write a symbol and a number in the same column.

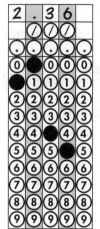 Although the number at the top of the grid is correct, the filled-in circles do not match the number.

Solve the following problems. Record your answers in the grids.

1. 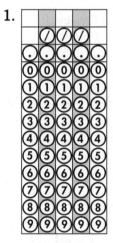 What fraction represents the shaded portion of the diagram below?

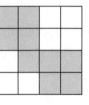

3. Regina has 24 cents in change in her pocket. What fraction of a dollar is 24 cents? Write your answer in lowest terms.

2. A small store spends $\frac{3}{5}$ of its budget on payroll. How would you write this fraction as a decimal?

4. 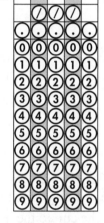 A package weighs one and twelve thousandths kilograms. How would you write the amount as a decimal number?

Answers start on page 203. **39**

Reading Fraction Measurements

Many common measuring tools require a knowledge of fractions. In this lesson, we'll look at the **measuring cup** and the **ruler.**

Reading a Measuring Cup

A standard measuring cup is used to measure detergent and ingredients such as sugar, flour, or water.

Marks on the side of a measuring cup indicate different fraction amounts. The cup on the right shows the fractions commonly listed on a measuring cup.

If:
your washing machine recommends $\frac{1}{2}$ cup of detergent per load

You would:
pour detergent in the cup until it reached the level marked $\frac{1}{2}$.

If:
a recipe calls for $1\frac{2}{3}$ cups water

You would:
fill the cup to the 1 cup level, pour the water in, then fill it to the $\frac{2}{3}$ mark and pour that water in.

Comparing fractions can be easy and interesting with a measuring cup. For example, which is greater, $\frac{1}{2}$ cup of milk or $\frac{2}{3}$ cup? If you filled the cup to the $\frac{2}{3}$ line, you'd have *more* milk than if you filled it to the $\frac{1}{2}$ line. $\frac{2}{3} > \frac{1}{2}$.

> **Remember:**
> \> means "is greater than"
> < means "is less than"

A. Use the measuring cup pictured above to decide which amount is greater. Write in the appropriate symbol (< or >).

1. $\frac{3}{4}$ _____ $\frac{2}{3}$

2. $\frac{1}{3}$ _____ $\frac{1}{2}$

3. Jan's recipe for chocolate chip cookies calls for $\frac{2}{3}$ cup of sugar. Belle's recipe calls for $\frac{3}{4}$ cup of sugar. Whose recipe has more sugar?

4. $\frac{2}{3}$ _____ $\frac{1}{4}$

5. $\frac{1}{4}$ _____ $\frac{1}{3}$

6. Martin added $\frac{1}{2}$ cup of water to a recipe that calls for $\frac{2}{3}$ cup of water. Did he add too much or too little water?

Reading a Ruler

The ruler below is 6 inches long. It is half the length of a standard 1-foot (12-inch) ruler. Below the ruler, write in the correct number of inches represented.

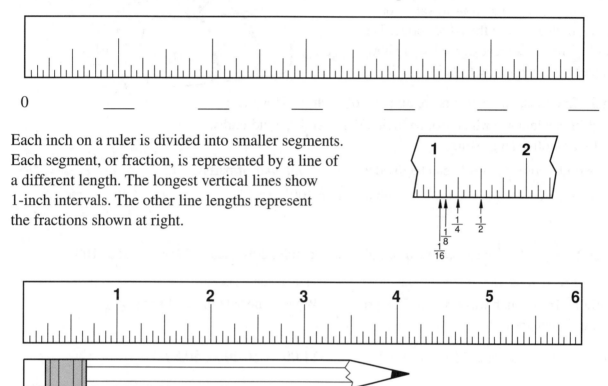

0 ___   ___   ___   ___   ___   ___

Each inch on a ruler is divided into smaller segments. Each segment, or fraction, is represented by a line of a different length. The longest vertical lines show 1-inch intervals. The other line lengths represent the fractions shown at right.

Example: How long is this pencil? You are correct if you measured $4\frac{1}{8}$ *inches.* Now measure your own pencil or pen. How long is it?

B. Write the correct measurement for each object.

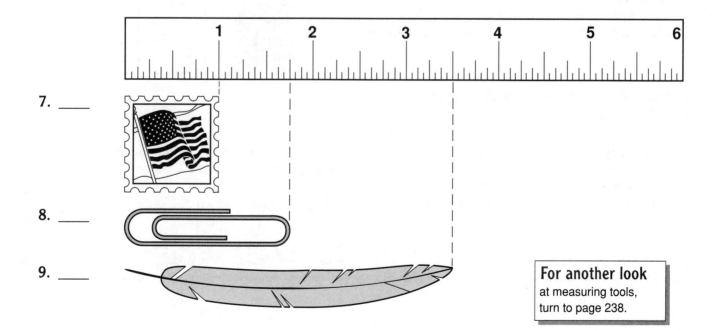

7. ___

8. ___

9. ___

| For another look |
| at measuring tools, turn to page 238. |

For another look at measuring tools, turn to page 238.

Understanding Percent

The **percent sign** (%) indicates a part of a whole.

When you buy a bag at a 20%-off sale, you are paying only a *part* of the *whole* price. The number before the percent sign tells you how large a part you *won't* have to pay.

Decimals, fractions, and percents are all parts of a whole. However:

- With decimals, a whole can be divided into tenths, hundredths, thousandths, and so on.
- With fractions, a whole can be divided into *any number* of parts.
- With percents, a whole is *always* divided into 100 parts.

▶ A percent sign (%) means *parts out of 100*. For example, 20% means 20 parts out of 100.

Example 1: How much was taken off the price of the bag shown above?

$1.00 is 100 pennies. You will save 20%, or $0.20.

What is the sale price of the bag?

$1.00 − $0.20 = $0.80.

Example 2: What percent of the box on the right is shaded?

You're right if you said 30%, because 30 of the 100 parts are shaded.
What percent is *not* shaded? If 70 squares out of 100 squares are *not* shaded, then **70% of the box is *not* shaded.**

Example 3: 60% of voters chose Romero Valdez for city council.

How many voters voted for Valdez?

The percent sign (%) means *out of 100*. 60% means *60 out of 100*. In this election, **60 out of every 100 voters** voted for Valdez.

What percent of the voters *did not* vote for Valdez?

$$100\% - 60\% = 40\%$$

↑ total voters   ↑ voted for Valdez   ↑ did not vote for Valdez

A. What percent of each figure is shaded? What percent is unshaded?

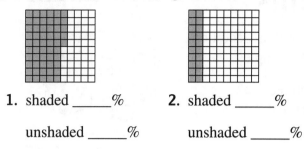 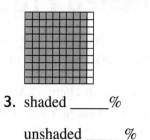 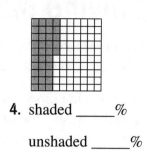

1. shaded _____%

unshaded _____%

2. shaded _____%

unshaded _____%

3. shaded _____%

unshaded _____%

4. shaded _____%

unshaded _____%

B. Answer each question below.

5. A family spends 28% of its income on rent. What percent of its income is left for other things?

(1) 100%

(2) 82%

(3) 72%

6. If 13% of all town residents voted for a larger police force, and 27% voted against it, what percent of residents did not vote?

(1) 87%

(2) 73%

(3) 60%

7. Twenty-five of the 100 students in a program are unemployed. What percent of the students are employed?

(1) 25%

(2) 75%

(3) 125%

8. An automated stamping system makes a print error on 3 of every 100 orders. What percent of orders are error-free?

(1) 100%

(2) 97%

(3) 3%

Making Connections: Relating Parts of a Whole

Suppose 57% of the paper produced at Recyclorama Inc. is made from recycled paper. What *fraction* of Recyclorama's paper is made from recycled paper? How is this number expressed as a *decimal?*

$$57\% = \frac{57}{100} = 0.57 \text{ (57 hundredths)}$$

percent   fraction   decimal

Write the correct fraction, decimal, or percent in each blank below.

1. 43% = _____ = _____
     fraction   decimal

2. $\frac{21}{100}$ = _____ = _____
     percent   decimal

3. 0.99 = _____ = _____
     fraction   percent

4. 33% = _____ = _____
     fraction   decimal

5. $\frac{67}{100}$ = _____ = _____
     decimal   percent

6. 0.13 = _____ = _____
     fraction   percent

Solving Multistep Problems

Sometimes a problem may involve more than one operation—addition, subtraction, multiplication, or division. Look at these examples:

When buying groceries, how much change should you receive? **Add** the prices of what you've bought. Then **subtract** that number from the amount you gave the clerk.

Can you figure out how many crates are filled per day at a factory? **Add** the number of crates filled per hour. Then **multiply** that number by the number of hours in the workday.

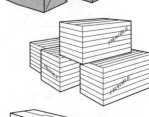

Using a receipt for 10 boxes of computer disks, can you figure the cost of 1 box? **Subtract** the tax. Then **divide** that number by the number of boxes purchased.

Solving Multistep Problems

Example: Of the 230 hand-embroidered napkins ordered, Carmen completed 41 in March, 49 in April, and 92 in May. How many more napkins does Carmen need to fill the order?

Step 1. Understand the question.	How many napkins does she have left to do?
Step 2. Decide what information is needed to solve the problem.	Need: 230 napkins in all 41, 49, and 92 napkins already done
Step 3. Think about how you might solve the problem.	To solve, I need two steps: (1) Add the numbers she's already done. (2) Subtract that number from the total she needs.
Step 4. Estimate an answer.	$40 + 50 + 90 = 180$ $230 - 180 = \mathbf{50}$
Step 5. Solve the problem and check your answer. Does it make sense?	Use the two operations:

$$\begin{array}{r} 41 \\ 49 \\ + \ 92 \\ \hline 182 \end{array} \qquad \begin{array}{r} 230 \\ - \ 182 \\ \hline \mathbf{48} \end{array}$$

48 napkins is close to your estimate and makes sense.

For each problem below, decide if you need one or more steps to solve it. Write how you would solve it. Finally, solve the problem.

1. Jamal sold 2 cars each day for 4 days in a row. His sales goal for the week is 10 cars. How many cars must he still sell to reach his sales goal?

   a. Single-step or Multistep

   b. How would you solve?

   _____

   _____

   c. Answer: _____

2. A baker uses 4 cups of flour for every loaf of bread he bakes. He estimates that he has about 18 cups of flour on hand. Does the baker have enough flour to make 5 loaves?

   a. Single-step or Multistep

   b. How would you solve?

   _____

   _____

   c. Answer: Yes or No

3. According to the data below, how many more phone books did Shift A deliver than Shift B this week?

	Shift A	Shift B
Saturday	120	110
Sunday	—	—
Monday	82	80
Tuesday	110	105
Wednesday	65	78
Thursday	100	100
Friday	90	85

   a. Single-step or Multistep

   b. How would you solve?

   _____

   _____

   c. Answer: _____

4. Last year, there were 20 children in Mrs. Hernandez's kindergarten class. She organized 6 field trips for the class. If each trip cost $5 per child, how much did the field trips cost in all?

   a. Single-step or Multistep

   b. How would you solve?

   _____

   _____

   c. Answer: _____

Unit 1 Review

A. Write the following decimal numbers.

1. twenty-five thousandths

2. ten and five tenths

3. eighty-nine hundredths

4. two tenths

5. one and forty-four thousandths

6. fifty-seven hundredths

B. Insert the correct symbol: <   >   =

7. 13.05 _____ 14.1

8. 10.3 _____ 10.21

9. 5.15 _____ 5.099

10. 120.1 _____ 120.100

11. 3.5 _____ 3.6

12. 0.20 _____ .200

C. Convert the following decimals to fractions.

13. .321   .87   .03   .001   .7

D. Write a fraction for each situation. Express fractions in lowest terms.

14. Juanita works 4 days per week. What fraction of a week does she work?

15. Of every 10 transistor boards that come off an assembly line, 2 are defective. What fraction of the boards are defective?

16. A meter is equal to 39 inches. What fraction of a meter is 13 inches?

17. LaTasha's take-home pay is $350 per week. She spends $50 of that on child care. What fraction of her pay does LaTasha spend on child care?

E. Write the correct fraction, decimal, or percent. Express fractions in lowest terms.

18. 20% = _____ = _____
       fraction   decimal

19. $\frac{45}{100}$ = _____ = _____
        decimal   percent

20. 0.50 = _____ = _____
        fraction   percent

21. 0.09 = _____ = _____
        fraction   percent

46

F. Grid in the answer to each problem.

22. 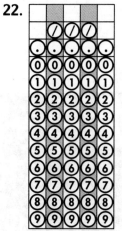 Paul and Margaret took a 100-mile trip to see their grandchildren. After they drove 60 miles, what fraction of their trip had they completed? Write your answer in lowest terms.

23. 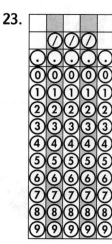 To find sales tax, Bruce multiplies the decimal form of the tax rate by the purchase price. If the sales tax rate is 8%, what is its decimal form?

G. Problems 24 through 28 refer to the chart below.

Household Supply, Inc.   Hand-Sewn Pot Holders   May 3

	Excellent	Passing	Rejected	Total
Line A	40	55	5	100
Line B	35	63	2	100
Line C	42	43	15	100

24. What fraction of the pot holders produced by Line A were excellent quality? Express in lowest terms.

25. What part of Line B's total pot holders were excellent quality? Express as a decimal.

26. a. What percent of Line C's pot holders were rejected?

b. Write this amount as a fraction reduced to lowest terms.

27. Of *all* pot holders produced on May 3 by the three lines, what fraction was excellent quality? (*Hint:* Add up the "total" column, then add up the "excellent" column.)

28. Of *all* pot holders produced on May 3 by the three lines, what fraction was rejected? (*Hint:* Add up the "total" column, then add up the "rejected" column.)

Working Together

1. Ask how many people in the class drove, were driven, took public transportation, or walked to class. Express each number as a fraction, a decimal, and a percent.

2. With a partner, brainstorm a list of where you would use fractions, decimals, and percents. Share your list with other groups to make a combined list for the class.

Unit 2

Decimals

Skills

Adding decimals

Subtracting decimals

Multiplying decimals

Dividing decimals

Tools

Rounding and estimating decimals

Calculator

Estimation

Equations

Problem Solvers

Understanding the question

Order of operations

Setup questions

Applications

Metric measurement

Checkbooks

Miles per gallon

A s you learned in Unit 1, the **decimal system** represents numbers smaller than one. A number that follows a decimal point has a value *less than 1*.

A money system based on dollars uses decimals. $10.50 means 10 *whole* dollars and 50 *hundredths* of a dollar.

In this unit, you'll work with money, and you will also see how decimals are used in other areas of our lives.

You may want to review these decimal lessons in Unit 1:

- Understanding Decimals ....page 14
- Reading Decimals ....page 16
- Writing Decimals ....page 18
- Comparing Decimals ....page 20

When Do I Use Decimals?

Each of the following situations involves decimals. Which ones sound familiar to you? Check off any experience that you've had.

- ☐ figuring travel mileage
- ☐ paying bills
- ☐ writing a check
- ☐ balancing a checkbook
- ☐ using a digital scale
- ☐ using the metric system for measurement (kilometers, centimeters, etc.)

If you've done any of the things above, you've used decimals. Describe some of these experiences on the lines below.

1. Describe a recent bill you paid. What were you paying for? Write the total amount, including cents. (Cents are a form of decimals.)

   _____

   _____

2. Now describe another time you've used money recently. It could be your last trip to the grocery store or the last time you rode the bus. Exactly how much money did you spend? Did you receive any change?

   _____

   _____

3. Have you ever used a car odometer to figure out how many miles you've driven? How are decimals used in an odometer?

   _____

   _____

4. Have you ever figured out how many miles a car could travel on a gallon of gas? If so, explain what you did.

   _____

   _____

Talk About It

When you make a purchase and receive change, you are working with cents—a form of decimals. How do you make sure you are getting the right change at a store or a restaurant? Discuss your methods with others.

Rounding and Estimating Decimals

What whole number is closest to 1.8? On the **number line,** you can tell that 1.8 is closer to 2 than to 1.

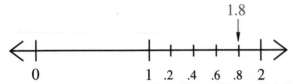

Rounding numbers is useful when you do not need an *exact* figure.

> ► **Symbol Used When Rounding Numbers**
>   ≈ means "is approximately equal to"

Example: You want to buy a bottle of shampoo for $3.59 and toothpaste for $2.89. You have $8 in your pocket. Do you have enough money?

To find the total cost, add $2.89 and $3.59. However, in this situation, you could **estimate,** since you don't need an exact number.

Round: $2.89 ≈ $3
         $3.59 ≈ $4

Add: $3
       + $4
       ─────
        $7

Rounding a Decimal to a Whole Number

Example: Round 3.39 and 3.75 to the nearest whole numbers.

Step 1. Circle the number in the tenths place.

3.③9   3.⑦5

Step 2. If the circled number is *less than 5,* round *down* to the nearest whole number.

3.③9 ⟶ **3**   3.⑦5 ⟶ **4**

If the circled number is *5 or more,* round *up* to the next whole number.

3.39 rounds to **3**; 3.75 rounds to **4.**

less than 5—round down   greater than 5—round up

A. Round the following decimals to the nearest whole number.

1. a. 10.9   1.7   4.09   **b.** 4.9   1.52   2.525

2. a. 900.5   900.4   12.925   **b.** 11.925   41.8   42.1

Rounding to a Decimal Place Value

What is 1.445 rounded to the nearest *tenth?* On a number line that shows hundredths, you can tell that 1.445 is closer to 1.4 than to 1.5.

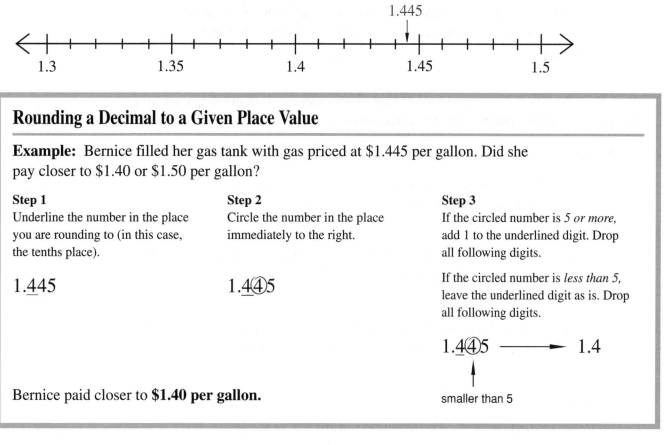

Rounding a Decimal to a Given Place Value

Example: Bernice filled her gas tank with gas priced at $1.445 per gallon. Did she pay closer to $1.40 or $1.50 per gallon?

Step 1
Underline the number in the place you are rounding to (in this case, the tenths place).

1.4̲45

Step 2
Circle the number in the place immediately to the right.

1.4④5

Step 3
If the circled number is *5 or more,* add 1 to the underlined digit. Drop all following digits.

If the circled number is *less than 5,* leave the underlined digit as is. Drop all following digits.

1.4④5 ———→ 1.4
↑
smaller than 5

Bernice paid closer to **$1.40 per gallon.**

B. Round the following decimals to the nearest *tenth.* **Visualize a number line to help you round, or follow the steps above.**

3. a. 1.93 ┌─ 1.95   4.092   **b.** 4.92   2.125   2.525

        Hint: What is 1 added to 9? Regroup the 1.

4. a. 0.78   0.82   10.95   **b.** 10.92   0.12   0.21

                      Hint: Regroup the 1.

C. Round each gas price to the nearest penny.

5.
> **BOB'S SAVE 'n SERVE**
> a. Regular............$1.219 per gallon
> b. Super...............$1.239 per gallon
> c. Supreme..........$1.289 per gallon

6.
> **PETRO-GAS STATION**
> a. Regular............$1.229 per gallon
> b. Super...............$1.439 per gallon
> c. Supreme..........$1.499 per gallon

Understanding the Question

Can you solve this problem?

> It takes Vera 15 minutes to drive Linny to school, 25 minutes to get from the school to work, and 5 minutes to get to her workstation to punch in for the morning.

There is no "problem" if there is no question. This example does not ask a question. Match each question below with the correct answer:

  a. Yes   **b.** 30 minutes   **c.** 45 minutes

1. How many minutes does it take Vera to get from home to her workstation each morning?

2. Will Vera get to work on time if she leaves the house at 8:05 and is required to punch in by 9:00?

> **Tip**
> To understand a problem well, *use your own words* to restate the question.

Did you answer 1. *c,* and 2. *a?* If so, you used the information correctly. To avoid mistakes, you must understand exactly what the question is asking.

A. In your own words, write what each question is asking you to find. Do not solve the problems. The first one is done for you.

1. A customer paid $14.99 for a classical music CD and $8.99 for a jazz cassette. She paid by check. For what amount should she make out the check, if it includes $1.49 tax?

   What are you being asked to find? <u>I need to find the total bill, including tax.</u>

2. A customer paid $14.99 for a classical music CD and $8.99 for a jazz cassette. She paid with two $20 bills. If there was $1.49 tax on the purchase, how much did she pay in all?

   What are you being asked to find? _____

3. A customer paid $14.99 for a classical music CD and $8.99 for a jazz cassette. She paid the clerk with two $20 bills. If there was $1.49 tax on the purchase, how much change should she get back?

   What are you being asked to find? _____

4. A customer paid $14.99 for a CD and $8.99 for a jazz cassette. She paid with two $20 bills. If there was $1.49 tax on the purchase, and the clerk gave her $13.53 in change, was she overcharged?

What are you being asked to find? _____

B. Match each problem with the question that belongs with it. Make sure that the question *can be answered* with the information given. Then solve each problem.

_____ **5.** The distance from Newton to Herald Square Mall is 24 miles. The distance from Newton to Shopper's Corner is 12 miles.

a. Can the distance between any 2 neighboring stations be more than 10 miles? (*Hint:* Draw a sketch before you try to answer this question.)

_____ **6.** Herald Square Mall has a land area of 24 square miles. Newton is about 40 square miles.

b. How many more miles does a Newton resident have to travel to shop at Herald Square Mall than to shop at Shopper's Corner?

_____ **7.** Andy drove 24 miles per hour from Newton to Shopper's Corner, a distance of 12 miles.

c. About how many minutes was the drive from Newton to Shopper's Corner?

_____ **8.** There are 4 gas stations evenly spaced along the 24-mile road between Newton and Herald Square Mall.

d. What is the combined area in square miles of Herald Square Mall and Newton?

C. Use the chart below to write two questions that *can be answered* with the information given. Then answer the questions.

9. Write an addition question.

_____

_____

_____

10. Write a subtraction question.

_____

_____

_____

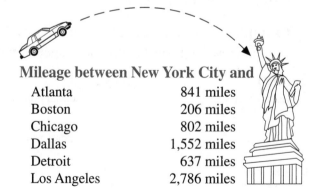

Mileage between New York City and

Atlanta	841 miles
Boston	206 miles
Chicago	802 miles
Dallas	1,552 miles
Detroit	637 miles
Los Angeles	2,786 miles

For another look at the five-step problem-solving plan, turn to page 235.

Adding Decimals

Adding decimals is like adding whole numbers. However, you need to line up the decimal points carefully.

Adding Decimals

Example: Marcus bought 1.45 pounds of Swiss cheese and .75 pound of cheddar cheese. How much cheese did he buy in all?

Step 1
Estimate first.

Step 2
Line up the decimal points.

Step 3
Bring the decimal point directly down in the answer.

Step 4
Add and regroup.

Regroup across decimal point.

Step 1	Step 2	Step 3	Step 4
$1.45 \approx 1$	1.45	1.45	¹ ¹ 1.45
$.75 \approx 1$	+ .75	+ .75	+ .75
$1 + 1 = 2$ pounds		.	**2.20 pounds**

Your answer, **2.2 pounds,** is close to your estimate of 2 pounds.

To add some decimals, you may need to use **placeholder zeros** to line up the decimal points correctly. Adding zeros *after* the last digit that follows a decimal point does *not* change the number's value.

Tip

A whole number has an "understood" decimal point after it.

$$9 = 9. = 9.0 = 9.00$$

Using Placeholder Zeros

Example: A costume designer fastened together 4 feet, 3.8 feet, and 5.25 feet of netting. How long was the fastened-together netting?

Step 1
Estimate first.

Step 2
Line up decimal points.

added zeros

Step 3
Bring the decimal point directly down in the answer.

Step 4
Add and regroup.

Regroup the 1.

Step 1	Step 2	Step 3	Step 4
$3.8 \approx 4$	4.00	4.00	¹ 4.00
$5.25 \approx 5$	3.80	3.80	3.80
$4 + 4 + 5 = 13$ feet	+ 5.25	+ 5.25	+ 5.25
		.	**13.05 feet**

Your answer, **13.05 feet,** is close to your estimate of 13 feet.

A. Add the following decimals. Write in zeros as necessary. The first one is started for you.

┌─ Add zero.

1.
$$\begin{array}{r} 2.8\overset{\downarrow}{0} \\ + 9.01 \\ \hline \end{array}$$
  $$\begin{array}{r} 10.25 \\ + 23 \\ \hline \end{array}$$
  $$\begin{array}{r} 60.5 \\ + .155 \\ \hline \end{array}$$
  $$\begin{array}{r} 90 \\ + 6.65 \\ \hline \end{array}$$

2. 1.2 + 4.05 + 12   5.7 + 7.8 + 2.3   0.9 + 7.07 + 4.5   0.5 + 3.5 + 0.08

B. Solve the following problems. Add zeros when necessary. To understand each problem, draw a picture if you'd like.

3. The perimeter (distance around) a square is found by adding the lengths of the 4 sides. If each side of a square is 1.5 inches, what is its perimeter?

4. A cyclist rides 4.3 miles from his home to Gate A of the forest preserve. He cycles an additional 5 miles on the trails there. Counting his return ride home from Gate A, how many miles did he ride?

5. Mr. Rodriguez bought a $5 box of paper and a $2.99 roll of ribbon. The tax was $.40. For what amount should he make out his check?

6. Mary walks 4 miles per hour. If she leaves her house at 9:00, can she walk to the grocery store, to the child-care center, and home again by 10:00?

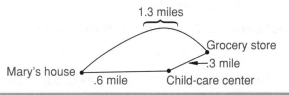

Making Connections: Grouping to Solve Problems

When adding a group of numbers, you may want to use strategies other than rounding.

Grouping Strategies

Example: 1.5 + 1.5 + 1.7 + 1.3 = ?

Strategy 1: Group halves.
.5 equals $\frac{1}{2}$. $\frac{1}{2}$ plus $\frac{1}{2}$ equals 1.

$$1.5 + 1.5 =$$
$$1 + 1 + 1 = 3$$

$$\begin{array}{r} 1.5 \\ 1.5 \end{array} \!\!= 3$$
$$\begin{array}{r} 1.7 \quad \approx 2 \\ + 1.3 \quad \approx 1 \\ \hline \approx 6 \end{array}$$

Strategy 2: Group "friendly numbers."
By grouping whole numbers that add up to 10, you can find decimals that add up to 1.

$$\begin{array}{r} 1.5 \\ 1.5 \end{array}\!\!= 3$$
$$\begin{array}{r} 1.7 \\ + 1.3 \\ \hline \end{array}$$ *Think:* 7 + 3 = 10
              So: .7 + .3 = 1

Exact answer: 1.7 + 1.3 = 3
               1.5 + 1.5 = 3
                   3 + 3 = **6**

Use the strategies above to add the following decimal numbers.

1. 4.5 + 8.5 + 10   **2.** 9.1 + 5.5 + 4.9 + 2.5   **3.** 42.6 + 38.4 + 19

Subtracting Decimals

To subtract decimals, first line up the decimal points. Then subtract as you do with whole numbers.

Subtracting Decimals

Example: An engineer's specs for a machine part call for a hole with a diameter of 3.8 centimeters. The current hole is 2.85 centimeters in diameter. By how much is the current hole off?

2.85 cm

Step 1
Estimate first.

Step 2
Line up decimal points.

Step 3
Bring the decimal point directly down in the answer.

Step 4
Regroup and subtract.

┌ Add zero.

┌ Regroup across decimal point.

$$3.8 \approx 4$$
$$-\,2.85 \approx 3$$
$$\approx 1 \text{ centimeter}$$

$$3.80$$
$$-\,2.85$$

$$3.80$$
$$-\,2.85$$

$$\overset{2\ \ 17}{3.8\!\!\diagup0}$$
$$-\,2.85$$
$$.95 \text{ centimeter}$$

Your answer, **.95 centimeter,** is close to your estimate of 1 centimeter.

A. Subtract the following decimals. The first one is started for you.

1.
$$2.000$$
$$-\ .011$$

$$3.5$$
$$-\ 2.9$$

$$10.925$$
$$-\ \ 8.5$$

$$5.025$$
$$-\ 4.1$$

2. $9.9 - 1.125$ $6.5 - 3$ $5.985 - 2.8$ $3.4 - 2.01$

3. $4.5 - 2.4$ $3.8 - 1.5$ $9 - 2.7$ $21.6 - 8.8$

B. To solve the following problems, subtract the second number from the first number. From that answer, subtract the third number to get a final answer. Use a calculator if you'd like. The first one is done for you.

4. $10 - 4.5 - 3.5$ $98.6 - 1 - 2.5$ $13.5 - 3.625 - 1.5$ $5.6 - 3.2 - 1.2$

Step 1   Step 2
$$10 \qquad 5.5$$
$$-\,4.5 \qquad -\,3.5$$
$$\overline{5.5} \qquad \overline{2.0}$$

5. $21.9 - 2.7 - 12$ $.125 - .001 - .001$ $5 - 2.3 - 1$ $104.50 - 31.25 - 2.25$

C. Solve the following problems. Estimate an answer first.

6. An engineering blueprint calls for a 10.5-foot clearance from some pipes to the wall. The pipes are currently 8.25 feet from the wall. How many feet will the pipes need to be moved?

7. The D-bus odometer showed this reading at the beginning of a trip from Indianapolis to Chicago:

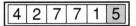

| 4 | 2 | 5 | 9 | 0 | 8 |

After the trip, the odometer read:

| 4 | 2 | 7 | 7 | 1 | 5 |

How many miles did the bus travel on this trip?

8. During an experiment, Patient A's body temperature went from 101.9° to 99.5°. Patient B's temperature went from 100° to 98.6°. Which patient showed the greater drop in temperature?

9. Naomi wants to order a tuna sandwich, milk, and chips. She has $6.50 in her purse, and she knows she'll need $1.20 for train fare to get home. Can she afford the lunch she wants?

Restaurant Prices
Burger $3.50
Tuna Sandwich $3.95
Turkey Club $5.95
Chips .... $.95
Soda $1.25
Milk .... $.95

Making Connections: Changing Fractions to Decimals

On page 35, you learned to change a fraction to a decimal. You can use that skill to add or subtract fractions.

Tip:
To change a fraction to a decimal, divide the numerator by the denominator.

$$\frac{4}{5} = 5\overline{)4.0} \quad (.8)$$

Example: Add $\frac{1}{2} + \frac{3}{4}$

Step 1
Change each fraction to a decimal. Divide the denominator into the numerator. You may use your calculator.

$\frac{1}{2} = 1 \div 2 = .50$

$\frac{3}{4} = 3 \div 4 = .75$

Step 2
Add or subtract the decimals.

$.50 + .75 = 1.25$

Step 3
Change the decimal to a fraction by putting the number over its place value. Reduce to lowest terms.

$1.25 = 1\frac{25}{100} = 1\frac{1}{4}$

↑ hundredths ↑ hundred

Add or subtract these fractions by first changing fractions to decimals.

1. $\frac{3}{5} - \frac{1}{4}$ **2.** $\frac{1}{4} + \frac{1}{2}$ **3.** $\frac{1}{5} + \frac{1}{4}$ **4.** $\frac{1}{2} - \frac{2}{5}$ **5.** $\frac{4}{5} - \frac{3}{4}$

Addition and Subtraction Equations

An **equation** is a mathematical sentence that contains an equal sign. In an equation, the value on one side of the equal sign is the same as the value on the other side.

Examples:

$$10 + 12 = 22 \qquad 2 + 1 = 1 + 2 \qquad 9 - 7 = 1 + 1$$

Many equations also use a variable, or letter, to stand for a number you do not know.

Examples:

$24 - x = 10$
(24 minus *something* equals 10.)

$n + 25 = 31$
(If you add 25 to *some number,* you get 31.)

Writing an equation can help you understand the relationship between numbers in a math problem. Use a variable to stand for a number you do not know.

Example 1: At the start of his weight loss plan, Mark weighed 185.5 pounds. At the end of three months, he weighed 179. How many pounds did Mark lose?

Write an equation:

$$\underset{\substack{\text{starting}\\\text{weight}}}{185.5} - \underset{\substack{\text{pounds}\\\text{lost}}}{x} = \underset{\substack{\text{new}\\\text{weight}}}{179}$$

or

$$\underset{\substack{\text{new}\\\text{weight}}}{179} + \underset{\substack{\text{pounds}\\\text{lost}}}{x} = \underset{\substack{\text{starting}\\\text{weight}}}{185.5}$$

Example 2: Mel paid Darlene the $12.75 he owed her. When Darlene put this amount in her pocketbook, she then had a total of $22.50. How much money did Darlene have before Mel repaid her?

Write an equation:

$$\underset{\substack{\text{amount she}\\\text{started with}}}{d} + \underset{\substack{\text{repaid}\\\text{loan}}}{\$12.75} = \underset{\substack{\text{total in her}\\\text{pocketbook}}}{\$22.50}$$

or

$$\underset{\substack{\text{total in her}\\\text{pocketbook}}}{\$22.50} - \underset{\substack{\text{amount she}\\\text{started with}}}{d} = \underset{\substack{\text{repaid}\\\text{loan}}}{\$12.75}$$

In each example above, the variable stands for the number you do *not* know. When writing an equation, you must first identify the value you do not know and assign a variable to that value.

A. Choose the correct equation for each problem below.

1. Beulah wrote a $41 check against her bank balance. Her new balance was $298. What was her balance before she wrote the check?

   (1) $x - 41 = \$298$

   (2) $x + 41 = \$298$

2. Beulah had $41 in her checking account. She made a deposit, and her new balance was $298. How much money did she deposit?

   (1) $\$41 + y = \$298$

   (2) $\$41 + \$298 = y$

3. Gary spent 45 minutes in the grocery store and 35 minutes getting his hair cut. How much total time did he spend on these two errands?

   (1) $m + 35 = 45$

   (2) $45 + 35 = m$

4. Gary spent 45 minutes in the grocery store and 35 minutes getting his hair cut. How much more time did he spend in the grocery store than the barber shop?

   (1) $t - 35 = 45$

   (2) $45 - 35 = t$

5. How many feet long is the gate pictured below?

   (1) $215 - 207 = g$

   (2) $215 + 207 = g$

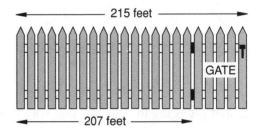

B. Write an addition or subtraction equation for each problem below. Remember that your first step is to let a variable stand for the value you do not know. Do not solve the problems.

6. A carpenter cut a 1.625-inch piece of wood from a piece of molding. The molding then measured 11.5 inches long. How long was the molding before he cut the piece?

   Equation: _____

7. Margo added 3.5 liters of water to a bowl. The bowl then contained 5.75 liters of liquid. How many liters of liquid were in the bowl to begin with?

   Equation: _____

8. A car traveled from Point A to Point C below, a total of 305.5 miles. How many miles is it from Point A to Point B?

   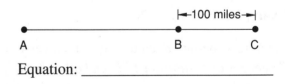

   Equation: _____

9. **Multiple Solutions** Write four equations for the following problem:

   Mike had 112 books in his science fiction collection. He added some new books, building the collection to 135 books. How many books did he add?

   Equations: _____

Solving Addition and Subtraction Equations

What is the value of x in the equation below?

$$75 + x = 125$$

To guess the value of x, you could try plugging in numbers and seeing if they make the equation true. Try plugging 25 into the first equation. Does it work?

$$75 + x \overset{?}{=} 125$$

$$75 + 25 \neq 125 \qquad \textbf{No, } x \textbf{ cannot equal 25.}$$

Can $x = 50$?

$$75 + 50 = 125 \qquad \textbf{Yes, } x = 50.$$

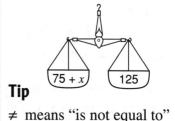
Guessing and plugging in values is one way to solve equations. A more efficient method is to solve the equation by *getting the variable alone on one side of the equal sign.* To do this, use **inverse operations.**

▶ **Addition** is the opposite, or inverse, of **subtraction.**

▶ **Subtraction** is the opposite, or inverse, of **addition.**

Notice how using inverse operations helps you get the variable alone on one side of the equal sign.

Example: $x + 15 = 70$

Since 15 is being *added* to x, use the inverse operation—**subtraction.**
To get x alone, *subtract 15 from both sides of the equation.*

Whatever you do to one side of the "balancing scale," you must do to the other.

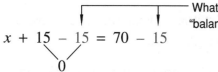

$$x + 15 - 15 = 70 - 15$$

Notice that subtracting 15 on the left side leaves x alone. The "scale" balances because you have taken the same number away from both sides of the equation. You now have the equation:

$$x = 70 - 15$$

$$x = 55$$

Solving a Subtraction or Addition Equation

Example: $x - 35 = 90$

Step 1
Decide what inverse operation to use to get the variable alone on one side of the equal sign.

Since 35 is being subtracted in the equation, use the inverse operation—
addition.

Step 2
Perform the inverse operation on *both sides* of the equal sign to get the *x* alone.

$$x - 35 + 35 = 90 + 35$$
$$0$$
Add 35 to both sides.

Step 3
Simplify to find the value of the unknown.

$$x = 90 + 35$$

$$x = 125$$

To check your work, plug your answer into the original equation:

$x - 35 = 90$; $125 - 35 = 90$; **yes,** $x = 125$

A. Solve the following addition and subtraction equations, using inverse operations when needed.

1. $x - 3.5 = 2.5$

2. $250 + h = 375$

3. $y + 4.2 = 6.2$

4. $x - .90 = 1.10$

5. $1.5 + z = 3$

6. $x - 10.5 = 3.1$

7. $10.6 - 3.6 = b$

8. $15 + 20.4 = h$

9. $p + 80 = 120$

10. $r + 12.5 = 12.8$

B. Write an equation for each problem below. Then solve the equation using inverse operations when needed.

11. Nina walked 6.5 miles over the weekend. Her total mileage for that week was 21.7 miles. How many miles did Nina walk before the weekend?

    Equation: _____

12. Esther cut a 1.5-pound piece from a leg of lamb. She had 3.75 pounds left over for stew. What was the total weight of the leg of lamb?

    Equation: _____

13. On his doctor's recommendation, Arturo cut 10 grams of fat from his daily diet. He now consumes only 25 grams of fat a day. How many grams was Arturo consuming before he cut his consumption?

    Equation: _____

14. Harry built his first table in 12.5 hours. He completed his second table in 10.5 hours. How much shorter is his second time?

    Equation: _____

Balancing a Checkbook

A **check** represents money in your checking account. If you write a check for more than the amount in your account, the check will bounce. You will owe the bank a fee and will still owe the amount of the check.

Balancing your checkbook regularly helps you avoid bouncing checks. Use a **check register** like the one shown below. Every time you write a check or make a deposit, record the **transaction** in your register.

Example: Pamela had a checking account balance of $832.40. On September 1, she wrote a check for her share of the rent: $320. On September 5, she paid $32.89 for groceries by check. On September 8, she **deposited** her paycheck of $458.75. This is her register:

		RECORD ALL CHARGES OR CREDITS THAT AFFECT YOUR ACCOUNT					
CHECK NUMBER	DATE	DESCRIPTION OF TRANSACTION	AMOUNT OF WITHDRAWAL	FEE (IF ANY)	✓ T	AMOUNT OF DEPOSIT	NEW BALANCE $832.40^1
#121	9/1	Peterson Rental Agency	$320^2				$512.40^3
#122	9/5	Giant Groceries	$32.89				$479.51^4
	9/8	paycheck deposit				$458.75^5	$938.26^6

To find the **new balance,** *subtract* the amount of a check that is written or *add* the amount of a deposit.

Example 1:

$832.40^1 balance before 9/1
− $320.00^2 rent check
$512.40^3 new balance

Example 2:

$479.51^4 balance before 9/8
+ $458.75^5 deposit (paycheck)
$938.26^6 new balance

A. On the check register on page 62, record the transactions from the story below. Find the new balance after each transaction.

On September 10, Pamela sent a $300 check (#123) to Townwide Savings Bank for this month's car payment. On the same day, she cashed a check for $25 (#124) at Corner Market. On September 17, Pamela deposited a $155 child support check from her ex-husband. She also wrote a check for $64.90 (#125) for groceries at Giant that same day. On September 20, Pamela paid $22.67 to Bell Telephone Company (#126), $12.73 to East Electric (#127), and $34.95 to Continental Cable Co. (#128).

B. Read the story below.

An Unexpected Windfall

Imagine that you receive a $3,000 bonus at work. You decide to pay off some bills and to buy some things you've been needing for a long time.

In the check register below, record some transactions you would make if you came upon such a windfall. Be sure to calculate the new balance after each transaction—and be sure there's enough money in your account before you write a check.

		RECORD ALL CHARGES OR CREDITS THAT AFFECT YOUR ACCOUNT					
CHECK NUMBER	DATE	DESCRIPTION OF TRANSACTION	AMOUNT OF WITHDRAWAL	FEE (IF ANY)	✓ T	AMOUNT OF DEPOSIT	NEW BALANCE $3,000.00

Multiplying Decimals

Multiplying decimals is like multiplying whole numbers. You just need to place the decimal point correctly in your answer.

Tip
Remember, a whole number has an "understood" decimal point to its right: $3 = 3. = 3.0$

Multiplying a Decimal

Example: Diego unloaded 12 cartons that each weigh 2.2 pounds. How many pounds do the cartons weigh altogether?

Step 1
Estimate first.

Step 2
Line numbers up at right.

Step 3
Multiply as with whole numbers.

Step 4
Count the digits following each decimal point in the problem. From the *right,* count out this same number of decimal places in the answer. Insert decimal point.

Step 1:
$$\begin{array}{r} 12 = 12 \\ \times\ 2.2 \approx\ 2 \\ \hline \approx 24 \text{ pounds} \end{array}$$

Step 2:
$$\begin{array}{r} 12 \\ \times\ 2.2 \\ \hline \end{array}$$

Step 3:
$$\begin{array}{r} 12 \\ \times\ 2.2 \\ \hline 24 \\ 240 \\ \hline 264 \end{array}$$

Step 4:
$$\begin{array}{r} 12 \quad\longleftarrow\quad 0 \text{ places} \\ \times\ 2.2 \quad\longleftarrow\quad +\ 1 \text{ place} \\ \hline 2\ 4 \qquad 1 \text{ place} \\ 24\ 0 \\ \hline \textbf{26.4 pounds} \end{array}$$
1 place

Your answer, **26.4 pounds,** is close to your estimate of 24 pounds.

Sometimes, when multiplying decimals, you must add a placeholder zero in your answer to keep the correct number of decimal places.

Multiplying with Placeholder Zeros

Example: What is 0.09×0.8?

Step 1
Estimate first.

Step 2
Line numbers up at right.

Step 3
Multiply as with whole numbers.

Step 4
Count the digits following each decimal point in the problem. From the *right,* count out this same number of decimal places in the answer. Insert decimal point.

Step 1:
$$\begin{array}{r} .09 \approx .1 \\ \times\ .8 \approx\ 1 \\ \hline \approx .1 \end{array}$$

Step 2:
$$\begin{array}{r} .09 \\ \times\ .8 \\ \hline \end{array}$$

Step 3:
$$\begin{array}{r} .09 \\ \times\ .8 \\ \hline 72 \end{array}$$

Step 4:
$$\begin{array}{r} .09 \quad\longleftarrow\quad 2 \text{ places} \\ \times\ .8 \quad\longleftarrow\quad +\ 1 \text{ place} \\ \hline .072 \qquad 3 \text{ places} \end{array}$$

Add this zero to get 3 places after the decimal point.

Your answer, **.072,** is close to your estimate of .1.

A. Put the decimal point in the correct place in each answer below. The first one is started for you.

1.
10.5 ← 1 place	2.1	.009	4.5	.5
× 5.5 ← + 1 place	× 9	× .4	× .001	× .1
5775 2 places	189	0036	0045	5

B. Multiply the following decimals. Estimate first. Be careful where you put your decimal point in your final answer.

2. .45 × 98   2.5 × 3.5   10.25 × 4   3.75 × 4.1   .18 × .2

3. .6 × 7.5   2.8 × 9.9   1.25 × 1.25   35 × 8.9   1.5 × 4.1

C. Solve the following problems. Remember to estimate first.

4. Hazel bought 15 birthday party favors priced at $.15 each. How much did she pay in all?

Estimate: _____ Answer: _____

5. A jeweler used 3 gold rings, each weighing 1.65 grams, to create a new piece of jewelry. What weight is this new piece?

Estimate: _____ Answer: _____

6. A shipping crate is filled with 18 containers of spring water. If each container holds 2.64 gallons, how many gallons of spring water are in the shipping crate?

Estimate: _____ Answer: _____

7. Ten metal washers each measuring 0.07 inch thick are stacked on the bolt pictured at right. Is any of the bolt left exposed?

}1 inch

Estimate: _____ Answer: Yes/No

D. Read these shortcuts for multiplying a decimal by 10, 100, or 1,000. Then multiply the decimals below.

- To multiply by 10, move the decimal point *1 place to the right.*   4.5 × 10 = 4.5 = 45

- To multiply by 100, move the decimal point *2 places to the right.*   4.5 × 100 = 4.50 = 450

Add 1 placeholder zero.

- To multiply by 1,000, move the decimal point *3 places to the right.*   4.5 × 1,000 = 4.500 = 4,500

Add 2 placeholder zeros.

8. 4.8 × 100   1.225 × 10   7.5 × 10   35 × 10   .62 × 1,000

9. 2.05 × 1,000   16.9 × 100   12.5 × 10   35.5 × 10   820 × 100

Gridding in Decimal Answers

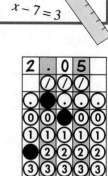
Some tests provide five-column **grids** for you to record your answers. The grid to the right shows the number 2.05. When you take such a test, your answers must fit in the grids provided. Always read the test instructions carefully to learn any special rules for entering decimals. Use the hints below to fit decimal answers in the grids for any test.

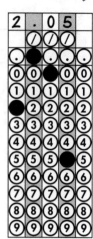

- Although you can start your answer in any column, start in the first column on the left. Then leave unused columns blank.

- Don't enter a leading zero before the decimal point. **Example:** Write .125 instead of 0.125.

- Drop any zeros that appear after the last digit in the decimal part of the answer. **Example:** Write .5 instead of 0.5000.

- If your answer has many digits, read the problem carefully for instructions about rounding your answer to a certain place value.

To enter decimal numbers in the answer grid, follow these steps:

1. Solve the problem.

2. Write the answer in the grid, with the decimal point in its own column.

3. Fill in the one correct circle in each column.

Filling in the Grid

Example: Michelle has a fever of 103.4°. After taking medication, her temperature drops 4.6°. What is her temperature in degrees now?

Step 1
Subtract the number of degrees the temperature fell to find the new temperature.

Subtract: 103.4
           − 4.6
           ‾‾‾‾‾
            98.8

After taking the medicine, her temperature is 98.8°.

Step 2
Write your answer in the top row of boxes. Put the decimal point in a box by itself. Do not write the degree symbol.

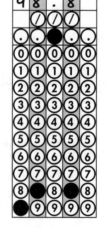

Step 3
Fill in the correct circles on the grid. Use the digits in the top row as a guide. Leave unused columns blank.

Study these examples to see how to fit decimal numbers in the grid.

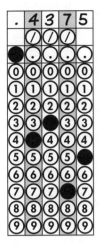 A calculator display shows the answer to a problem as 0.4375. Drop the leading zero.

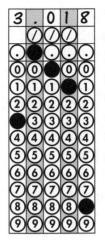 The sum of two decimals is 3.0180. Drop the zero to the right of the 8. This does not change the value of the answer.

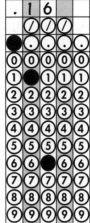 The answer to a problem is 0.15625. The instructions say to round the answer to the nearest hundredth. Enter .16.

Solve the following problems. Record your answers in the grids.

1. 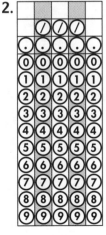 Each link in a large chain weighs 0.125 kilogram. If the chain contains 15 links, how many kilograms does the chain weigh?

2.  Tammy expected a job to take 10 hours. Instead, she finished the job in 7.75 hours. How many hours less was the actual time than her estimate?

3.  Troy walked 0.8 mile from home to school, 1.4 miles from school to soccer practice, and 2.1 miles from soccer practice to home. How many miles did Troy walk in all?

4. A sheet of plastic is 0.0125 meter thick. If you stack 40 sheets of plastic, what is the total thickness of the stack in meters?

Mixed Review

A. Round the following decimals to the nearest *whole number*.

1. 5.5   100.7   101.11   99.4   9.31

2. 2.7   2.441   87.29   87.59   0.51

B. Round the following numbers to the given place value.

3. 5.51 to the nearest *tenth*   82.908 to the nearest *hundredth*   12.329 to the nearest *tenth*

C. Do the following calculations. Estimate an answer first. Do the first problem in each row with a calculator if you'd like.

4. $6.5 + 8.9$ 3.5×5.5 $100.625 - 10.5$

5. $105.9 + 10.8$ 20.7×8 $21.9 - 16.9$

6. $34 + 16.9$ 21.9×4.225 $25 - 4.85$

7. $201.15 + 54.5$ 1.5×100 $210 - 35.005$

D. Change each fraction to a decimal by dividing the numerator by the denominator. You may use your calculator. Round each decimal to the nearest *hundredth*.

8. a. $\frac{2}{3}$ **b.** $\frac{4}{5}$ **c.** $\frac{1}{8}$ **d.** $\frac{9}{10}$ **e.** $\frac{7}{10}$ **f.** $\frac{3}{4}$ **g.** $\frac{5}{6}$

E. Change each fraction to a decimal, using a calculator if you'd like. Then complete the calculations. Write your final answer as a fraction. See page 57 if you need a refresher.

9. $\frac{1}{2} + \frac{3}{4}$ $\frac{4}{5} + \frac{1}{4}$ $\frac{2}{5} + \frac{1}{2}$

10. $\frac{1}{2} \times \frac{1}{4}$ $\frac{9}{10} - \frac{3}{5}$ $\frac{3}{10} \times \frac{3}{4}$

F. Solve the following equations.

11. $p + 250 = 495$ $x - 26 = 44$ $\$1.99 + d = \$19.99$

12. $\$12.50 - \$2.00 = p$ $g - 14.7 = 10.1$ $750 + m = 1{,}000$

G. Solve the following problems.

13. The perimeter of a triangle is found by adding the lengths of its three sides. What is the perimeter of the triangle below?

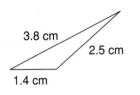

3.8 cm

2.5 cm

1.4 cm

14. Rita began the week with a $760.40 bank balance. She wrote two checks: one for $43.55 and one for $100.09. She also deposited $200. What is her new bank balance?

15. The area of a rectangle is found by multiplying the length by the width. The resulting number is expressed in *square units*. How many square inches is the rectangle below?

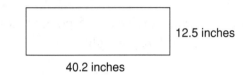

12.5 inches

40.2 inches

16. Explain Mrs. Abromovitz got $11.14 change back from a purchase totalling $3.86. If she gave the clerk a check for $16, did she get the correct change? How do you know?

H. Grid in the answer to each problem.

17.

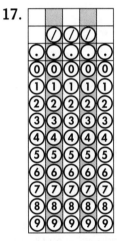

A container holds 1.5 liters of a chemical mixture. A scientist pours 0.85 liter of the mixture into a new container. How many liters are left in the first container?

18.

A carpenter glues two sheets of wood together to make a tabletop. The sheets are 1.4 and 2.85 centimeters thick. If the tabletop is supposed to be 4.2 centimeters thick, how many centimeters too thick is the construction?

I. Find the new balance after each transaction below.

CHECK NUMBER	DATE	DESCRIPTION OF TRANSACTION	AMOUNT OF WITHDRAWAL	FEE (IF ANY)	✓ T	AMOUNT OF DEPOSIT	NEW BALANCE $629.43
1415	5/10	Super-K Foods	$63.93				$565.50
1416	5/13	Bank of the States (car payment)	$282.88				
	5/15	deposit (paycheck)				$795.85	
1417	5/15	Bette's Boutique	$82.14				
1418	5/17	Citizen's Gas	$49				
	5/20	deposit				$250.00	

RECORD ALL CHARGES OR CREDITS THAT AFFECT YOUR ACCOUNT

Dividing a Decimal by a Whole Number

When dividing a decimal by a whole number, be sure you place the
decimal point in the correct place in the answer.

Dividing a Decimal by a Whole Number

Example: Ms. Kato divides a 3.5-pound box of candy into 5 equal bags.
How much does each bag weigh?

Step 1
Estimate first.

$3.5 \approx 4$

$5\overline{)4}$ is a little less than 1.

Step 2
Set up the division
problem.

$5\overline{)3.5}$

Step 3
Place a decimal point directly
above the decimal point in the
number being divided.

Bring the decimal
point directly up.

$5\overline{)3.5}$

Step 4
Divide just as with whole
numbers.

$$\begin{array}{r} .7 \text{ pound} \\ 5\overline{)3.5} \\ \underline{3\ 5} \\ 0 \end{array}$$

Your answer, **.7 pound,** is close to your estimate of a little less than 1 pound.

Adding Zeros to Divide

Example: A carpenter divided an 8.3-meter board into 4 equal shelves. How long is
each shelf?

Step 1
Estimate first.
$8.3 \approx 8$

$$\begin{array}{r} 2 \text{ meters} \\ 4\overline{)8} \end{array}$$

Step 2
Set up. Place a decimal
point directly above.

$4\overline{)8.3}$

Step 3
Start dividing just as you
would whole numbers.

$$\begin{array}{r} 2.0 \\ 4\overline{)8.3} \\ \underline{8} \\ 0\ 3 \end{array}$$
Since 4
cannot go
into 3, put
zero here.

Step 4
Continue dividing. Add
zeros if necessary.

$$\begin{array}{r} 2.075 \text{ meters} \\ 4\overline{)8.300} \\ \underline{8} \\ 0\ 30 \\ \underline{28} \\ 20 \\ \underline{20} \\ 0 \end{array}$$
Add zeros
and bring
them down.

Your answer, **2.075 meters,** is very close to your estimate of 2 meters.

A. Do the following division problems. Follow the steps above.

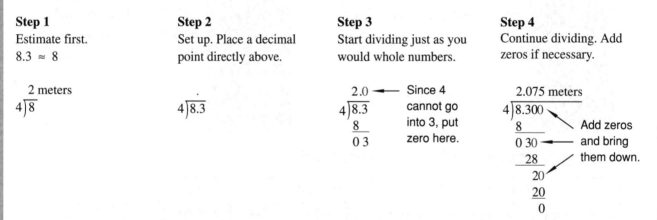

1. $4\overline{)4.5}$ $2\overline{)8.92}$ $7\overline{)10.57}$ $12\overline{)2.28}$

2. $13.5 \div 6$ $1.75 \div 25$ $204 \div 8$ $90.35 \div 5$

means "divided by"

B. Solve the following problems. Remember to estimate first.

Problems 3 and 4 refer to this information.

> To find an **average,** *add* a group of numbers, then *divide* this total by the number of numbers in the group.
>
> **Example:** What is the average of 1.3, 2.5, and 0.1?
>
> 1.3 + 2.5 + .1 = 3.9   3.9 ÷ 3 = 1.3
>
> The average is **1.3.**

3. Mr. Bertino's class recorded these weights in pounds during an experiment:

   26.5   50.4   25.25   30.1   42.9

   What was the average weight?

4. What is the average workday on this time card?

Monday	4.5 hours
Tuesday	8.25 hours
Wednesday	8.5 hours
Thursday	10.25 hours
Friday	7.5 hours

5. A janitor wanted to divide 8.5 liters of cleaning solution evenly into 4 buckets. Each bucket holds 2.2 liters. Will these buckets hold the solution?

6. Bridget and her 3 friends decided to split a $16.04 lunch bill evenly among themselves. How much will each person pay?

7. **Label** Alison cut a 10.5-foot rope into 3 equal segments, shown below. Label each segment with its length.

   Segment A ⟨〰〰〰〰〰〰⟩
   Segment B ⟨〰〰〰〰〰〰⟩
   Segment C ⟨〰〰〰〰〰〰⟩

C. Use the shortcuts on page 65 for multiplying decimals by 10, 100, or 1,000 to help you think of shortcuts for *dividing decimals.* (*Hint:* Dividing is the *opposite* of multiplying.)

8. To multiply by 10, move the decimal point *1 place to the right.*

   To divide by 10, move the decimal point _____ _____.

9. To multiply by 100, move the decimal point *2 places to the right.*

   To divide by 100, move the decimal point _____ _____.

10. To multiply by 1,000, move the decimal point *3 places to the right.*

    To divide by 1,000, move the decimal point _____ _____.

D. Use your new shortcut rules to solve the following division problems.

11. 34.5 ÷ 10   203.56 ÷ 1,000   1.5 ÷ 100

    Hint: Add zeros when necessary.

Dividing by a Decimal

When dividing a number by a decimal, first *change the divisor to a whole number.*
Then divide as you learned in the last lesson.

Dividing a Decimal by a Decimal

Example: $3.5\overline{)15.75}$

Step 1
Estimate first.

$15.75 \approx 16$
$3.5 \approx 4$

$16 \div 4$ is 4.

Step 2
Change the divisor to a whole number. Move the decimal point in the divisor to the right until the divisor becomes a whole number.

divisor

$3.5\overline{)15.75}$

one place

Step 3
Move the decimal point in the dividend *the same number of places.*

dividend

$35.\overline{)157.5}$

one place

Step 4
Bring the decimal point directly up from its *new* position. Divide as usual.

$$35\overline{)157.5} \quad \begin{array}{r} 4.5 \\ \hline 140 \\ \hline 17\ 5 \\ 17\ 5 \\ \hline 0 \end{array}$$

Your answer of **4.5** is close to your estimate of 4.

Pay close attention to how you use zeros with decimals.

Using Zeros to Divide Decimals

Example: A bakery employee divided 9 pounds of fudge into 1.25-pound boxes. How many boxes did she fill?

Step 1
Estimate first.

$1.25 \approx 1$

$1\overline{)9}$ → 9 boxes

Note: Actually, fewer than 9 boxes will be filled because 1.25 is greater than 1.

Step 2
Move the decimal point in the divisor to the right until the divisor becomes a whole number.

$1.25\overline{)9.}$

A whole number is understood to have a decimal point *after* it.

Step 3
Move the decimal point in the dividend *the same number of places.*

$125.\overline{)900.}$

Add zeros so you can move the decimal point the correct number of places.

Step 4
Bring the decimal point directly up from its *new* position. Divide as usual.

$$125\overline{)900.0} \quad \begin{array}{r} 7.2 \\ \hline 875.0 \\ \hline 25\ 0 \\ 25\ 0 \\ \hline 0 \end{array}$$

Add zero.

The employee could fill **7 boxes.** Ignore the remaining .2 because the problem asks for the number of *filled* boxes. Your answer is close to your estimate of *fewer than 9* boxes.

A. Solve the following division problems.

1. $.24\overline{)48}$ $.24\overline{).48}$ $2.4\overline{)4.8}$ $2.4\overline{).48}$

2. $.925 \div .25$ $92.5 \div .25$ $92.5 \div 2.5$ $.925 \div 2.5$

3. $.63 \div .3$ $6.39 \div .3$ $.639 \div .03$ $6.39 \div .03$

B. Solve the following division problems.

4. $2.8\overline{)5.6}$ $2.8\overline{)56}$ $.28\overline{)5.6}$ $.28\overline{)56}$ $.28\overline{).56}$

5. $.125 \div 625$ $12.5 \div 6.25$ $1.25 \div 62.5$ $1.25 \div .625$ $12.5 \div 625$

C. Solve the following word problems. Estimate an answer first.

6. Suppose Roland's Deli charged you $7.24 for 3.5 pounds of sandwich meat. How much did you pay per pound? Round your answer to the nearest penny.

7. The times in the chart below were recorded during a radiation experiment. Find the average time elapsed. (If you need to review averages, turn back to page 71.)

Exposure #	Time Elapsed
101	2.25 seconds
102	2.05 seconds
103	2.5 seconds
104	1.175 seconds
105	1.5 seconds

8. One serving of the crackers below is 1.2 ounces. How many servings are in the box?

Snackee Crackers
Net Wt. 12 oz.

9. In March it rained 3.65 inches. In April it rained 4.5 inches. In the first half of May, it rained 3.25 inches. What was the average rainfall per month for these 2.5 months?

10. Louis lost 22.5 pounds in 6 months. How many pounds did he lose per month, on average?

11. A man owed $351.75. If he paid back the loan in installments of $50.25 per week, how many weeks did it take him to pay off the loan?

12. **Explain** Thelma paid $126.35 for 3 tablecloths and some napkin rings. The napkin rings were priced at $.95 each. If the tablecloths cost $114.95 total, how many napkin rings did Thelma buy? Explain how you arrived at your answer.

Metric Measurement

Metric measurement is a measurement system based on the decimal system. Most countries in the world use the metric system. However, the United States uses the English system of measurement. Contrast the metric with the English system:

	English System	Metric System
Basic unit of length	foot	meter
Basic unit of weight	pound	gram
Basic unit of volume	quart	liter

Fill in as many facts below as you can. The metric facts are completed.

English System		Metric System	
Number of inches in a foot:	_____	Number of centimeters in a meter:	100
Number of feet in a yard:	_____	Number of millimeters in a meter:	1,000
Number of inches in a yard:	_____	Number of millimeters in a centimeter:	10
Number of feet in a mile:	_____	Number of meters in a kilometer:	1,000
Number of ounces in a pound:	_____	Number of milligrams in a gram:	1,000
Number of pounds in a ton:	_____	Number of grams in a kilogram:	1,000

Do you see any pattern in the English system? Probably not. You should have written in *12, 3, 36, 5,280, 16,* and *2,000.*

What is the pattern in the metric system? Each number is a multiple of 10 (10, 100, 1,000). The chart below compares the basic units of metric measurement—**meter, gram,** and **liter**—to other metric units. Each unit is 10 times larger or smaller than the units closest to it.

× 1,000	× 100	× 10	× 1	× .1	× .01	× .001
kilometer	**hecto**meter	**deko**meter	METER	**deci**meter	**centi**meter	**milli**meter
kilogram	**hecto**gram	**deko**gram	GRAM	**deci**gram	**centi**gram	**milli**gram
kiloliter	**hecto**liter	**deko**liter	LITER	**deci**liter	**centi**liter	**milli**liter

To **convert** one measurement unit into another, move the decimal point

- to the **left** to convert to a *larger* unit
- to the **right** to convert to a *smaller* unit

Converting to a Larger Unit

Example: Suppose a chemist added 4 grams to 330 milligrams. What is the combined weight in grams? (*Hint:* First convert milligrams to grams.)

Step 1. Find **milligrams** on the chart on page 74.	Gram	Deci	Centi	(Milli)

Gram   Deci   Centi   (Milli)

Step 2. Count how many places **grams** are *to the left*.

Gram   Deci   Centi   (Milli)
③places ②places ①place

Step 3. Move the decimal point the *same number of places* in the *same direction*.

.330 milligrams = .330 or .33 gram

Step 4. Add grams to grams.

4 grams + .33 gram = **4.33 grams**

The combined weight is **4.33 grams.**

Converting to a Smaller Unit

Example: Change 22.5 meters to centimeters.

Step 1.
Find **meters** on the chart on page 74.

(Meter)   Deci   Centi   Milli

Step 2.
Count how many places **centimeters** are *to the right*.

(Meter)   Deci   Centi   Milli
①place ②places

Step 3.
Move the decimal point the *same number of places* in the *same direction*.

22.50 meters = **2,250 centimeters**

Add a zero.

The answer is **2,250 centimeters.**

A. Solve the following conversion problems.

1. 2,500 milliliters = _____ liters

2. 1.4 kilograms = _____ grams

3. 90 meters = _____ centimeters

4. 8.2 liters = _____ milliliters

5. 50 grams = _____ kilograms

6. 90 centimeters = _____ meter

B. Solve the following problems. Convert the units first.

7. A carpenter has a 6-meter-long board that he wants to cut into 30-centimeter lengths. How many of these lengths can he cut?

8. A seamstress cut 25.5 centimeters from a roll of cloth tape that was 2 meters long. How many centimeters were left on the roll?

Estimating with Friendly Numbers

Dividing can be messy because of remainders. Even when you round numbers, the division may not come out even. For example, estimate a solution to this problem:

$$7.1\overline{)36}$$

Even if you round 7.1 to 7 and 36 to 40, your division does not get easier. This is because 7 does not go into 40 evenly.

To estimate an answer, you can use "friendly" or compatible numbers. **Friendly numbers** are easy to add, subtract, multiply, and divide.

Example 1: Estimate: 36 ÷ 7.1 = ?

Think: What number *close* to 36 does 7 divide into evenly?

7 × 1	7 × 2	7 × 3	7 × 4	7 × 5	7 × 6
7	14	21	28	35	42

35 ÷ 7 = 5, so **36 ÷ 7.1 ≈ 5.**

In this next example, you can ignore the decimal point at first.

Example 2: Estimate: 51.1 ÷ 2.4 = ?

Think: What are friendly numbers close to 51 and 24 ?

50 and 25 are friendly numbers because 50 ÷ 25 = 2.

Set up the problem using your friendly numbers and divide.

$$2.5\overline{)50.0} = 20.$$

51.1 ÷ 2.4 ≈ 20

Notice why these pairs of friendly numbers are easy to work with:

1.4 and 280	45 and 9.0	1.25 and 6.25
(28 ÷ 14 = 2)	(90 ÷ 45 = 2)	(625 ÷ 125 = 5)

A. Change one number in each pair below to make the numbers friendly. Remember—you should be able to divide with no remainders. The first one is done for you.

1. 1.4 and 2.9 *become* __1.4__ and __2.8__

2. 10.4 and 33 *become* _____ and _____

3. 2.1 and 40 *become* _____ and _____

4. 1.8 and 35 *become* _____ and _____

B. Estimate an answer to the following problems. Use rounding, friendly numbers, or both. Use your estimate to choose the answer from the choices given.

5. A customer bought 4.7 pounds of cheese at a total price of $9.12. How much was the cheese per pound?

   (1) $1.94
   (2) $1.40
   (3) $1.20

6. What is 519 milligrams divided into 25.5-milligram weights?

   (1) 20.35
   (2) 40
   (3) 45

7. Dolores bought 5.2 yards of fabric on sale for $1.98 per yard. How much did she pay in all?

   (1) $26.05
   (2) $10.30
   (3) $3.50

8. One inch is equal to 2.54 centimeters. How many inches are there in 51.2 centimeters?

   (1) about 20
   (2) about 10
   (3) about 5

Making Connections: Estimating with 10s

Friendly numbers are numbers that are easy to work with. For example, when you divide by 11, numbers like 22, 33, and 44 are friendly. When you divide by 2, even numbers such as 4, 6, 8, and 10 are friendly.

One of the friendliest numbers to work with is 10. To multiply or divide by 10, just move the decimal place to the right or left. To add, you can use groups of 10. Study two other ways to use the number 10:

Example 1: $5 \times 12.7 \times 2 = ?$

Think:
$5 \times 2 = 10$
$10 \times 12.7 = \mathbf{127}$

Example 2: About how many 9.4-minute filmstrips can be shown in 60 minutes?

Think:
Change 9.4 to 10, and divide:
$60 \div 10 = \mathbf{6\ filmstrips}$

Use "easy 10s" to do the following problems.

1. $44.6 + 22.5 + 11.5 + 2.4$

2. $75 \times 5 \times 2$

3. Estimate: $80 \div 9.3$ is about _____.

4. Estimate: $12.5 \div 98$ is about _____.

Order of Operations

Sometimes you may have to do more than one operation to solve a math problem. To do so, follow the rules at right.

> ► **Order of Operations**
> 1. First, do any operation in parentheses.
> 2. Next, do multiplication and/or division.
> 3. Finally, do addition and/or subtraction.

Using the Order of Operations

Example: $60 + 165 \div (6 + 9) = ?$

Step 1
Do the operation in parentheses.

Step 2
Next, do the division.

Step 3
Finally, do the addition.

$60 + 165 \div (6 + 9)$

$60 + 165 \div 15$

$60 + 11$

71

The correct answer is **71**. If you had done the operations from left to right, you could have come up with 46.5, which is incorrect. This shows how important it is to follow the order of operations.

A. Use the order of operations to find the value of each expression.

1. $950 - 25 + (14 \times 3)$

2. $20 \times 4 + 6$

3. $20 \times (4 + 6)$

4. $100 \div (10 - 5)$

5. $64 + 16 \div (13 + 7)$

6. $(12 \times 5) \div (5 - 4)$

7. $5 \times 4 \times 3 \times 2 - 6$

8. $(5 \times 4) \times (3 \times 2) - 6$

9. $100 \div 10 - 5$

To solve some problems, you may need to write your own expression.

> **Tip**
> In math expressions, division can be shown with a ÷ or a fraction bar.
>
> $(2 - 1) \div 3 = \dfrac{2 - 1}{3}$

Writing an Expression

Example: Glenda took 1 cup of flour from a 10-cup bag. She divided the remaining flour into 3-cup tins. Write an expression to show how many tins of flour she had.

Step 1
Write an expression for the subtraction. Put it in parentheses.

$(10 - 1)$

↑   ↑
bag   cup removed

Step 2
Add the expression for the division step. Use parentheses to keep operations separate.

$\left(10 - 1\right) \div 3 = \dfrac{10 - 1}{3}$

3-cup tin ⌐

B. Write an expression for each problem below.

Problems 10 and 11 refer to the following menu.

Grilled Cheese $2.25
Turkey Club $5.95
Hamburger $3.20
Cheeseburger $3.85
Milk/Soda .... $.85
Coffee .... $.70

10. Danielle paid for a lunch order of 3 turkey clubs, 1 cheeseburger, and 4 coffees. Write an expression that shows how much she paid.

11. Mr. Martinez paid for 1 grilled cheese and 2 sodas with a $10 bill. Write an expression that shows how much change he should receive.

Sometimes you'll have to recognize the correct expression, or **setup.**

Example: Chien has a checking account balance of $325. He writes a check for 4 pairs of socks, each pair priced at $5.49 including tax. Which expression shows his new bank balance?

   (1) ($325 − $5.49) × 4

   (2) $325 + ($5.49 × 4)

   (3) $325 − ($5.49 × 4)

Choice **(3)** is correct: first, find the total amount paid for the socks ($5.49 × 4); then subtract that total from the balance ($325).

C. Choose the correct expression for each problem below.

12. Paulo bought a box of nails for $4.99 and a can of paint for $13. He received $2.01 in change. Which expression represents the amount of money Paulo gave the clerk?

   (1) $4.99 + $13

   (2) $13 − $4.99 − $2.01

   (3) $4.99 + $13 + $2.01

13. Beatriz soldered a 6.8-meter pipe to a 3.5-meter pipe, then divided the new pipe into 2 equal pieces. Which expression shows the length of each new pipe?

   (1) 6.8 − (3.5 ÷ 2)

   (2) (6.8 + 3.5) × 2

   (3) (6.8 + 3.5) ÷ 2

14. It takes most assembly workers .6 minute to wrap a package. Which expression shows how many packages 2 workers can wrap in an hour (60 minutes)?

   (1) (60 ÷ .6) × 2

   (2) (60 ÷ .6) ÷ 2

   (3) 60 ÷ (.6 × 2)

15. One pint is equal to 16 fluid ounces. Which expression represents the number of fluid ounces in a mixture of 3 pints juice and .5 pint water?

   (1) 16 ÷ (3 + .5)

   (2) 16 × (3 + .5)

   (3) 16 × 3 + .5

Calculators and Decimal Answers

Working with decimals on a calculator is easy and can save you time. Suppose you and 2 friends decide to evenly split the cost of a gift to another friend.

The gift, including tax, costs $24.50.

decimal point

Key in:

| 2 | 4 | • | 5 | 0 | ← Always enter the number *being divided* first.

÷

3

=

Your display reads:

| 24.50 |
| 24.5 |
| 3. |
| 8.1666666 |

How much money *is* that?

Repeating Decimals

When you divide 24.5 by 3, your calculator display reads 8.1666666. This is called a **repeating decimal.** The digit 6 could repeat itself forever. Your calculator drops any digits that do not fit in its display window.

For another look at the scientific calculator, see pages 239–240.

To figure out how much each friend will pay for the gift, round the repeating decimal to the hundredths place:

8.1666666 rounds to **$8.17**

└ Greater than 5, so round up.

Notice that when you round up to $8.17 and multiply by 3, you actually get a penny more than you need.

80

Decimal Series

Other division problems result in decimals that repeat a **series** of digits.

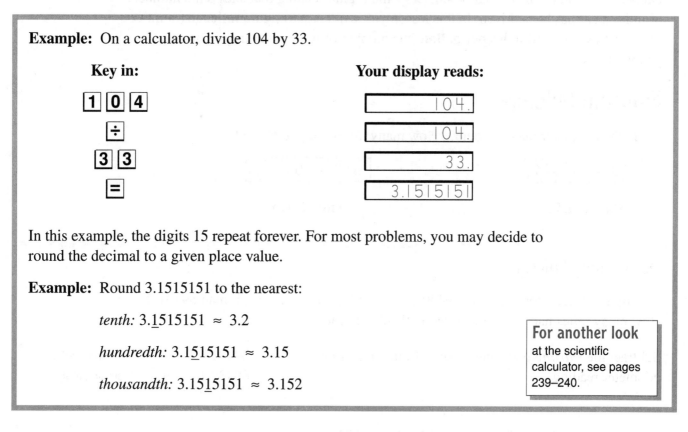

Example: On a calculator, divide 104 by 33.

Key in:	Your display reads:

Key in:
1 0 4
÷
3 3
=

Your display reads:
104.
104.
33.
3.1515151

In this example, the digits 15 repeat forever. For most problems, you may decide to round the decimal to a given place value.

Example: Round 3.1515151 to the nearest:

tenth: 3.1515151 ≈ 3.2

hundredth: 3.1515151 ≈ 3.15

thousandth: 3.1515151 ≈ 3.152

> **For another look**
> at the scientific calculator, see pages 239–240.

A. Do the following problems with your calculator. Write the repeating digits to the *ten thousandths* place.

1. 5 ÷ 6

Repeating digit:

—.— — — —

2. 525 ÷ 77

Repeating digits:

—.— — — —

3. 121 ÷ 90

Repeating digit:

—.— — — —

B. Solve the following problems. Round the repeating decimals as indicated. Round money to the nearest cent.

4. Rosa and her 2 sisters divided up the cost of their parents' anniversary party evenly. The total cost of the party was $695. How much should each woman pay?

5. To the nearest tenth, what is 124 divided by 82?

6. To the nearest thousandth, what is 7 ÷ 3?

7. Carl bought 6 portable CD players for $958 total. How much did he pay for each, to the nearest cent?

8. Estimate What is $300 divided evenly among 9 people? Use your calculator to check the estimate. Was it close?

Mileage and Miles per Gallon

On page 22, you learned about odometers—the digital reading that shows the number of miles a car has been driven. In this lesson you will learn to figure **mileage** (number of miles traveled) and **miles per gallon** (the number of miles a car travels on one gallon of gas).

Figuring Mileage

Study the odometer readings below. How many miles did you travel?

| 6 | 9 | 4 | 3 | 9 | 1 |

start of trip

| 6 | 9 | 4 | 9 | 1 | 8 |

end of trip

Determining Mileage

Example: A car odometer read 69439.1 on Monday. On Thursday, it read 69491.8. How many miles had this car traveled in this time span?

Subtract the *starting* odometer reading from the *ending* odometer reading.

$$
\begin{array}{r}
69491.8 \quad \longleftarrow \text{ ending reading}\\
-\ 69439.1 \quad \longleftarrow \text{ starting reading}\\
\hline
52.7
\end{array}
$$

The car traveled **52.7 miles** between Monday and Thursday.

A. Determine mileage from the following odometer readings. Use a calculator if you'd like.

	Starting Reading	Ending Reading	Miles Traveled
1.	9 9 8 1 2 1	9 9 8 5 0 0	_____
2.	1 7 6 5 2 9	2 0 8 0 9 1	_____
3.	5 0 0 2 0 3	5 1 0 9 0 9	_____
4.	3 5 5 5 5 3	4 0 3 4 5 8	_____
5.	4 6 2 9 8 7	4 6 9 8 7 1	_____

Figuring Miles per Gallon

Car buyers often look for cars that get good mileage—that is, cars that can travel as many miles as possible on one gallon of gas.

> **Tip**
>
> To find miles per gallon (MPG), divide:
>
> $$\frac{\text{total number of miles driven}}{\text{number of gallons used}} = \text{MPG}$$

Determining Miles per Gallon

Example: Joan's 6.2-gallon gas tank was full and her odometer read 77,761.2 at the start of her trip. At the end of her trip, the odometer read 77,940.9 and her tank was empty. To the nearest tenth, how many miles did she get per gallon?

Step 1
To figure out *mileage* (number of miles driven), subtract the starting odometer reading from the ending reading.

```
  77,940.9
- 77,761.2
  ────────
   179.7 miles
```

Step 2
To figure *miles per gallon,* divide the miles driven by the number of gallons used.

179.7 ÷ 6.2 = 28.98 MPG

miles   gallons

Step 3
The problem asks for the miles rounded to the nearest tenth.

28.98 ≈ **29.0 MPG**

Joan's car got about **29.0 miles per gallon** on this trip.

B. Answer the following problems. Use a calculator if you'd like.

Martha left Philadelphia for Atlanta at 5 P.M. Thursday with a full tank of gas. When she started, the odometer reading was 34,781.1. At the end of the first leg of her trip, the odometer reading was 35,121.1.

6. **a.** How many miles did Martha travel on the first leg of her trip?

   b. When she recorded the ending odometer reading above, Martha refilled her gas tank with 12.5 gallons. To the nearest mile, how many miles per gallon did she get on this leg of her trip?

   c. When Martha refilled her gas tank, she paid $1.299 per gallon of gas. What total amount did she pay to refill the tank?

Unit 2 Review

A. **Solve the following problems. Estimate an answer first. Do the first problem in each row with a calculator if you'd like.**

1. $3.74 - 1.5$ $200.5 - 89.9$ $30.05 - 26$

2. $1.75 + 3.25$ $50.125 + 5.75$ $21.04 + 1.275$

3. 3.5×1.25 5.55×6 80.9×2.05

4. $6 \div 1.5$ $2.09 \div 4$ $125.5 \div .125$

5. $4.5 \times (75.25 + 100.75)$ $90.25 \div (90.5 - 85.5)$ $(5.4 \times 3) + (2.8 \times 9)$

B. **Choose the best answer to each word problem below. Remember to estimate an answer first.**

6. One pound of ground beef at Nellie's Meats costs \$2.48. How much will a $\frac{1}{2}$-pound package cost?

   (1) \$5.96
   (2) \$1.24
   (3) \$.62
   (4) \$.59
   (5) \$.48

7. Put the following lengths in order, from *longest* to *shortest*:

   A: 0.425 meters   D: 0.075 meters
   B: 0.42 meters   E: 0.75 meters
   C: 1.25 meters

   (1) C, A, D, E, B
   (2) C, D, A, B, E
   (3) A, C, D, E, B
   (4) A, B, D, E, C
   (5) C, E, A, B, D

8. Five housemates will split a \$108.79 grocery bill evenly. To the nearest penny, how much will each person pay?

   (1) \$20.00
   (2) \$21.00
   (3) \$21.70
   (4) \$21.76
   (5) \$21.80

9. Before a big race, a runner jogs 3 times around a .25-mile track to warm up. She then runs 8.5 miles. Which of the following expressions represents the total miles she covers?

   (1) $(3 + .25) + 8.5$
   (2) $3 \times (.25 \times 8.5)$
   (3) $(.25 + 8.5) \times 3$
   (4) $(.25 \times 3) + 8.5$
   (5) $.25 + 8.5$

C. Grid in the answer to each problem.

10.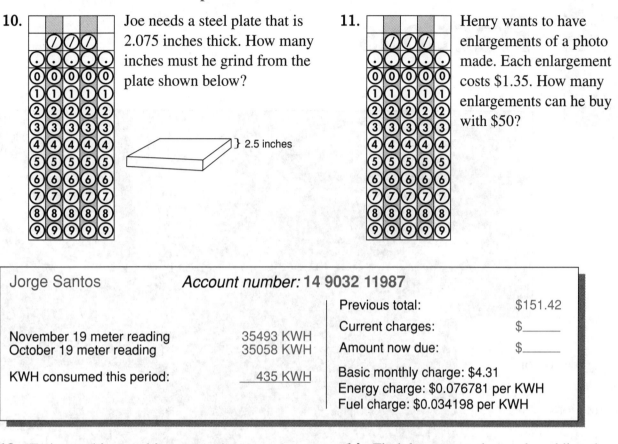

Joe needs a steel plate that is 2.075 inches thick. How many inches must he grind from the plate shown below?

} 2.5 inches

11. Henry wants to have enlargements of a photo made. Each enlargement costs $1.35. How many enlargements can he buy with $50?

Jorge Santos   *Account number:* **14 9032 11987**

November 19 meter reading	35493 KWH
October 19 meter reading	35058 KWH
KWH consumed this period:	435 KWH

Previous total:	$151.42
Current charges:	$_____
Amount now due:	$_____

Basic monthly charge: $4.31
Energy charge: $0.076781 per KWH
Fuel charge: $0.034198 per KWH

---

12. Estimate this month's energy charge. Multiply the kilowatt-hours (KWH) consumed this period by the energy charge rounded to the nearest cent.

13. Estimate this month's fuel charge. Multiply the KWH consumed this period by the fuel charge rounded to the nearest cent.

14. Find the current charges by adding the basic monthly charge plus this month's energy and fuel charges.

15. Find the amount now due by adding the previous total and the current charges.

Working Together

Bring a newspaper with grocery sales advertisements to class. With a partner, design a shopping list for a week's groceries for yourself or your family with $75. Base the list on the grocery sales ads and calculate the subtotal. Next, decide whether sales tax applies to any items on the list. If so, calculate the total using your local sales tax. Compare your shopping list with others in the class. How did others spend the money?

Fractions

Skills

Estimating the size of fractions

Adding fractions

Subtracting fractions

Finding common denominators

Multiplying fractions

Using cancellation

Dividing fractions

Tools

Calculator

Equations

Problem Solvers

Choosing necessary information

Drawing a picture

Multiply or divide?

Applications

Measuring distances

Fractions and money

Knowing how to work with **fractions** can help you in many situations in your life. In this unit, you'll learn how to do things such as:

- find the total amount of liquid if you add *half* $\left(\frac{1}{2}\right)$ a cup of water to *one-third* $\left(\frac{1}{3}\right)$ cup oil
- subtract *three-eighths* $\left(\frac{3}{8}\right)$ of a pie from one *whole* (1) pie
- divide a $92\frac{1}{2}$-mile trip into 3 equal segments
- find the total length of stair railing made up of 12 pieces of lumber, each $3\frac{3}{4}$ feet long

You may want to review these fraction lessons in Unit 1:

- Understanding Fractions ....page 30
- The Size of Fractions ....page 32
- Forms of Fractions ....page 34
- Equivalent Fractions ....page 36

When Do I Use Fractions?

Each of the following situations involves fractions. Check off any experiences you've had.

- ☐ adding or subtracting fractions when measuring for sewing, carpentry, or cooking
- ☐ using fractional measurements with a ruler or yardstick
- ☐ using fractions to express distances—for example, $\frac{9}{10}$ *of a mile* or $\frac{2}{3}$ *of the way*
- ☐ using fractions to represent a part of a group—for example, $\frac{3}{5}$ *of the people*
- ☐ using fractions when talking about time—for example, $\frac{1}{2}$ *hour* or $\frac{3}{4}$ *hour*
- ☐ multiplying or dividing fractions when changing a mixture at home or at work

Now describe some of your experiences with fractions.

1. Describe something you have measured using fractions. What object did you measure? What was the weight, height, or length of the object?

   _____

   _____

   _____

2. Describe a situation in which you used fractions in cooking and measuring. What numbers did you use? Why?

   _____

   _____

   _____

3. Do you ever add fractions that represent time, such as $\frac{1}{2}$ hour or $1\frac{3}{4}$ hours? Describe why and how you do this.

   _____

   _____

   _____

Talk About It

As a class, brainstorm a list of specific times in which class members have used fractions. What did each person do? What tools or instruments were used?

Then describe individually whether working with fractions is hard or easy for you. Tell what you hope to learn from this unit. How will what you learn be useful in your life?

Estimating the Size of Fractions

Your work with fractions will make a lot more sense if you know about how large a fraction is. A fraction is a number smaller than 1. But is it *a lot* smaller than 1, close to $\frac{1}{2}$, or *very close* to 1?

Fractions Close to 1

Example: What numerator would make this fraction *close to,* but *less than,* 1?

$$\frac{\blacksquare}{12}$$

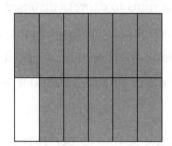

One whole box is divided into 12 sections. $\frac{11}{12}$ of the box is *almost* 1 whole box.

Think: A numerator of 12 would make the fraction $\frac{12}{12}$, which is equal to 1. The number just less than 12 is 11. Try this as the numerator.

$$\frac{11}{12}$$

► The closer in value a numerator and denominator are, the closer the fraction is to 1.

Circle the fractions below that are close to 1.

$\frac{5}{6}$ $\qquad$ $\frac{12}{25}$ $\qquad$ $\frac{11}{30}$ $\qquad$ $\frac{1}{5}$ $\qquad$ $\frac{8}{9}$ $\qquad$ $\frac{4}{5}$ $\qquad$ $\frac{13}{15}$

Did you circle $\frac{5}{6}$, $\frac{8}{9}$, $\frac{4}{5}$, and $\frac{13}{15}$? The numerator and denominator in each of these fractions are close in value.

Fractions Close to $\frac{1}{2}$

A fraction is less than $\frac{1}{2}$ if its denominator is *more than 2 times its numerator.* $\frac{1}{3}$ is less than $\frac{1}{2}$ because 2×1 (the numerator) is less than 3 (the denominator).

$\frac{1}{3}$ $\quad$ $2 \times 1 = 2$
$\phantom{\frac{1}{3}}$ $\quad$ 2 is less than 3.

► A fraction is close to $\frac{1}{2}$ if its denominator is *close to 2 times the numerator.*

Example 1: Is $\frac{5}{9}$ close to $\frac{1}{2}$?

$\frac{5}{9}$ $\quad$ $2 \times 5 = 10$
$\phantom{\frac{5}{9}}$ $\quad$ 10 is close to 9.

Yes, $\frac{5}{9}$ is close to $\frac{1}{2}$.

Example 2: Is $\frac{3}{10}$ close to $\frac{1}{2}$?

$\frac{3}{10}$ $\quad$ $2 \times 3 = 6$
$\phantom{\frac{3}{10}}$ $\quad$ 6 is not close to 10.

No, $\frac{3}{10}$ is not close to $\frac{1}{2}$.

Circle the fractions below that are close to $\frac{1}{2}$:

$\frac{9}{11}$ $\qquad$ $\frac{4}{7}$ $\qquad$ $\frac{15}{31}$ $\qquad$ $\frac{12}{17}$ $\qquad$ $\frac{2}{5}$

Did you circle $\frac{4}{7}$, $\frac{15}{31}$, and $\frac{2}{5}$? Each of these fractions has a denominator that is close to twice its numerator.

A. Complete the following fractions so that each is close or equal in value to $\frac{1}{2}$. There is more than one right answer for most of the fractions.

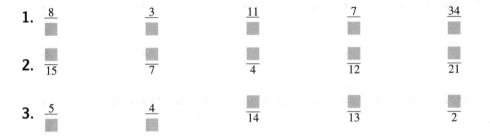

1. $\frac{8}{\blacksquare}$ $\qquad$ $\frac{3}{\blacksquare}$ $\qquad$ $\frac{11}{\blacksquare}$ $\qquad$ $\frac{7}{\blacksquare}$ $\qquad$ $\frac{34}{\blacksquare}$

2. $\frac{\blacksquare}{15}$ $\qquad$ $\frac{\blacksquare}{7}$ $\qquad$ $\frac{\blacksquare}{4}$ $\qquad$ $\frac{\blacksquare}{12}$ $\qquad$ $\frac{\blacksquare}{21}$

3. $\frac{5}{\blacksquare}$ $\qquad$ $\frac{4}{\blacksquare}$ $\qquad$ $\frac{\blacksquare}{14}$ $\qquad$ $\frac{\blacksquare}{13}$ $\qquad$ $\frac{\blacksquare}{2}$

B. Complete the following fractions so that each is close to, *but not equal to*, 1. There is more than one right answer for most of the fractions.

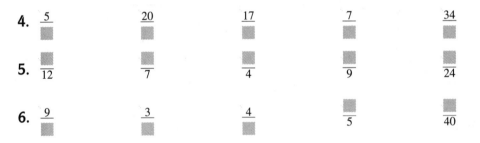

4. $\frac{5}{\blacksquare}$ $\qquad$ $\frac{20}{\blacksquare}$ $\qquad$ $\frac{17}{\blacksquare}$ $\qquad$ $\frac{7}{\blacksquare}$ $\qquad$ $\frac{34}{\blacksquare}$

5. $\frac{\blacksquare}{12}$ $\qquad$ $\frac{\blacksquare}{7}$ $\qquad$ $\frac{\blacksquare}{4}$ $\qquad$ $\frac{\blacksquare}{9}$ $\qquad$ $\frac{\blacksquare}{24}$

6. $\frac{9}{\blacksquare}$ $\qquad$ $\frac{3}{\blacksquare}$ $\qquad$ $\frac{4}{\blacksquare}$ $\qquad$ $\frac{\blacksquare}{5}$ $\qquad$ $\frac{\blacksquare}{40}$

C. Think of the *size* of each fraction. Then solve the following problems.

7. Mel shaved $\frac{1}{10}$ centimeter off a disk. About how much did he shave off?

   (1) much less than a centimeter

   (2) about $\frac{1}{2}$ centimeter

   (3) close to 1 centimeter

8. Cat lost the race by $\frac{5}{6}$ of a second. By about how much did she lose?

   (1) much less than 1 second

   (2) about $\frac{1}{2}$ second

   (3) close to 1 second

9. $\frac{3}{5}$ of the committee missed the meeting. About how many were absent?

   (1) almost no one

   (2) about $\frac{1}{2}$ the members

   (3) almost all the members

10. **Estimate** Li wanted to buy $\frac{11}{12}$ foot of ribbon. Estimate the length of the ribbon.

   (1) much less than 1 foot

   (2) about $\frac{1}{2}$ foot

   (3) close to 1 foot

Adding and Subtracting Like Fractions

Like fractions are fractions that have the same denominator. For example, $\frac{1}{3}$ and $\frac{2}{3}$ are like fractions, while $\frac{1}{3}$ and $\frac{1}{2}$ are **unlike fractions.** To add like fractions, just add the numerators. The denominator remains the same.

$$\frac{1}{3} + \frac{1}{3} = \frac{2}{3} \longleftarrow \quad 1 + 1 = 2$$

Adding fractions can result in an **improper fraction**—a fraction with a numerator larger than the denominator. Be sure to change the improper fraction to a mixed number. Review page 34 if you need to.

Adding Like Fractions

Example: Marta glued a $\frac{4}{5}$-inch-thick board to a $\frac{2}{5}$-inch-thick one. What was the total thickness of the two boards?

Step 1
Add the numerators.

Step 2
Place the result over the denominator.

Step 3
Change to a mixed number if necessary.

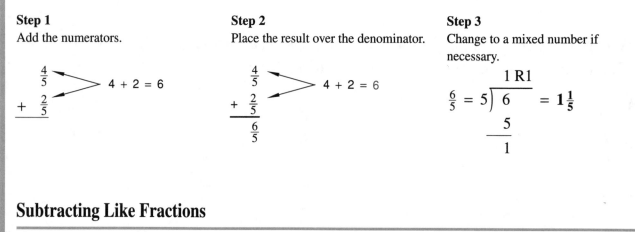

Subtracting Like Fractions

Example: Bolt A is $\frac{1}{8}$ inch shorter than Bolt B. If Bolt B is $\frac{3}{8}$ inch long, how long is Bolt A?

Step 1
Subtract the numerators.

Step 2
Place the result over the denominator.

Step 3
Simplify if necessary.*

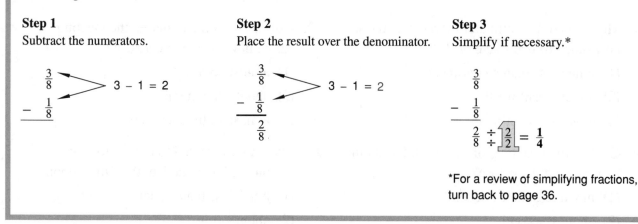

*For a review of simplifying fractions, turn back to page 36.

A. Add or subtract the following fractions. Express fractions in lowest terms. Change any improper fractions to mixed numbers.

1. $\frac{9}{10} - \frac{3}{10}$ $\frac{6}{11} - \frac{4}{11}$ $\frac{2}{3} - \frac{1}{3}$ $\frac{5}{8} - \frac{3}{8}$

2. $\frac{1}{7} + \frac{3}{7}$ $\frac{5}{9} + \frac{4}{9}$ $\frac{5}{8} + \frac{7}{8}$ $\frac{5}{12} + \frac{11}{12}$

B. Solve the following word problems. Pay careful attention to whether you should add or subtract.

3. Naomi glued a $\frac{1}{8}$-inch-thick laminate to a $\frac{3}{8}$-inch-thick platform. What is the thickness of the laminated platform?

(1) $\frac{1}{4}$ inch

(2) $\frac{1}{2}$ inch

(3) 1 inch

4. An instructor added a $\frac{1}{4}$-hour class discussion to her $\frac{3}{4}$-hour lecture. How long is the class now?

(1) $\frac{1}{4}$ hour

(2) $\frac{1}{2}$ hour

(3) 1 hour

5. What is $\frac{7}{16}$ of an inch less than $\frac{12}{16}$ inch?

(1) $1\frac{3}{16}$ inches

(2) $\frac{9}{16}$ inch

(3) $\frac{5}{16}$ inch

6. Salvador recorded a light flash lasting $\frac{7}{10}$ of a second. This was $\frac{4}{10}$ of a second longer than his last entry. How long was the last entry?

(1) $1\frac{1}{10}$ seconds

(2) 1 second

(3) $\frac{3}{10}$ second

7. What is $\frac{10}{21}$ less than $\frac{20}{21}$?

(1) $1\frac{9}{21}$

(2) $\frac{10}{21}$

(3) $\frac{9}{21}$

8. Marina poured $\frac{7}{8}$ cup of water into $\frac{5}{8}$ cup of vinegar. How much liquid did she have altogether?

(1) $1\frac{1}{2}$ cups

(2) 1 cup

(3) $\frac{3}{8}$ cup

C. Use the clocks to solve the following problems.

9.  Angel left his office at the time shown on the left. It took him $\frac{3}{4}$ hour to get home. What time did he get home?

10.  Glenda needs to pick up her daughter at school at the time shown on the clock. If it takes her $\frac{1}{2}$ hour to get to the school, what time should she leave?

Choosing Necessary Information

Part of solving any problem is finding the information you need. What information do you need to solve the problems below?

Example 1: Mr. Assad drives only $\frac{7}{10}$ of a mile to work each day. His wife walks $\frac{9}{10}$ of a mile to work. How many miles does Mr. Assad drive to and from work each day?

Necessary information: $\frac{7}{10}$ mile to and from work

Extra information: $\frac{9}{10}$ mile (the distance the wife walks)

Example 2: A delivery truck traveled from Bolten Apartments to Renville High to Creighton College, then back to Bolten. How many miles in all did it travel?

What information is necessary?

_____

What information is extra?

_____

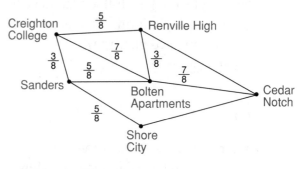

distances in miles

Necessary information includes $\frac{3}{8}$, $\frac{5}{8}$, and $\frac{7}{8}$ *mile.* Other distances shown on the map are extra information.

A. Use the map above to solve the following problems. First write down the information that is necessary.

1. How much farther is a trip from Bolten Apartments to Creighton College than a trip from Bolten Apartments to Renville High?

   Necessary information: _____

   Answer: _____

2. Is the distance from Cedar Notch to Bolten Apartments more or less than $\frac{1}{2}$ mile?

   Necessary information: _____

   Answer: _____

3. If you walk from Creighton College to Sanders to Shore City, how far will you walk in all?

   Necessary information: _____

   Answer: _____

4. How much farther is the distance from Sanders to Shore City than from Creighton College to Sanders?

   Necessary information: _____

   Answer: _____

Not Enough Information

Sometimes you may have more information than you need to solve a problem. Other times, you may not have enough information.

Example: According to the map on page 92, how long will it take to get from Bolten Apartments to Cedar Notch?

You can see that the map gives only information about distance and no information about speed of travel. The answer to this question is "Not enough information is given."

B. Solve the following problems. Use only the information needed. If you do not have enough information to solve a problem, write "Not enough information is given."

5. Mrs. Sheldon spent $\frac{1}{4}$ hour driving to the mall, $\frac{3}{4}$ hour shopping, and another $\frac{1}{4}$ hour driving home. How many hours did she spend driving?

6. Billie paid $1.99 for a remnant of cloth $\frac{7}{8}$ yard wide. From it, she cut a strip $\frac{3}{8}$ yard wide. How wide is the remaining piece?

7. A carpenter cut a hole $\frac{3}{16}$ inch in diameter into the 14-inch width of a rack. The dowel for this hole is $\frac{7}{16}$ inch. How much more does the carpenter need to expand the hole?

8. A recipe calls for $\frac{1}{3}$ cup molasses to be added to $\frac{2}{3}$ cup butter. How many cookies can be made with this recipe?

Making Connections: Adding Measurements

You know that 1 foot is equal to 12 inches. Therefore, when you add or subtract inches, you can express your answer in inches or as a fraction of a foot.

$$1 \text{ inch} = \tfrac{1}{12} \text{ foot}$$

Example: How much is 8 inches plus 5 inches?

Method 1: Inches

8 inches + 5 inches = 13 inches

Method 2: Fraction of a Foot

$\frac{8}{12}$ foot + $\frac{5}{12}$ foot = $\frac{13}{12}$ **feet** *or* $1\frac{1}{12}$ **feet**

Add the following measurements. Express your answer in inches *and* as a fraction of a foot.

For another look at the five-step problem-solving plan, turn to page 235.

1. 11 inches + 10 inches

2. 5 inches + 6 inches

3. 4 inches + 14 inches

Writing Equivalent Fractions

Unlike fractions are fractions with different denominators. Before you add or subtract unlike fractions, you must work to give them the same denominator. To do this, write **equivalent fractions.**

On page 36, you learned that you can multiply both numerator and denominator of a fraction by the same number *without changing the value of that fraction.*

> **Tip**
> Any number over itself is equal to 1. Multiplying $\frac{1}{6} \times \frac{4}{4}$ is the same as multiplying $\frac{1}{6} \times 1$.

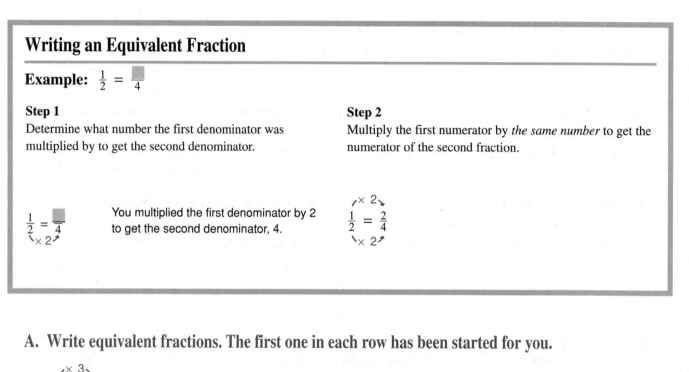

Writing an Equivalent Fraction

Example: $\frac{1}{2} = \frac{\blacksquare}{4}$

Step 1
Determine what number the first denominator was multiplied by to get the second denominator.

$\frac{1}{2} = \frac{\blacksquare}{4}$
$\times 2$

You multiplied the first denominator by 2 to get the second denominator, 4.

Step 2
Multiply the first numerator by *the same number* to get the numerator of the second fraction.

$\overset{\times 2}{\frac{1}{2}} = \frac{2}{4}$
$\times 2$

A. Write equivalent fractions. The first one in each row has been started for you.

1. $\overset{\times 3}{\underset{\times 3}{\frac{3}{4}}} = \frac{\blacksquare}{12}$ $\frac{4}{5} = \frac{\blacksquare}{10}$ $\frac{1}{7} = \frac{\blacksquare}{21}$ $\frac{7}{8} = \frac{\blacksquare}{32}$ $\frac{2}{3} = \frac{\blacksquare}{30}$

2. $\overset{\times 3}{\underset{\times 3}{\frac{1}{6}}} = \frac{\blacksquare}{18}$ $\frac{2}{5} = \frac{\blacksquare}{40}$ $\frac{1}{9} = \frac{\blacksquare}{36}$ $\frac{6}{7} = \frac{\blacksquare}{28}$ $\frac{9}{10} = \frac{\blacksquare}{100}$

3. $\underset{\times 10}{\frac{1}{2}} = \frac{\blacksquare}{20}$ $\frac{3}{8} = \frac{\blacksquare}{80}$ $\frac{4}{9} = \frac{\blacksquare}{18}$ $\frac{2}{3} = \frac{\blacksquare}{63}$ $\frac{2}{5} = \frac{\blacksquare}{100}$

Choosing a Common Denominator

You can use your knowledge of equivalent fractions to find a **common denominator** for two or more fractions.

Finding a Common Denominator

Example: What is a common denominator for $\frac{1}{6}$ and $\frac{3}{8}$?

Step 1
List the multiples of each denominator.

$\frac{1}{6}$ multiples of 6:
6, 12, 18, 24, 30, 36

$\frac{3}{8}$ multiples of 8:
8, 16, 24, 32, 40, 48

Step 2
Choose the lowest common multiple for both fractions.

$\frac{1}{6}$ 6,   12,   18,   (24,)   30,   36
    (× 1) (× 2) (× 3) (× 4) (× 5) (× 6)

$\frac{3}{8}$ 8,   16,   (24,)   32,   40,   48
    (× 1) (× 2) (× 3) (× 4) (× 5) (× 6)

Step 3
Write equivalent fractions using this new denominator. Use the multiplier for each.

$$\frac{1}{6} = \frac{4}{24} \qquad \frac{3}{8} = \frac{9}{24}$$

(× 4)   (× 3)

The new denominator, 24, is the lowest multiple both fractions have in common.

B. For each number in the pairs below, list the first five multiples, or more if necessary. Circle the common multiple. The first one is done for you.

4. 4: _4, 8, 12, 16, (20)_   2: _____   7: _____

     5: _5, 10, 15, (20), 25_   6: _____   3: _____

5. 3: _____   4: _____   6: _____

     5: _____   7: _____   9: _____

6. 9: _____   10: _____   3: _____

     5: _____   4: _____   4: _____

C. For each pair of fractions below, find a common denominator, then use it to write equivalent fractions. The first one is started for you.

7. $\frac{1}{2}$ and $\frac{3}{5}$ $\frac{3}{4}$ and $\frac{1}{12}$ $\frac{2}{9}$ and $\frac{3}{7}$ $\frac{1}{8}$ and $\frac{1}{3}$

     $\frac{1}{2} = \frac{\blacksquare}{10}$ $\frac{3}{5} = \frac{\blacksquare}{10}$

8. $\frac{1}{4}$ and $\frac{2}{5}$ $\frac{3}{10}$ and $\frac{5}{6}$ $\frac{1}{10}$ and $\frac{1}{3}$ $\frac{2}{3}$ and $\frac{3}{4}$

9. $\frac{4}{5}$ and $\frac{1}{3}$ $\frac{7}{8}$ and $\frac{1}{5}$ $\frac{8}{9}$ and $\frac{1}{3}$ $\frac{5}{6}$ and $\frac{1}{8}$

Answers start on page 212.   **95**

Adding Unlike Fractions

Now that you know how to make *unlike* fractions into *like* fractions, you can add unlike fractions.

Adding Unlike Fractions

Example: Add $\frac{2}{3}$ and $\frac{4}{5}$.

Step 1
Choose a common denominator by using multiples.

$$\frac{2}{3} \quad 3, 6, 9, 12, \boxed{15}$$
$$\qquad\qquad (\times 5)$$
$$+ \quad \frac{4}{5} \quad 5, 10, \boxed{15}, 20$$
$$\qquad\qquad (\times 3)$$

Step 2
Write equivalent fractions using the new denominator.

$$\overset{\times 5}{\frac{2}{3}} = \frac{10}{15}$$
$$\underset{\times 5}{}$$
$$+ \overset{\times 3}{\frac{4}{5}} = \frac{12}{15}$$
$$\underset{\times 3}{}$$

Step 3
Add the like fractions.

$$\frac{10}{15}$$
$$+ \frac{12}{15}$$
$$\overline{\quad \frac{22}{15}}$$

Step 4
Simplify and write a mixed number as necessary.

$$\frac{22}{15} = 15\overline{)22}^{\,1\,R7} = 1\frac{7}{15}$$
$$\qquad\qquad \underline{15}$$
$$\qquad\qquad\quad 7$$

A. Add the following unlike fractions. Some have been started for you.

1. $\frac{5}{6} + \frac{1}{3}$ $\qquad$ $\frac{2}{3} + \frac{2}{5}$ $\qquad$ $\frac{1}{8} + \frac{3}{4}$ $\qquad$ $\frac{6}{7} + \frac{4}{5}$

$\quad\dfrac{\blacksquare}{6} + \dfrac{\blacksquare}{6}$

2. $\frac{1}{8} + \frac{1}{5}$ $\qquad$ $\frac{2}{7} + \frac{2}{5}$ $\qquad$ $\frac{4}{9} + \frac{2}{3}$ $\qquad$ $\frac{1}{7} + \frac{3}{14}$

$\quad\dfrac{\blacksquare}{40} + \dfrac{\blacksquare}{40}$

3. $\frac{4}{5} + \frac{3}{8}$ $\qquad$ $\frac{1}{3} + \frac{1}{4}$ $\qquad$ $\frac{3}{7} + \frac{1}{2}$ $\qquad$ $\frac{3}{4} + \frac{1}{8}$

4. $\frac{2}{3} + \frac{1}{10}$ $\qquad$ $\frac{3}{4} + \frac{9}{10}$ $\qquad$ $\frac{1}{8} + \frac{1}{3}$ $\qquad$ $\frac{4}{5} + \frac{9}{10}$

5. $\frac{1}{2} + \frac{2}{8}$ $\qquad$ $\frac{5}{6} + \frac{2}{3}$ $\qquad$ $\frac{3}{7} + \frac{5}{21}$ $\qquad$ $\frac{5}{6} + \frac{1}{18}$

6. $\frac{2}{5} + \frac{7}{10}$ $\qquad$ $\frac{1}{4} + \frac{1}{3}$ $\qquad$ $\frac{3}{8} + \frac{3}{4}$ $\qquad$ $\frac{2}{9} + \frac{2}{3}$

B. Solve the following word problems. Be careful to use only the necessary information.

7. Claudia worked $\frac{1}{2}$ hour on her office's filing system, then $\frac{3}{4}$ hour on the computer. How much time did she spend on these two jobs?

8. Esteban put a $\frac{3}{8}$-inch pad underneath a carpet that is $\frac{3}{4}$ inch thick. What is the total thickness of rug and pad?

9. A customer bought $\frac{9}{10}$ pound of deli meat at $3.99 per pound. He also bought $\frac{1}{4}$ pound of cheese at $1.99 per pound. How many pounds of meat and cheese did he buy?

10. A machinist laid the metal strips below side by side. What is the total width of the metal strips fastened together?

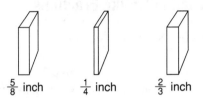

$\frac{5}{8}$ inch $\frac{1}{4}$ inch $\frac{2}{3}$ inch

11. To test the strength of her paper bag, Yuki filled it with the 2 heaviest weights below to see if it would break. What total weight did she put in her bag?

$\frac{3}{4}$ pound oranges	$\frac{1}{8}$ pound grapes
$\frac{7}{10}$ pound grapefruit	$\frac{7}{8}$ pound tomatoes
$\frac{2}{5}$ pound apples	

C. Explain For each problem below, write a short paragraph that explains, step-by-step, how to solve it. All questions refer to the following figure.

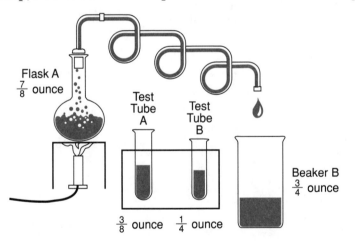

Flask A
$\frac{7}{8}$ ounce

Test Tube A

Test Tube B

Beaker B
$\frac{3}{4}$ ounce

$\frac{3}{8}$ ounce $\frac{1}{4}$ ounce

12. If you combined the contents of Test Tube A with the contents of Test Tube B, how much liquid would you have altogether?

13. Once all of the liquid from Flask A reaches Beaker B, what total amount of liquid will be in Beaker B?

14. If you combined all the liquid from all the containers, what total amount would you have?

Subtracting Unlike Fractions

Now that you can make *unlike* fractions into *like* fractions, you will be able to subtract unlike fractions.

Subtracting Unlike Fractions

Example: Subtract $\frac{1}{12}$ from $\frac{3}{4}$.

Step 1
Choose a common denominator by using multiples.

$$\frac{3}{4} \quad \underset{(\times 1)}{4,} \; \underset{(\times 2)}{8,} \; \underset{(\times 3)}{\boxed{12}}$$
$$-\frac{1}{12} \quad \underset{(\times 1)}{\boxed{12,}} \; \underset{(\times 2)}{24,} \; \underset{(\times 3)}{36,}$$

Step 2
Write equivalent fractions using the new denominator.

$$\overset{\times 3}{\frac{3}{4}} = \frac{9}{12}$$
$$\underset{\times 3}{}$$
$$-\frac{1}{12} = \frac{1}{12}$$

Step 3
Subtract the like fractions.

$$\frac{9}{12}$$
$$-\frac{1}{12}$$
$$\overline{\frac{8}{12}}$$

Step 4
Simplify and write a mixed number as necessary.

$$\frac{8}{12} \div \frac{4}{4} = \frac{2}{3}$$

A. Subtract the following unlike fractions. Some have been started for you.

1. $\frac{7}{8} - \frac{2}{5}$ $\frac{5}{12} - \frac{5}{16}$ $\frac{4}{15} - \frac{1}{10}$ $\frac{2}{3} - \frac{1}{2}$

$$\frac{\blacksquare}{40} - \frac{\blacksquare}{40}$$

2. $\frac{4}{7} - \frac{1}{5}$ $\frac{3}{8} - \frac{1}{10}$ $\frac{5}{6} - \frac{1}{3}$ $\frac{7}{8} - \frac{1}{16}$

$$\frac{\blacksquare}{35} - \frac{\blacksquare}{35}$$

3. $\frac{9}{10} - \frac{1}{4}$ $\frac{11}{12} - \frac{2}{3}$ $\frac{3}{5} - \frac{1}{6}$ $\frac{8}{9} - \frac{1}{3}$

4. $\frac{3}{4} - \frac{3}{16}$ $\frac{3}{4} - \frac{1}{8}$ $\frac{4}{5} - \frac{1}{3}$ $\frac{1}{3} - \frac{1}{4}$

5. $\frac{4}{5} - \frac{1}{10}$ $\frac{2}{9} - \frac{1}{12}$ $\frac{1}{8} - \frac{1}{16}$ $\frac{5}{12} - \frac{1}{24}$

6. $\frac{7}{10} - \frac{1}{5}$ $\frac{4}{7} - \frac{3}{14}$ $\frac{15}{16} - \frac{1}{8}$ $\frac{5}{9} - \frac{4}{10}$

B. Solve the following word problems. Be sure to use only the information that is necessary to answer the question.

7. A researcher estimated that $\frac{2}{5}$ of the people in her survey ate buttered popcorn, $\frac{1}{10}$ ate plain popcorn, and the rest ate popcorn with salt. What fraction of the group ate salted popcorn?

8. Jorge's ring finger is $\frac{3}{16}$ inch smaller around than his brother Tomas's. If Tomas's ring finger is $\frac{7}{8}$ inch around, how many inches around is Jorge's?

9. Mei-yu would like to lengthen a skirt so that the hem is only $\frac{1}{2}$ inch. The hem now is $\frac{7}{8}$ inch. How much will Mei-yu have to adjust the hem?

10. A boy walked $\frac{1}{4}$ mile from his home toward the grocery store. How much farther does he have to walk to get to the store?

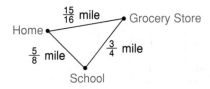

Making Connections: Number Sense with Fractions

Use what you know about the size of fractions to get an idea of how big or small an addition or subtraction answer will be.

Example: What is $\frac{9}{10} + \frac{1}{8}$?

Think: You know that $\frac{9}{10}$ is very close to 1 ($\frac{10}{10} = 1$). You also know that $\frac{1}{8}$ is a very small number (since 1 and 8 are not very close in value). So, if you add a number close to 1 to a very small number, your answer will still be close to 1.

Now decide if your answer will be more or less than 1.

Think: $\frac{9}{10}$ is $\frac{1}{10}$ away from 1. $\frac{1}{8}$ is *greater than* $\frac{1}{10}$. (Remember why? See page 32.) $\frac{9}{10} + \frac{1}{8}$ will be *more than 1* because $\frac{9}{10}$ plus a number greater than $\frac{1}{10}$ is more than 1.

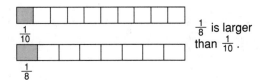

Use your number sense with fractions. Estimate the size of each answer: close to $\frac{1}{2}$, close to 1, and so on. Do not solve the problems.

1. $\frac{1}{2} + \frac{1}{10}$

2. $\frac{4}{5} + \frac{4}{7} + \frac{1}{10}$

3. $\frac{1}{9} + \frac{2}{5}$

4. $\frac{5}{9} + \frac{7}{8} + \frac{1}{2}$

5. $\frac{1}{2} + \frac{9}{10}$

6. $\frac{1}{6} + \frac{3}{7}$

7. $\frac{4}{9} + \frac{3}{5}$

8. $\frac{7}{8} + \frac{1}{5}$

Adding Mixed Numbers

A **mixed number** is a whole number and a fractional amount together.
To add mixed numbers, add the fractions, then add the whole numbers.

Adding Mixed Numbers

Example: Add $4\frac{1}{4} + 9\frac{1}{3}$.

Step 1
Find a common denominator and write equivalent fractions, if necessary.

$$4\frac{1}{4} = 4\frac{3}{12}$$
$$+\ 9\frac{1}{3} = 9\frac{4}{12}$$

Step 2
Add the fractions.

$$4\frac{3}{12}$$
$$+\ 9\frac{4}{12}$$
$$\overline{\frac{7}{12}}$$

Step 3
Add the whole numbers.

$$4\frac{3}{12}$$
$$+\ 9\frac{4}{12}$$
$$\overline{13\frac{7}{12}}$$

If the fractions add up to more than 1, write a mixed number and add it to the whole numbers.

Adding and Regrouping with Mixed Numbers

Example: Add $12\frac{7}{8} + 1\frac{3}{4}$.

Step 1
Find a common denominator and write equivalent fractions, if necessary.

$$12\frac{7}{8} = 12\frac{7}{8}$$
$$+\ 1\frac{3}{4} = 1\frac{6}{8}$$

Step 2
Add the fractions. Change the improper fraction to a mixed number.

$$12\frac{7}{8}$$
$$+\ 1\frac{6}{8}$$
$$\overline{\frac{13}{8} = 1\frac{5}{8}}$$

Step 3
Add the whole numbers. Then add the mixed number to the whole number.

$$12\frac{7}{8}$$
$$+\ 1\frac{6}{8}$$
$$\overline{13\ \ +\ 1\frac{5}{8}\ =\ \mathbf{14\frac{5}{8}}}$$

A. Add the following mixed numbers.

1.

$$3\frac{1}{2}$$
$$+\ 1\frac{1}{3}$$

$$16\frac{3}{7}$$
$$+\ 4\frac{3}{8}$$

$$9\frac{1}{10}$$
$$+\ \ \frac{2}{5}$$

$$27\frac{4}{7}$$
$$+\ 10\frac{1}{14}$$

$$1\frac{2}{3}$$
$$+\ 5\frac{1}{4}$$

2. $100\frac{1}{4} + 104\frac{4}{5}$ $3\frac{1}{8} + 4\frac{1}{6}$ $6\frac{3}{4} + 6\frac{2}{3}$

B. Solve the following word problems.

3. At birth, Spencer was $19\frac{3}{8}$ inches long. He has grown $5\frac{1}{2}$ inches. How long is the baby now?

4. Prison officials ordered a $4\frac{1}{2}$-foot fence to be erected on top of an existing $10\frac{3}{4}$-foot wall. What will the total height of the barrier now be?

5. Lucretia poured the contents of Cup A below into the contents of Cup B. What total amount of liquid is now in Cup B?

$\frac{1}{3}$ cup {

Cup A   **Cup B** $1\frac{3}{4}$ cups

Problems 6 and 7 refer to this chart.

Rainfall in Carver County

Monday..........................	$\frac{1}{4}$ inch
Tuesday..........................	$\frac{1}{2}$ inch
Wednesday..........................	$\frac{1}{8}$ inch
Thursday..........................	$\frac{3}{4}$ inch
Friday..........................	$\frac{1}{8}$ inch
Saturday..........................	$1\frac{1}{8}$ inches
Sunday..........................	$\frac{1}{4}$ inch

6. How many total inches of rain fell in Carver County *before the weekend?*

7. **Estimate** How many total inches of rain fell in Carver County for the 7 days listed?

C. Write Write some mixed number addition problems of your own, based on weights and measures shown below. Then solve your word problems. The first one is started for you.

8. For a stew, Mrs. Hayashi combined the

beef with the pork.

_____

_____

Beef	**Chicken**	**Pork**
$1\frac{3}{4}$ pounds	$3\frac{3}{8}$ pounds	$2\frac{1}{3}$ pounds

Olive Oil	**Vinegar**	**Salad Oil**
$4\frac{1}{2}$ pints	$6\frac{1}{3}$ pints	$1\frac{3}{4}$ pints

9. _____

_____

_____

_____

10. _____

_____

_____

_____

Subtracting Mixed Numbers

Subtracting mixed numbers follows the same pattern as adding mixed numbers: first subtract the fractions, then subtract the whole numbers.

Subtracting Mixed Numbers

Example: Subtract $2\frac{1}{2}$ from $9\frac{7}{8}$.

Step 1
Find a common denominator and write equivalent fractions, if necessary.

$$9\frac{7}{8} = 9\frac{7}{8}$$
$$- 2\frac{1}{2} = 2\frac{4}{8}$$

Step 2
Subtract the fractions.

$$9\frac{7}{8}$$
$$- 2\frac{4}{8}$$
$$\overline{\quad\frac{3}{8}}$$

Step 3
Subtract the whole numbers.

$$9\frac{7}{8}$$
$$- 2\frac{4}{8}$$
$$\overline{7\frac{3}{8}}$$

If the fraction being subtracted is greater than the other fraction, you have to borrow from the whole number.

Regrouping with Mixed Numbers

Example: Subtract $5\frac{3}{4}$ from $7\frac{1}{3}$.

Step 1
Find a common denominator and write equivalent fractions, if necessary.

$$7\frac{1}{3} = 7\frac{4}{12}$$
$$- 5\frac{3}{4} = 5\frac{9}{12}$$

Step 2
Subtract the fractions. If you cannot subtract, regroup 1 from the whole number and write it as a fraction with the same denominator.

$$7\frac{4}{12} = 6\frac{12}{12} + \frac{4}{12}$$
$$- 5\frac{9}{12} = 5\frac{9}{12}$$

Step 3
Combine into a new mixed number. Subtract the fractions.

$$6\frac{16}{12}$$
$$- 5\frac{9}{12}$$
$$\overline{\quad\frac{7}{12}}$$

Step 4
Subtract the whole numbers.

$$6\frac{16}{12}$$
$$- 5\frac{9}{12}$$
$$\overline{1\frac{7}{12}}$$

A. Subtract the mixed numbers below. The first one is started for you.

1.
$$10\frac{1}{3} = 9\frac{3}{3} + \frac{1}{3} = 9\frac{4}{3}$$
$$- 8\frac{2}{3} \qquad\qquad\qquad - 8\frac{2}{3}$$

$$9\frac{2}{7}$$
$$- 1\frac{5}{7}$$

$$1\frac{1}{4}$$
$$- \frac{3}{4}$$

B. Subtract the mixed numbers below. Some will require borrowing; some will not. Find a common denominator first, if necessary.

2. $3\frac{2}{5}$ $\qquad$ $7\frac{3}{8}$ $\qquad$ $4\frac{1}{6}$ $\qquad$ $14\frac{1}{2}$

$\quad\ \underline{-\ 2\frac{3}{5}}$ $\qquad$ $\underline{-\ \ \frac{3}{4}}$ $\qquad$ $\underline{-\ 2\frac{5}{6}}$ $\qquad$ $\underline{-\ 12\frac{1}{4}}$

3. $2\frac{1}{4}$ $\qquad$ $3\frac{3}{4}$ $\qquad$ $15\frac{1}{5}$ $\qquad$ $4\frac{2}{3}$

$\quad\ \underline{-\ 1\frac{1}{2}}$ $\qquad$ $\underline{-\ 3\frac{1}{2}}$ $\qquad$ $\underline{-\ 3\frac{1}{5}}$ $\qquad$ $\underline{-\ 3\frac{2}{3}}$

4. $2\frac{1}{4}$ $\qquad$ $4\frac{4}{7}$ $\qquad$ $8\frac{3}{4}$ $\qquad$ $12\frac{3}{8}$

$\quad\ \underline{-\ \ \frac{1}{2}}$ $\qquad$ $\underline{-\ 3\frac{1}{2}}$ $\qquad$ $\underline{-\ 3\frac{1}{4}}$ $\qquad$ $\underline{-\ 9\frac{1}{2}}$

Making Connections: Estimating with Mixed Numbers

When estimating with mixed numbers, try to round at least one of the numbers in the problem to a whole number. If you round *up,* round the other fraction *down.* If you round *down,* round the other fraction *up.*

Example: Estimate: $10\frac{5}{8} - 3\frac{3}{4}$.

> **Tip**
> When estimating with mixed numbers, whole numbers and the fraction $\frac{1}{2}$ are easiest to work with.

Think: You know that $\frac{5}{8}$ is close to $\frac{1}{2}$, and that $\frac{3}{4}$ is pretty close to 1. Round $3\frac{3}{4}$ to 4.

$3\frac{3}{4} \approx 4$

Since you rounded $3\frac{3}{4}$ *up* to 4, round $10\frac{5}{8}$ *down* to $10\frac{1}{2}$.

$10\frac{5}{8} \approx 10\frac{1}{2}$

Subtract. Your estimate is $\mathbf{6\frac{1}{2}}$.

$10\frac{1}{2} - 4 = \mathbf{6\frac{1}{2}}$

Estimate an answer to the following mixed-number problems. Remember to round one number up and the other down.

1. $57\frac{1}{8} + 20\frac{4}{5}$ $\qquad$ $12\frac{1}{2} - 2\frac{1}{3}$ $\qquad$ $3\frac{5}{12} + 4\frac{7}{8}$

2. $17\frac{5}{8} - 5\frac{5}{6}$ $\qquad$ $4\frac{3}{4} + 3\frac{4}{9}$ $\qquad$ $9\frac{9}{10} - 1\frac{1}{3}$

Working with Distances

Calculating **distances,** such as miles or kilometers, requires an understanding of mixed numbers. In this lesson, you'll use your fraction and mixed-number skills to add and subtract distances.

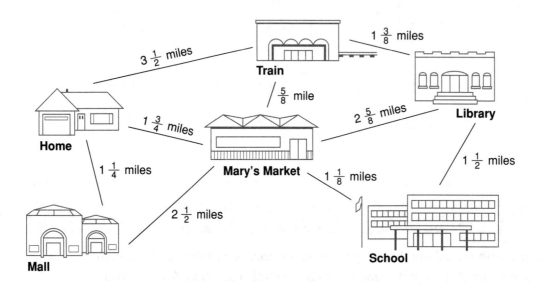

Adding or Subtracting Distances

Example 1: According to the map above, how many miles would you walk if you went from home to Mary's Market to the train station and home again?

$$1 \tfrac{3}{4} \text{ (home to Mary's Market)} = 1 \tfrac{6}{8}$$
$$\tfrac{5}{8} \text{ (market to train station)} \quad\quad \tfrac{5}{8}$$
$$+\; 3 \tfrac{1}{2} \text{ (train station to home)} \quad +\; 3 \tfrac{4}{8}$$
$$\overline{\phantom{+\; 3 \tfrac{1}{2} \text{ (train station to home)}}}$$
$$4 \tfrac{15}{8} = \mathbf{5 \tfrac{7}{8}}$$

Example 2: How much farther is it from home to the train station than it is from home to the mall?

To find the answer, subtract the two distances:

$$3 \tfrac{1}{2} = 3 \tfrac{4}{8}$$
$$-\; 1 \tfrac{1}{4} \quad -\; 1 \tfrac{2}{8}$$
$$\overline{\phantom{-\; 1 \tfrac{1}{4} \quad -\; 1 \tfrac{2}{8}}}$$
$$2 \tfrac{2}{8} = \mathbf{2 \tfrac{1}{4} \text{ miles}}$$

A. Answer the following questions based on the map on page 104.

1. Which is a shorter distance: from home to the train station to the library, or from home to Mary's Market to school to the library?

2. How many miles is it from the mall to Mary's Market to the train station?

3. How much farther is it from Mary's Market to the library than from Mary's Market to home?

4. How many miles do schoolchildren walk to get from the train station to school, if they stop at Mary's Market on the way?

B. Write Write four questions based on the map below. Then answer your questions, or exchange questions with someone else in your class. The first one has been started for you.

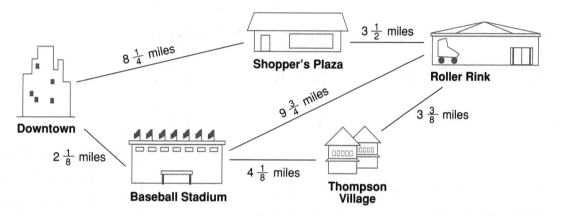

5. How much farther is it from the roller

    rink to the baseball stadium than it is

    from the roller rink to

    _____

6. _____

    _____

    _____

    _____

7. Make this a multistep problem.

    _____

    _____

    _____

    _____

8. Make this a multistep problem.

    _____

    _____

    _____

    _____

Mixed Review

A. Circle the answer that best describes each fraction below.

1. $\frac{4}{5}$ less than $\frac{1}{2}$ close to $\frac{1}{2}$ close to 1   greater than 1

2. $\frac{1}{4}$ less than $\frac{1}{2}$ close to $\frac{1}{2}$ close to 1   greater than 1

3. $\frac{5}{9}$ less than $\frac{1}{2}$ close to $\frac{1}{2}$ close to 1   greater than 1

4. $\frac{15}{8}$ less than $\frac{1}{2}$ close to $\frac{1}{2}$ close to 1   greater than 1

B. Add or subtract. Simplify or write a mixed number if necessary.

5. $\frac{7}{8} - \frac{3}{8}$ $\frac{9}{10} + \frac{1}{10}$ $\frac{11}{12} - \frac{4}{12}$ $\frac{2}{5} + \frac{1}{5}$

6. $\frac{3}{5} + \frac{4}{5}$ $\frac{3}{2} - \frac{2}{2}$ $\frac{3}{8} + \frac{4}{8}$ $\frac{5}{7} - \frac{2}{7}$

> **Tip**   1 foot = 12 inches
> 1 cup = 8 fluid ounces
> 1 yard = 3 feet

C. Convert the following measurements. Write your answers as mixed numbers, proper fractions, or whole numbers.

7. 12 fluid ounces = _____ cups   23 inches = _____ feet   2 feet = _____ yard

8. 3 feet + 4 feet = _____ yards   4 fluid ounces + 1 fluid ounce = _____ cup

9. 10 feet − 3 feet = _____ yards   27 inches − 3 inches = _____ feet

D. Write equivalent fractions.

10. $\frac{2}{3} = \frac{\blacksquare}{12}$ $\frac{5}{7} = \frac{\blacksquare}{21}$ $\frac{3}{4} = \frac{6}{\blacksquare}$ $\frac{7}{8} = \frac{28}{\blacksquare}$

11. $\frac{5}{7} = \frac{10}{\blacksquare}$ $\frac{9}{10} = \frac{\blacksquare}{100}$ $\frac{3}{5} = \frac{18}{\blacksquare}$ $\frac{2}{9} = \frac{10}{\blacksquare}$

E. Add or subtract the following fractions. Simplify if necessary.

12. $\frac{2}{3} + \frac{5}{6}$ $\frac{3}{5} + \frac{9}{10}$ $\frac{1}{2} + \frac{5}{8}$ $\frac{3}{4} + \frac{1}{8}$

13. $\frac{6}{7} - \frac{1}{3}$ $\frac{9}{10} - \frac{2}{5}$ $\frac{4}{5} - \frac{2}{3}$ $\frac{7}{10} - \frac{3}{5}$

14. $\frac{1}{8} + \frac{1}{5}$ $\frac{3}{4} + \frac{1}{6}$ $\frac{1}{3} + \frac{1}{4}$ $\frac{5}{6} + \frac{5}{8}$

F. Add or subtract the following mixed numbers. Simplify all fractions.

15. $14\frac{1}{2} + 1\frac{1}{3}$ $12\frac{7}{8} + 2\frac{4}{5}$ $3\frac{3}{5} + 4\frac{1}{4}$

16. $1\frac{4}{7} - \frac{3}{4}$ $5\frac{5}{6} - 1\frac{1}{3}$ $3\frac{9}{10} - 2\frac{4}{5}$

G. Grid in the answer to each problem.

17. 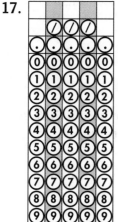 A door frame has a border that is $2\frac{3}{8}$ inches. DeShawn wants a border that is $3\frac{1}{4}$ inches. How many inches wider does DeShawn need to make the border?

18. 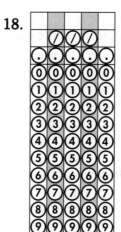 Jane spent $\frac{2}{3}$ of an hour helping a customer exchange an unwanted gift. Then she spent $\frac{1}{4}$ hour giving a customer a refund. What fraction of an hour did she spend helping both customers?

H. Solve the following word problems. Some problems may have extra information or not enough information.

19. Buffalo received $1\frac{1}{4}$ inches of snow on Thursday, $1\frac{1}{2}$ inches on Friday, and $3\frac{1}{2}$ inches on Saturday. How many more inches of snowfall did this city receive than Detroit?

  (1) $6\frac{1}{4}$

  (2) $7\frac{1}{2}$

  (3) Not enough information is given.

20. From the bolt of cloth pictured below, Bev cut $5\frac{1}{3}$ yards for a cape and $2\frac{1}{3}$ yards for a scarf. How many total yards did she cut off?

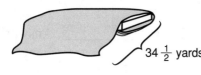

$34\frac{1}{2}$ yards

  (1) 3

  (2) $7\frac{2}{3}$

  (3) $26\frac{5}{6}$

Problems 21 and 22 refer to this chart.

Mighty Messengers Service Mileage 9/23

Bike #12	$2\frac{1}{8}$ miles	Bike #17	$4\frac{1}{2}$
Bike #13	$3\frac{1}{10}$	Bike #18	$9\frac{1}{10}$
Bike #14	$3\frac{3}{4}$	Bike #19	$9\frac{9}{10}$
Bike #15	$5\frac{5}{6}$	Bike #20	$6\frac{1}{2}$
Bike #16	$7\frac{1}{10}$		

21. Use your fraction sense skills to determine *approximately* how many miles were ridden in all on 9/23. Don't find an exact answer.

  (1) about 41

  (2) about 53

  (3) about 62

22. How many more miles was Bike #19 ridden than Bike #20?

  (1) $3\frac{2}{5}$

  (2) $16\frac{2}{5}$

  (3) Not enough information is given.

Multiplying Whole Numbers and Fractions

When you multiply by a fraction, you are finding a *part* of something. For example, when you find $\frac{1}{3}$ of a lunch bill, you are finding *part* of the bill. Another way to find a part is to *divide by a whole number*. In fact, multiplying by a fraction is like dividing by a whole number.

Finding a Part of a Whole

Example: You and 2 friends agree to share equally the cost of a $33.06 lunch bill. What is your share?

Strategy 1
Multiplying by a Fraction

You can look at it this way: you know that *your share is $\frac{1}{3}$* of the bill.

To find $\frac{1}{3}$ of $33.06, you can multiply:

$\frac{1}{3} \times \$33.06 = \mathbf{\$11.02}$

Strategy 2
Dividing by a Whole Number

Your number sense also tells you that you can divide the bill by 3, the number of people sharing the cost.

$$\overset{\textbf{\$11.02}}{3\overline{)\$33.06}}$$

Example 1: What is $\frac{1}{2}$ of 10?

Another way to ask this question is $\frac{1}{2} \times 10 = ?$

When multiplying a whole number by a fraction with a numerator of 1, divide by the denominator:

$\frac{1}{2} \times 10 = 10 \div 2 = \mathbf{5}$

Tip
The word *of* frequently means "multiply."

► Multiplying a number by $\frac{1}{2}$ is the same as dividing by 2.

Example 2: Find $\frac{1}{3}$ of 39.

$$\frac{1}{3} \times 39 = 39 \div 3 = \mathbf{13}$$

► Multiplying a number by $\frac{1}{3}$ is the same as dividing by 3.

A. Rewrite the fraction multiplication problems below as division problems. Then answer the problem. The first one is done for you.

1. $\frac{1}{4} \times 16 = \underline{\quad 16 \div 4 \quad}$ Answer: $\underline{\quad 4 \quad}$

2. $\frac{1}{8} \times 64 = \underline{\quad\quad\quad}$ Answer: $\underline{\quad\quad}$

3. $\frac{1}{5} \times 20 = \underline{\quad\quad\quad}$ Answer: $\underline{\quad\quad}$

4. $\frac{1}{6} \times 96 = \underline{\quad\quad\quad}$ Answer: $\underline{\quad\quad}$

Fractions with Numerators Other than 1

Example 1: What is $\frac{2}{3}$ of 18?

Think: You know how to find $\frac{1}{3}$ of 18. You divide 18 by 3, and get **6.**

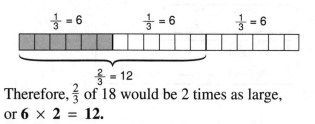

Therefore, $\frac{2}{3}$ of 18 would be 2 times as large, or **6 × 2 = 12.**

Example 2: What is $\frac{3}{4} \times 8$?

Think: You know that $\frac{1}{4}$ of 8 = 8 ÷ 4 = **2.**

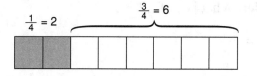

Therefore, $\frac{3}{4}$ of 8 is 3 times as large, or **2 × 3 = 6.**

B. Find the fraction of each whole number as indicated. The first one is done for you.

5. $\frac{7}{8} \times 16$ Since $\frac{1}{8} \times 16 = \underline{16} \div \underline{8} = \underline{2}$, then $\frac{7}{8} \times 18 = \underline{2} \times \underline{7} = \underline{14}$.

6. $\frac{3}{5} \times 15$ Since $\frac{1}{5} \times 15 = \underline{\hphantom{00}} \div \underline{\hphantom{00}} = \underline{\hphantom{00}}$, then $\frac{3}{5} \times 15 = \underline{\hphantom{00}} \times \underline{\hphantom{00}} = \underline{\hphantom{00}}$.

7. $\frac{7}{9} \times 27$ Since $\frac{1}{9} \times 27 = \underline{\hphantom{00}} \div \underline{\hphantom{00}} = \underline{\hphantom{00}}$, then $\frac{7}{9} \times 27 = \underline{\hphantom{00}} \times \underline{\hphantom{00}} = \underline{\hphantom{00}}$.

8. $\frac{2}{3} \times 21$ Since $\frac{1}{3} \times 21 = \underline{\hphantom{00}} \div \underline{\hphantom{00}} = \underline{\hphantom{00}}$, then $\frac{2}{3} \times 21 = \underline{\hphantom{00}} \times \underline{\hphantom{00}} = \underline{\hphantom{00}}$.

C. Solve the following word problems.

9. Marcia needs to approve $\frac{9}{10}$ of the labels addressed by her staff. If the last batch was 950 labels, how many does Marcia have to approve?

10. A carpenter cut off $\frac{3}{8}$ of the length of the board pictured below. How many inches did she cut?

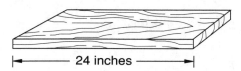

|←   24 inches   →|

11. $\frac{3}{4}$ of a 220-mile trip is completed. How many miles *remain* in the trip?

12. $\frac{3}{5}$ of the club members must be present at voting time. How many of the club's 75 members must be present to vote?

13. Of the 24 people on a committee, $\frac{2}{3}$ voted for a tax cut. How many voted in favor of the cut?

14. **Multiple Solutions** Jeff has typed $\frac{1}{3}$ of his 66-page report. How many pages must he still type? Use both strategies shown on page 108 to find the answer.

Answers start on page 214. **109**

Multiplying Fractions

When you multiply a fraction by a fraction, you find a *part of a fraction*. If both fractions are less than 1, your answer will be *smaller* than the fractions you started with.

Example: What is $\frac{1}{2}$ of $\frac{2}{3}$?

$\frac{1}{2} \times \frac{2}{3} = ?$

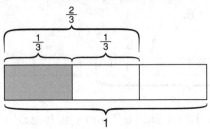

Can you see from the picture that $\frac{1}{2} \times \frac{2}{3} = \frac{1}{3}$?
Can you also see that $\frac{1}{2} \times \frac{2}{3}$ is less than either $\frac{1}{2}$ or $\frac{2}{3}$?

Multiplying a Fraction by a Fraction

Example: What is $\frac{1}{2}$ of $\frac{2}{3}$?

Step 1
Multiply numerators.

$\frac{1}{2} \times \frac{2}{3} = \frac{2}{}$ ⟵ 1 × 2

Step 2
Multiply denominators.

$\frac{1}{2} \times \frac{2}{3} = \frac{2}{6}$ ⟵ 1 × 2
⟵ 2 × 3

Step 3
Simplify if necessary.

$\frac{2}{6} = \frac{1}{3}$

Here's a shortcut that can help make multiplying fractions much easier.

Canceling Once

Example: $\frac{3}{8} \times \frac{4}{5} = ?$

Step 1
If a numerator of one fraction and a denominator of the other fraction can be divided by the same number, divide both by the same number.

4 ÷ 4 = 1

$\frac{3}{\overset{1}{\cancel{8}}} \times \frac{\overset{}{\cancel{4}}}{5} =$

8 ÷ 4 = 2

Step 2
Multiply the new numerators and denominators.

$\frac{3}{8} \times \frac{4}{5} = \frac{3}{10}$

A. Multiply the following fractions. Use cancellation as a first step if possible.

1. $\frac{1}{2} \times \frac{3}{4}$ $\frac{1}{8} \times \frac{3}{5}$ $\frac{2}{5} \times \frac{3}{7}$ $\frac{1}{10} \times \frac{3}{4}$

2. $\frac{5}{6} \times \frac{1}{2}$ $\frac{7}{8} \times \frac{3}{4}$ $\frac{3}{4} \times \frac{1}{8}$ $\frac{9}{10} \times \frac{3}{4}$

3. $\frac{2}{3} \times \frac{3}{5}$ $\frac{9}{10} \times \frac{1}{3}$ $\frac{1}{5} \times \frac{2}{3}$ $\frac{1}{9} \times \frac{3}{8}$

4. $\frac{3}{4} \times \frac{7}{9}$ $\frac{1}{12} \times \frac{4}{7}$ $\frac{8}{9} \times \frac{1}{10}$ $\frac{3}{4} \times \frac{12}{13}$

Sometimes you can cancel both sets of numerator and denominator.

Canceling Twice

Example: Multiply $\frac{5}{6}$ by $\frac{18}{25}$.

Step 1
Divide the numerator of one fraction and the denominator of the other fraction by the *same* number.

$$\overset{1}{\cancel{5}} \times \underset{5}{\frac{18}{\cancel{25}}} =$$

Divide both by 5.

Step 2
Divide the other numerator and the other denominator by the same number.

$$\underset{1}{\overset{1}{\cancel{\frac{5}{6}}}} \times \underset{5}{\overset{3}{\cancel{\frac{18}{25}}}} =$$

Divide both by 6.

Step 3
Multiply across.

$$\underset{1}{\overset{1}{\cancel{\frac{5}{6}}}} \times \underset{5}{\overset{3}{\cancel{\frac{18}{25}}}} = \frac{3}{5}$$

What would happen if you did not cancel the fractions before multiplying? You could still get the correct answer, but you'd have a complicated fraction to simplify in the end. Here's an example:

$$\frac{5}{6} \times \frac{18}{25} = \frac{90}{150}$$

multiplying fractions without canceling

$$\frac{90}{150} \div \frac{30}{30} = \frac{3}{5}$$

simplifying large fraction to get final answer

It is easier to simplify fractions *before* multiplying than *after*.

B. Multiply the fractions below. Use canceling where you can to make the work easier. If you do not use canceling, be sure to simplify your answers.

5. $\frac{4}{5} \times \frac{15}{16}$ $\frac{2}{3} \times \frac{3}{8}$ $\frac{2}{5} \times \frac{10}{11}$ $\frac{3}{4} \times \frac{5}{6}$

6. $\frac{1}{8} \times \frac{24}{25}$ $\frac{3}{10} \times \frac{5}{9}$ $\frac{1}{2} \times \frac{4}{5}$ $\frac{3}{8} \times \frac{8}{9}$

7. $\frac{6}{7} \times \frac{5}{12}$ $\frac{4}{9} \times \frac{1}{2}$ $\frac{2}{5} \times \frac{3}{5}$ $\frac{9}{10} \times \frac{3}{5}$

C. Solve the following word problems.

8. Harry planted corn in $\frac{1}{2}$ of his $\frac{3}{4}$-acre field. In how much of an acre did he plant corn?

9. A tailor used $\frac{2}{3}$ of a piece of cloth for design work. The cloth was $\frac{9}{10}$ yard long. How much cloth did she use for design?

10. Samouk ate $\frac{3}{4}$ of the leftover pie pictured below. What fraction of the *whole* pie did he eat?

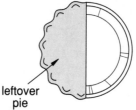

leftover pie

Multiplying Whole and Mixed Numbers

On page 109, you learned to find a fraction of a whole number this way:

Example: Two-thirds of the cargo in the wharf warehouse $\frac{2}{3} \times 6 = ?$ is industrial supplies. The total cargo weighs about 6 tons. How many tons are industrial supplies?

Think: You know how to find $\frac{1}{3}$ of 6. You divide 6 by 3, and get 2. Therefore, $\frac{2}{3}$ of 6 would be 2 times as large, or **2 × 2 = 4 tons.**

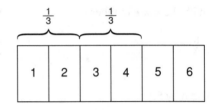

Here's another way to look at the same problem:

Multiplying a Fraction by a Whole Number

Example: What is $\frac{2}{3}$ of 6?

Step 1
Write the whole number as a fraction with a denominator of 1.

$\frac{2}{3} \times \frac{6}{1}$ ⟵ Any whole number is equal to itself over 1. $6 = \frac{6}{1}$

Step 2
Cancel if possible. Multiply the numerators, then multiply the denominators.

$\frac{2}{\cancel{3}_1} \times \frac{\cancel{6}^2}{1} = \frac{4}{1}$

Step 3
Simplify if necessary.

$\frac{4}{1} = \mathbf{4}$

A. **Multiply the following fractions and whole numbers. First, write the whole numbers as fractions. Cancel if possible, then multiply. The first row is started for you.**

1. $\frac{5}{6} \times 4$ $\qquad$ $3 \times \frac{3}{4}$ $\qquad$ $\frac{1}{2} \times 7$ $\qquad$ $\frac{1}{10} \times 5$

   $\frac{5}{6} \times \frac{4}{1} =$ $\qquad$ $\frac{3}{1} \times \frac{3}{4} =$ $\qquad$ $\frac{1}{2} \times \frac{7}{1} =$ $\qquad$ $\frac{1}{10} \times \frac{5}{1} =$

2. $9 \times \frac{1}{3}$ $\qquad$ $4 \times \frac{1}{2}$ $\qquad$ $2 \times \frac{2}{3}$ $\qquad$ $4 \times \frac{1}{6}$

3. $10 \times \frac{1}{10}$ $\qquad$ $\frac{3}{5} \times \frac{4}{7}$ $\qquad$ $12 \times \frac{3}{4}$ $\qquad$ $4 \times \frac{5}{6}$

Multiplying by Mixed Numbers

In this problem, a fraction is multiplied by a mixed number: $\frac{4}{7} \times 5\frac{1}{4} = ?$

Before you can multiply, you need to convert the mixed number to an improper fraction (with a numerator larger than the denominator).

Changing a Mixed Number to an Improper Fraction

Example: Change $5\frac{1}{4}$ to an improper fraction.

Step 1
Multiply the whole number by the denominator of the fraction.

$5\frac{1}{4} = \frac{20}{4}$ ◄—— $5 \times 4 = 20$

Step 2
Add the numerator to the product of Step 1.

$5\frac{1}{4} = \frac{20}{4} + \frac{1}{4} = \frac{21}{4}$

Once you've converted the mixed number, you can multiply: $\overset{1}{\underset{1}{\cancel{\frac{4}{7}}}} \times \overset{3}{\underset{1}{\cancel{\frac{21}{4}}}} = \frac{3}{1} = 3$

B. Multiply the following mixed numbers, fractions, and whole numbers. Change mixed numbers and whole numbers to fractions as a first step. Cancel if possible. Some have been started for you.

4. $1\frac{1}{3} \times 8 =$

   $\frac{4}{3} \times \frac{8}{1} =$

   $\frac{3}{4} \times 2\frac{1}{2} =$

   $\frac{3}{4} \times \frac{5}{2} =$

   $5\frac{5}{6} \times 4$

   $\frac{35}{6} \times \frac{4}{1} =$

   $2\frac{2}{3} \times 3\frac{1}{3}$

5. $4\frac{1}{4} \times \frac{1}{3}$

   $6\frac{1}{2} \times \frac{1}{4}$

   $1\frac{1}{2} \times 1\frac{1}{2}$

   $5\frac{1}{2} \times 8$

6. $12\frac{1}{2} \times 1\frac{1}{2}$

   $\frac{3}{5} \times 1\frac{1}{10}$

   $2\frac{3}{4} \times \frac{3}{4}$

   $1\frac{1}{8} \times 3$

C. Solve the following problems. Remember, to find a *part* of something, multiply.

7. Annie has hiked $\frac{3}{4}$ of the 16-mile trail. How many miles has she hiked?

8. Professor Howard Cohen usually lectures for $\frac{1}{2}$ his class time. If his class runs $1\frac{1}{2}$ hours, how long does he lecture?

9. Zach is $4\frac{1}{2}$ feet tall. His sister Maddie is $\frac{3}{4}$ that height. How tall is Maddie?

10. A carpenter will use $\frac{5}{8}$ of the board below. How many inches will he use?

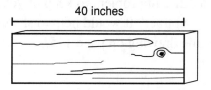

40 inches

Drawing a Picture

Have you ever been confused by a math problem? Many times, the words and numbers in math problems don't seem real. You can't picture what's going on.

It may help to draw a picture. Don't worry—you don't need to be an artist. Your sketch will be useful *as long as it is meaningful to you.*

Example 1: Carl paid $12 for an 8-foot board. How much did he pay *per foot?*

Should you add, subtract, multiply, or divide to find your answer? To "see" the problem, two different students drew these pictures:

Student #1

"Here's the board that he bought for $12."

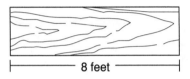

8 feet

"I need to know the cost of **part** of this board—this shaded part."

1 foot

"If this whole piece cost $12, then it looks like I should **divide** to find the cost of this little piece."

$12 ÷ 8 = $1.50

Student #2

"The 8-foot board and the $12 are equal in value; for $12, I get 8 feet of board, and 8 feet of board cost me $12."

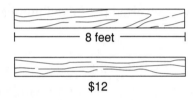

8 feet

$12

"Since I want to know how much **1** foot costs, I have to divide the board up into 8 pieces."

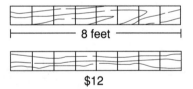

8 feet

$12

"So, I should also divide the money up into 8 pieces."

$12 ÷ 8 = $1.50

Example 2: A portable dance floor from Cramer Catering is $10\frac{1}{4}$ yards long and $8\frac{1}{2}$ yards wide. The band takes up $3\frac{1}{2}$ yards of the length of the floor. How much of the length of the floor is left for dancing?

This is a difficult problem to keep in your head. How do you know what numbers to add or subtract? It would help to sketch the dance floor and the dimensions given. Look at the drawing on page 115.

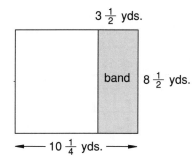

3 ½ yds.

band | 8 ½ yds.

10 ¼ yds.

Now can you see more clearly what you should do?

Subtract $3\frac{1}{2}$ from $10\frac{1}{4}$:

$$10\ \frac{1}{4} = 10\ \frac{1}{4}$$
$$-\ 3\ \frac{1}{2} =\ 3\ \frac{2}{4}$$
$$\overline{\quad\quad\quad\ \ 6\ \frac{3}{4}}$$

The length of the space available for dancing is **$6\frac{3}{4}$ yards.**

Draw Try drawing pictures to help you solve the following problems. Remember—there is more than one way to picture a solution.

Draw your pictures here.

1. The distance from Neston to Marblerock is $22\frac{3}{4}$ miles. From Marblerock to Talton is $\frac{1}{2}$ of that distance. How far is it from Marblerock to Talton?

2. Jeannette bought 9 yards of fabric for $27.18. How much did she pay *per yard?*

3. A community playground is 56 meters long. Its width is $\frac{3}{4}$ the length. How wide is the playground?

Dividing Fractions

On page 110 you learned that when you *multiply* a fraction by a fraction, your answer is *smaller* than either number.

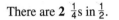

$$\frac{1}{2} \text{ of } \frac{1}{4} = \frac{1}{8}$$

When you multiply by a fraction, you are finding a *part of* another number. The answer is *smaller* than the original fractions in the problem.

Example: $\frac{1}{2} \times \frac{1}{4} = \frac{1}{8}$

What happens when you *divide* a fraction by a fraction? Will your answer be *larger* or *smaller* than the original fractions?

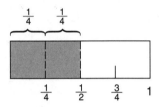

There are **2** $\frac{1}{4}$s in $\frac{1}{2}$.

Example: $\frac{1}{2} \div \frac{1}{4} = 2$

When you divide by a fraction, you find *how many* of that fraction there are in the number being divided up (in this case, how many $\frac{1}{4}$s there are in $\frac{1}{2}$). The answer is usually *larger* than the original fractions in the problem.

► Dividing a fraction by a fraction usually produces a *larger* number.

► Dividing a fraction by a whole number produces a *smaller* number.

Dividing by a Fraction

Example: What is $\frac{3}{4} \div \frac{1}{2}$?

Step 1
Invert the divisor (the number you are dividing *by,* the number *following* the division sign).

$\frac{3}{4} \div \frac{1}{2}$ $\frac{1}{2}$ inverts to $\frac{2}{1}$.

To *invert* means to turn the fraction upside down.

Step 2
Change the ÷ to a ×.

$\frac{3}{4} \div \frac{1}{2} = \frac{3}{4} \times \frac{2}{1}$

Step 3
Cancel if possible and multiply. Change improper fractions to mixed numbers.

$\frac{3}{\overset{2}{4}} \times \frac{\overset{1}{2}}{1} = \frac{3}{2} = 1\frac{1}{2}$

There are $1\frac{1}{2}$ $\frac{1}{2}$s in $\frac{3}{4}$.

Dividing a Fraction by a Whole Number

Example: What is $\frac{1}{3} \div 4$?

Step 1
Write the whole number as a fraction with a denominator of 1. Then invert the fraction.

$\frac{1}{3} \div 4$ $\frac{4}{1}$ inverts to $\frac{1}{4}$.

Step 2
Change the ÷ to a ×.

$\frac{1}{3} \times \frac{1}{4}$

Step 3
Multiply.

$\frac{1}{3} \times \frac{1}{4} = \frac{1}{12}$

A. Invert the following fractions and whole numbers. To invert a whole number, first write it as a fraction by putting it over the number 1. The first two are done for you.

1. a. $\frac{1}{4} \longrightarrow \frac{4}{1}$ $10 = \frac{10}{1} \longrightarrow \frac{1}{10}$ $\frac{2}{3}$ $\frac{4}{7}$ **b.** $\frac{3}{4}$ $\frac{9}{10}$ $\frac{7}{100}$ 11 15

B. Divide the following fractions and whole numbers. Some hints are given in the first row.

2. $\frac{2}{3} \div \frac{1}{2}$ $\frac{1}{2} \div 4$ $\frac{4}{5} \div \frac{1}{8}$ $\frac{3}{4} \div \frac{1}{2}$

   Invert: $\frac{1}{2} \to \frac{2}{1}$ Invert: $4 \to \frac{1}{4}$ Invert: _____   Invert: _____

   Multiply: _____   Multiply: _____   Multiply: _____   Multiply: _____

3. $\frac{5}{7} \div \frac{1}{3}$ $\frac{1}{6} \div \frac{1}{3}$ $\frac{3}{4} \div \frac{1}{8}$ $\frac{1}{7} \div \frac{1}{3}$

4. $5 \div \frac{1}{3}$ $6 \div \frac{1}{4}$ $\frac{1}{10} \div \frac{1}{8}$ $\frac{2}{9} \div \frac{2}{3}$

Making Connections: Estimating with Fractions

To estimate when you are multiplying and dividing fractions, you can't always round to $\frac{1}{2}$ or 1 as you did earlier in this unit.

Example 1: Estimate an answer to $\frac{4}{5} \times \frac{1}{8}$.

You can round $\frac{4}{5}$ to 1 because they are close in value. What about $\frac{1}{8}$?
It's closer to 0 than it is to 1. But if you round to 0, this happens:

$\frac{4}{5} \times \frac{1}{8} \approx 1 \times 0 \approx \mathbf{0}$

Zero is *not* a good estimate. Instead, follow this rule:

▶ When estimating in a multiplication or division problem, leave small fractions as they are. Round fractions that are close to $\frac{1}{2}$ or 1.

Example 2: Estimate an answer to $\frac{4}{5} \times \frac{1}{8}$.
$\frac{4}{5} \approx 1$ $\frac{4}{5} \times \frac{1}{8} \approx 1 \times \frac{1}{8} \approx \frac{1}{8}$

Check: $\frac{4}{5} \times \frac{1}{8} = \frac{1}{10}$ Your answer, $\mathbf{\frac{1}{10}}$, is close to the estimate of $\frac{1}{8}$.

Estimate an answer to each of the following problems.

1. $\frac{1}{2} \times \frac{1}{10}$ **2.** $\frac{6}{7} \times \frac{1}{12}$ **3.** $\frac{9}{10} \times \frac{2}{3}$ **4.** $\frac{1}{7} \times \frac{5}{6}$

Dividing with Mixed Numbers

Dividing mixed numbers is the same as dividing fractions—there's just one additional step. You must change all mixed numbers to improper fractions.

Dividing Mixed Numbers

Example: $3\frac{3}{4} \div 1\frac{2}{3} = ?$

Step 1	**Step 2**	**Step 3**	**Step 4**
Change mixed numbers to fractions.	Invert the divisor and change the $\div$ to a $\times$.	Cancel if possible and multiply.	Change improper fractions to mixed numbers.

Step 1

$$3\frac{3}{4} = \frac{15}{4} \xleftarrow{\quad} (3 \times 4) + 3$$

$$1\frac{2}{3} = \frac{5}{3} \xleftarrow{\quad} (3 \times 1) + 2$$

Step 2

divisor

$$\frac{15}{4} \div \frac{5}{3} =$$

$$\frac{15}{4} \times \frac{3}{5} =$$

Step 3

$$\frac{\overset{3}{\cancel{15}}}{4} \times \frac{3}{\underset{1}{\cancel{5}}} = \frac{9}{4}$$

Step 4

$$\frac{9}{4} = 2\frac{1}{4}$$

A. Divide the following fractions, whole numbers, and mixed numbers.
Convert all numbers into fractions first. The first two are started for you.

1. $1 \div \frac{2}{3}$ $\qquad$ $3\frac{1}{4} \div 4$ $\qquad$ $10\frac{1}{2} \div 2\frac{1}{2}$ $\qquad$ $5\frac{3}{5} \div 1\frac{1}{2}$

$\quad 1 \times \frac{3}{2} =$ $\qquad\quad$ $3\frac{1}{4} \times \frac{1}{4} =$

2. $3\frac{1}{8} \div \frac{1}{3}$ $\qquad$ $\frac{1}{4} \div 4$ $\qquad$ $5\frac{1}{2} \div 2$ $\qquad$ $9 \div 1\frac{1}{2}$

3. $\frac{1}{3} \div 3$ $\qquad$ $1\frac{1}{4} \div 8$ $\qquad$ $10\frac{1}{2} \div 5$ $\qquad$ $2\frac{2}{5} \div \frac{1}{2}$

4. $\frac{1}{3} \div 6$ $\qquad$ $3\frac{1}{2} \div 3$ $\qquad$ $10 \div 2\frac{1}{2}$ $\qquad$ $5 \div 2\frac{1}{2}$

5. $4 \div \frac{1}{3}$ $\qquad$ $\frac{1}{8} \div 2$ $\qquad$ $\frac{1}{2} \div \frac{1}{2}$ $\qquad$ $\frac{1}{2} \div 10$

B. Solve the following problems.

6. How many $\frac{7}{8}$-inch pieces can be cut from the wire pictured below?

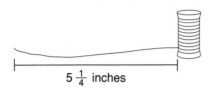

5 $\frac{1}{4}$ inches

7. Arturo piled $1\frac{1}{2}$-inch-thick boards on top of one another. The stack was 120 inches high. How many boards were in the stack?

8. A video producer has $10\frac{1}{2}$ minutes to fill on a tape. How many $1\frac{1}{2}$-minute segments can she fit on the tape?

9. How many stops will you make if you divide the distance below into $1\frac{1}{3}$-mile segments?

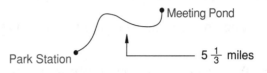

Meeting Pond

Park Station

5 $\frac{1}{3}$ miles

10. It takes $1\frac{1}{8}$ yards of fabric to make a vest. How many vests can a tailor make with the $11\frac{1}{4}$ yards he has in stock?

11. Larissa has $4\frac{1}{2}$ cups of sugar in her kitchen. How many batches of fudge can she make if each batch calls for $2\frac{1}{4}$ cups of sugar?

Making Connections: Estimating with Mixed Numbers

When multiplying or dividing, estimating with mixed numbers can be simple or tricky. It depends on how close an estimate you need.

Example: Estimate an answer to $55\frac{1}{2} \times 9\frac{9}{10}$.

Method 1
Round both numbers to whole numbers.

$55\frac{1}{2} \approx 56$

$9\frac{9}{10} \approx 10$

$56 \times 10 = \textbf{560}$
$55\frac{1}{2} \times 9\frac{9}{10} \approx \textbf{560}$

Method 2
Round only one number to a whole number.

$9\frac{9}{10} \approx 10$

$$55\frac{1}{2} \times 10 = (55 \times 10) + (\tfrac{1}{2} \times 10)$$
$$= 550 + 5$$
$$= \textbf{555}$$

$55\frac{1}{2} \times 9\frac{9}{10} \approx \textbf{555}$

The actual answer to $55\frac{1}{2} \times 9\frac{9}{10}$ is $\textbf{549}\frac{9}{20}$. When you round only one mixed number, your estimate is a little closer to the actual answer.

Use both estimation methods for each of the following problems.

1. $3\frac{3}{4} \times 1\frac{1}{4}$

2. $10\frac{1}{4} \times 2\frac{1}{4}$

3. $15\frac{1}{8} \times 5\frac{1}{4}$

4. $6\frac{1}{4} \times 3\frac{1}{2}$

5. $6\frac{5}{6} \times 1\frac{1}{2}$

6. $2\frac{3}{4} \times 4\frac{1}{6}$

Multiply or Divide?

Solving fraction problems can be confusing because the difference between multiplication and division can be difficult to see. It can be hard to see that to find a part of something, you multiply.

Fraction problems are solved like whole number problems:

► To find 2 of something, **multiply by 2.**

► To find $\frac{1}{2}$ of something, **multiply by $\frac{1}{2}$.**

► To find how many 2s are in another number, **divide by 2.**

► To find how many $\frac{1}{2}$s are in another number, **divide by $\frac{1}{2}$.**

Example 1: Tommy bought a $\frac{3}{4}$-pound bag of candy and ate $\frac{1}{4}$ of it. What part of a pound did he eat?

Multiply or divide?

Think: To find a *part of* a pound, multiply.

$\frac{1}{4} \times \frac{3}{4} = \frac{3}{16}$ **pound**

$\frac{3}{16}$ is the amount Tommy *ate.*

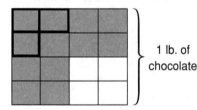
1 lb. of
chocolate

The shaded amount is the amount Tommy *bought.*

Example 2: Tommy has $\frac{3}{4}$ pound of candy. How many $\frac{1}{4}$-pound bags can he fill?

Multiply or divide?

Think: To find *how many* $\frac{1}{4}$s are in $\frac{3}{4}$, divide.

$\frac{3}{4} \div \frac{1}{4} = \frac{3}{4} \times \frac{4}{1} = \frac{3}{1}$ or **3 bags**

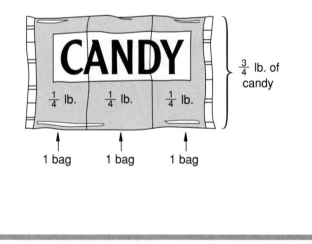

$\frac{3}{4}$ lb. of candy

Think about what size your answer should be:

► When you *multiply* a whole number by a proper fraction, your answer will be *smaller* than the number you started with.

► When you *divide* a whole number by a proper fraction, your answer will be *larger.*

Example 1: How many $\frac{3}{4}$-acre parcels of land are there in 12 acres?

Think: There are going to be *more* than 12 parcels if each parcel is less than an acre. To get an answer *larger than* 12, I need to *divide.*

$$\frac{12}{1} \div \frac{3}{4} =$$

$$\frac{\overset{4}{\cancel{12}}}{1} \times \frac{4}{\underset{1}{\cancel{3}}} = \frac{16}{1} \text{ or } \textbf{16 parcels}$$

Example 2: Three-fourths of Mahaney's Farm is cultivated forest. The farm is 12 acres total. How many acres are forest?

Think: I know that *fewer* than 12 acres are forest. ($\frac{3}{4}$ is less than the whole.) To get a *smaller* number than 12, *multiply.*

$$\frac{\overset{3}{\cancel{12}}}{1} \times \frac{3}{\underset{1}{\cancel{4}}} = \frac{9}{1} \text{ or } \textbf{9 acres}$$

Think about what size your answer should be. Then solve the problems below. Use estimation whenever possible.

1. The Grzeckis spend $\frac{2}{5}$ of their income on house and car payments. If their monthly income is $2,200, what are their monthly house and car payments?

   (1) $25

   (2) $880

   (3) $5,500

2. A study showed that $\frac{1}{2}$ of people surveyed were satisfied in their jobs. Of the 750 people surveyed, how many were satisfied?

   (1) 375

   (2) 700

   (3) 1,500

3. There are $11\frac{1}{2}$ tons of garbage that need to be moved from an industrial area. How many truckloads is that if each load is $\frac{1}{2}$ ton?

   (1) 5.75

   (2) 12

   (3) 23

4. One-third of Marcia's homemade salad dressing is vinegar. Of the dressing pictured below, how much is vinegar?

   (1) $\frac{1}{4}$ cup

   (2) $\frac{4}{9}$ cup

   (3) $1\frac{1}{12}$ cups

   } $\frac{3}{4}$ cup

5. How many $\frac{3}{4}$-minute slots are there in a $3\frac{3}{4}$-minute commercial break?

   (1) 2

   (2) 3

   (3) 5

6. **Label** Jack's house is exactly halfway between the 2 towns below. Label the distance between Jack's house and each town.

   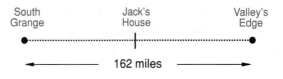

Multiplication and Division Equations

As you learned in Unit 2, equations can help you understand the relationship between numbers. Can you see that the value on one side of each equation below is equal to the value on the other side?

Examples:

$$3 \times 2 = 6 \times 1 \qquad\qquad \tfrac{1}{2} \times \tfrac{1}{2} = \tfrac{1}{4} \qquad\qquad 10 \times \tfrac{2}{5} = 16 \div 4$$

You can also use a **variable,** or letter, to stand for a number you do not know.

Examples:

$\tfrac{3}{4} \times d = 9$ (Three-fourths of *some number* is equal to 9.)

$10 \div x = 5$ (Ten divided by *some number* will give you 5.)

Writing equations can help you understand multiplication and division problems more clearly. Let's see how.

Example 1: A chef divided a pot of steamed vegetables into $6\tfrac{1}{2}$-ounce servings. She got 18 servings from the pot. How many ounces of vegetables did the pot contain in all?

Write an equation:

$$x \div 6\tfrac{1}{2} = 18$$

total ounces | ounces per serving | number of servings

The number being divided goes first in the equation.

Example 2: Two-fifths of the people at the meeting were police officers. If there were 20 police officers at the meeting, how many people attended the meeting in all?

Write an equation:

$$\tfrac{2}{5} \times p = 20$$

fraction that were police officers | total people | number of police officers

In these examples, the variable stands for the number you do not know—the number you are looking for.

122

A. Choose the correct equation for each problem below.

1. Yoshi divided all the strawberries he picked among 3 friends. Each friend received $3\frac{1}{2}$ pints. How many pints of strawberries did Yoshi pick?

   (1) $p \times 3 = 3\frac{1}{2}$

   (2) $p \times 3\frac{1}{2} = 3$

   (3) $p \div 3 = 3\frac{1}{2}$

   (4) $3\frac{1}{2} \div p = 3$

2. A company estimates that $\frac{1}{4}$ of its catalog mailings results in sales. If the company mails 185,000 catalogs a year, how many catalog sales result?

   (1) $185,000 \div r = \frac{1}{4}$

   (2) $\frac{1}{4} \times 185,000 = r$

   (3) $r \times 185,000 = \frac{1}{4}$

   (4) $\frac{1}{4} \div r = 185,000$

3. City Cleaners charges between $1.50 and $2.50 per stair to clean carpeted stairs. If the total bill came to $150.00 and there were 60 stairs, how much did they charge per stair for this job?

   (1) $60 \div \$150 = c$

   (2) $c \times \$150 = 60$

   (3) $\$150 \div 60 = c$

   (4) $c \div 60 = \$150$

4. Pedro drove 250 miles in $4\frac{1}{2}$ hours. How many miles per hour did Pedro drive?

   (1) $4\frac{1}{2} \times 250 = m$

   (2) $4\frac{1}{2} \div m = 250$

   (3) $m \div 4\frac{1}{2} = 250$

   (4) $250 \div 4\frac{1}{2} = m$

B. Write an equation for each problem below. Remember that your first step is to assign a letter to the number you do not know. Do not solve the problems.

5. Farad weighs $3\frac{1}{2}$ times the weight of his daughter. If Farad weighs 175 pounds, how many pounds does his daughter weigh?

   Equation: _____

6. The total height of the drums below is $12\frac{3}{4}$ feet. How tall is one drum?

   Equation: _____

7. Kieran paid $43.80 for a dress at a $\frac{1}{2}$-off sale. What was the original price of the dress?

   Equation: _____

8. How many $3\frac{1}{2}$-minute film clips can be shown in 21 minutes?

   Equation: _____

Solving Multiplication and Division Equations

Can you guess the value of *g* in the equation below?

$$\tfrac{1}{2} \times g = 10$$

Try plugging in some values to see if they work.

Does 5 work?

$$\tfrac{1}{2} \times 5 \neq 10 \qquad \textbf{No, } \tfrac{1}{2} \times 5 = 2\tfrac{1}{2}.$$

Can *g* = 20?

$$\tfrac{1}{2} \times 20 = 10 \qquad \textbf{Yes, } g = 20.$$

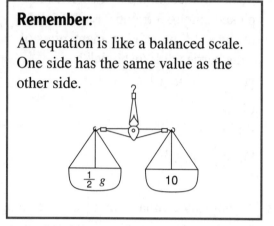

Remember:

An equation is like a balanced scale. One side has the same value as the other side.

Just as with addition and subtraction equations, there is an easy way to find out what value will solve a multiplication or division equation. To solve multiplication and division equations, use these **inverse operations:**

▶ **Multiplication** is the opposite, or inverse, of division.

▶ **Division** is the opposite, or inverse, of multiplication.

As with addition and subtraction equations, your goal is to *get the unknown alone on one side of the equal sign.*

Example: $z \times 5 = 105$

Since *z* is being *multiplied* by 5, use the inverse operation—**division.**
To get *z* alone, *divide both sides of the equation by 5.*

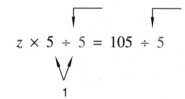

Whatever you do to one side of the "balancing scale" you must do to the other.

Can you see that dividing by 5 on the left side leaves *z* alone?

$z \times 1$ is one *z* or just *z*. The "scale" balances because you have divided by the same number on *both* sides of the equation. You now have this equation:

$$z = 105 \div 5$$

$$z = 21$$

Solving a Multiplication or Division Equation

Example: $a \div 3 = 14$

Step 1
Decide what inverse operation to use to get the variable alone on one side of the equal sign.

*Since a is being divided by 3 in the equation, then **multiplication** would be the correct inverse operation.*

Step 2
Perform the inverse operation *on both sides of the equal sign.*

$a \div 3 \times 3 = 14 \times 3$

1

Multiply both sides by 3.

Step 3
Simplify to find the value of the unknown.

$a = 14 \times 3$

$a = 42$

To check your work, plug your answer into the original equation:

$a \div 3 = 14; 42 \div 3 = 14;$ **Yes,** $a = 42$.

A. Solve the following multiplication and division equations, using inverse operations when needed.

1. $y \times \frac{1}{2} = 4$

2. $\frac{9}{10} \times t = 90$

3. $p \div \frac{3}{4} = 20$

4. $q \div 5 = \frac{8}{15}$

5. $3\frac{1}{2} \div \frac{1}{2} = b$

6. $y \times 12 = 6$

7. $5 \times t = 1,100$

8. $p \div \frac{2}{3} = 30$

9. $q \div \frac{1}{2} = \frac{1}{4}$

10. $5 \div \frac{1}{2} = b$

B. Write an equation for each problem below, then solve the equation using inverse operations when needed.

11. A mother divided her $4.12 in spare change evenly among her children. Each child received $1.03. How many children did the mother have?

    Let s = _____ Equation: _____

12. Ursula split her car trip into 4 segments, each consisting of 40 miles. How many miles in all was her trip?

    Let s = _____ Equation: _____

13. Troy is 3 times as old as his son. Troy is 30 years old. How old is his son?

    Let s = _____ Equation: _____

14. One-third of all women in Rosalita's support group are single. There are 13 single women in the group. How many women are in the group altogether?

    Let s = _____ Equation: _____

Fractions and Your Calculator

Calculators use the decimal system to represent number values. To work with fractions on a calculator, *convert the fractions to decimals.*

▶ To change a fraction to a decimal, divide the numerator by the denominator.

Example: Change $\frac{4}{5}$ to a decimal.

On your calculator:

$$\frac{4}{5} = 5\overline{)4.0}^{\,.8} \qquad \frac{4}{5} = \mathbf{.8}$$

| 4 | ÷ | 5 | = | | 0.8 |

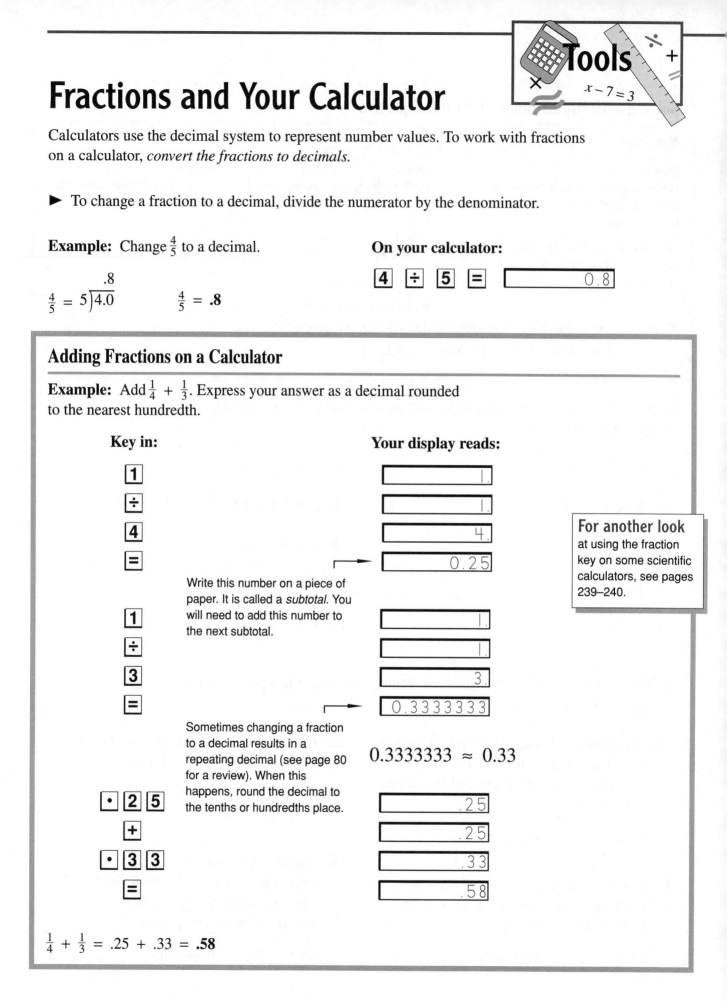

Adding Fractions on a Calculator

Example: Add $\frac{1}{4} + \frac{1}{3}$. Express your answer as a decimal rounded to the nearest hundredth.

Key in: **Your display reads:**

1	1.
÷	1.
4	4.
=	0.25

Write this number on a piece of paper. It is called a *subtotal*. You will need to add this number to the next subtotal.

1	1.
÷	1.
3	3.
=	0.3333333

Sometimes changing a fraction to a decimal results in a repeating decimal (see page 80 for a review). When this happens, round the decimal to the tenths or hundredths place.

$$0.3333333 \approx 0.33$$

• 2 5	.25
+	.25
• 3 3	.33
=	.58

For another look at using the fraction key on some scientific calculators, see pages 239–240.

$$\frac{1}{4} + \frac{1}{3} = .25 + .33 = \mathbf{.58}$$

Mixed Numbers on a Calculator

To work with mixed numbers on a calculator, change the fraction part to a decimal, then combine it with the whole number.

Subtracting Fractions on a Calculator

Example: Subtract $3\frac{1}{4}$ from $5\frac{1}{8}$.

Step 1. Change $\frac{1}{4}$ to a decimal with your calculator: $\qquad \frac{1}{4} = 0.25$

Step 2. Combine the decimal with whole number: $\qquad 3.25$

Step 3. Do the same with any other mixed number: $\qquad \frac{1}{8} = .125$

$$5\frac{1}{8} = 5.125$$

Step 4. Do the computation with your calculator: $\qquad 5.125 - 3.25 = \mathbf{1.875}$

> **Tip**
> On page 240, you can see how to use the fraction key that is provided on some scientific calculators.

A. Use a calculator to do the following problems.

1. $5\frac{1}{4} \times 3$ $\qquad\qquad$ $\frac{5}{8} + \frac{2}{5}$ $\qquad\qquad$ $7\frac{1}{2} \times 2\frac{1}{2}$

2. $10\frac{2}{3} - 4\frac{1}{2}$ to the nearest *tenth* $\qquad\qquad$ $\frac{1}{3} \div \frac{3}{4}$ to the nearest *hundredth*

B. Solve the following problems. Use a calculator.

3. Tina bought $2\frac{3}{4}$ pounds of grapes, $3\frac{4}{5}$ pounds of oranges, and a $1\frac{1}{2}$-pound pineapple. How many pounds of fruit did she buy?

4. One-third of the area of the school gym can be used for a science exhibit. If the whole gym is 3,400 square feet, how many square feet can be used for the exhibit, rounded to the nearest hundredth?

5. What is the perimeter of the rectangle below? (*Hint:* Add the four sides together.)

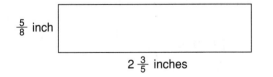

$\frac{5}{8}$ inch

$2\frac{3}{5}$ inches

6. How many $1\frac{1}{8}$-inch metal rings can be cut from a 6-inch metal pipe?

7. What is the area of the square below? (*Hint:* Multiply length × width.)

$3\frac{1}{2}$ cm

$3\frac{1}{2}$ cm

8. How many times can a $5\frac{1}{3}$-minute filmstrip be shown in its entirety during a $\frac{1}{2}$-hour exhibition?

9. **Discuss** With a partner, discuss how to solve this problem: Wanda earns $4.70 an hour, but gets paid $5.50 *extra* in overtime for each hour over 40 hours. She worked $46\frac{3}{4}$ hours last week. How much overtime pay will she receive for the time over 40 hours she worked?

Fractions and Money

When you work with fractions and money, you are actually using both fractions and decimals at the same time. It's usually easiest to change the fractions to decimals before you do any calculating.

Example: Tanisha worked $37\frac{1}{2}$ hours and earns $7.16 per hour. How much did she earn, before taxes?

Tanisha J. White	SSN 440-00-3205
Employee # 312-13	Week ending 4/27/02
Gross Pay ▬▬▬	FICA ▬▬▬
Net Pay ▬▬▬	State Tax ▬▬▬
Medical ▬▬▬	Union ▬▬▬

Total Hours $37\frac{1}{2}$

Working with Fractions and Money

Example: What is $37\frac{1}{2} \times \$7.16$?

Step 1
Estimate first by rounding to whole numbers.

$37\frac{1}{2} \approx 38$

$\$7.16 \approx \$7$

$$\begin{array}{r} 38 \\ \times\ \$7 \\ \hline \$266 \end{array}$$

Step 2
Change fractions to decimals by dividing the denominator into the numerator.

$37\frac{1}{2} = 37.5$

$\frac{1}{2} = 2\overline{)1.0}\ \ .5$

Step 3
Do the calculations.

$$\begin{array}{r} 37.5 \\ \times\ \$7.16 \\ \hline \$268.50 \end{array}$$

Your answer of **$268.50** is very close to the estimate $266.

A. **Use a calculator to do the following problems. As a first step, change each fraction to a decimal by dividing the numerator by the denominator. Round money values to the nearest *cent*.**

1. $\$3.10 \times \frac{3}{4} =$ _____

2. $\$5.50 \times \frac{1}{2} =$ _____

3. $1\frac{1}{2} \times \$10 =$ _____

4. $4\frac{3}{8} \times \$.89 =$ _____

5. $\$1.75 \times \frac{3}{5} =$ _____

6. $\$.50 \times \frac{1}{10} =$ _____

7. $\frac{1}{5} \times \$2.10 =$ _____

8. $1\frac{1}{2} \times \$5 =$ _____

B. Using the information on the payroll ledger below, determine how much money Franklin Company will pay in employee wages this week. Use a calculator if you'd like, and round to the nearest *cent*.

FRANKLIN COMPANY
Employee Wages – Week of 8/20/02

J. Thompson	F. Alvarez	T. Rico	S. Kim	L. Delgado
$25 \frac{3}{4}$ hours	$30 \frac{1}{2}$ hours	$38 \frac{1}{4}$ hours	$39 \frac{1}{2}$ hours	$35 \frac{3}{4}$ hours
@ $5.91 per hour	@ $9.45 per hour	@ $5.50 per hour	@ $6.75 per hour	@ $5.25 per hour

Thompson _____

Alvarez _____

Rico _____

Kim _____

Delgado _____

Total Wages: _____

C. Take a shopping trip in Evita's Exotic Fruit Market. Using the prices per pound and the weights shown, determine how much this customer will spend on the produce. Use a calculator if you'd like, and round to the nearest cent.

$1.39	$1.89	$1.99	$2.59	$2.19	$2.29
Mangoes	Papaya	Breadfruit	Jackfruit	Kiwi	Kumquats
$\frac{3}{4}$ pound	$\frac{7}{8}$ pound	$1 \frac{1}{2}$ pounds	$\frac{1}{2}$ pound	$\frac{1}{4}$ pound	$1 \frac{1}{3}$ pounds

Mangoes: _____

Papaya: _____

Breadfruit: _____

Jackfruit: _____

Kiwi: _____

Kumquats: _____

Total Amount Spent: _____

Answers start on page 217.

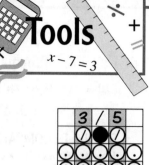

Gridding in Fraction Answers

You can grid in a fraction using one of the slash marks from the second row of the standard five-column grid. The slash mark is a form of the fraction bar. For example, the fraction $\frac{3}{5}$ would be entered as 3/5 on the grid. See the sample grid shown to the right.

There are important rules to remember when entering fractions on a grid.

- You <u>cannot</u> enter mixed numbers. Convert any mixed number to an improper fraction before you grid it.

- You do not have to write a fraction in lowest terms unless the problem tells you to do so. However, you may have to write it in lower terms so that it will fit in five columns.

- Do not leave any columns blank within your answer.

To enter fractions in the answer grid, follow these steps:

1. Solve the problem. If the answer is a mixed number, convert it to an improper fraction.

2. Write the answer beginning with the numerator. Write the slash mark in its own column. Finally, write the denominator. Do not leave blank columns between the parts of the fraction.

3. Fill in the one correct circle in each column.

Filling in the Grid

Example: A hiking trail is $3\frac{1}{2}$ miles long. Jenna hiked $1\frac{3}{5}$ miles in 75 minutes. How many miles does she have left to hike?

Step 1
Solve the problem.

$$\begin{array}{r} 3\frac{1}{2} = 3\frac{5}{10} = 2\frac{15}{10} \\ \text{Subtract:} \quad - 1\frac{3}{5} = 1\frac{6}{10} = 1\frac{6}{10} \\ \hline 1\frac{9}{10} \end{array}$$

Write as an improper fraction:
$1\frac{9}{10} = \frac{19}{10}$

Step 2
Write your answer in the top row of boxes. Use the slash for the fraction bar.

Step 3
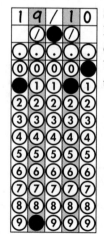
Fill in the correct circles on the grid. Use the digits in the top row as a guide.

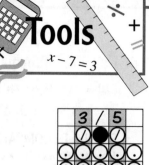

130

Study these examples to see how to fit your answers in the grid.

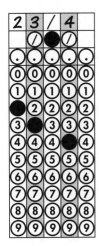 The answer to a problem is $5\frac{3}{4}$. You must convert it to an improper fraction. Then enter it in the grid.

$$5\frac{3}{4} = \frac{23}{4}$$

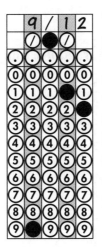 The answer to a problem is $\frac{9}{12}$. You don't have to spend time writing the fraction in lowest terms unless the question asks you to.

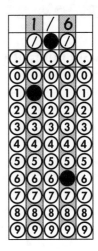 The answer to a problem is $\frac{25}{150}$. Write the fraction in lowest terms to fit it in five columns.

$$\frac{25}{150} \div \frac{25}{25} = \frac{1}{6}$$

Solve the following problems. Record your answers in the grids.

1.  The Gersons have driven $9\frac{3}{4}$ hours of a $12\frac{1}{2}$-hour drive. How many more hours do they have to go?

3. 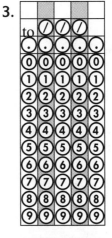 Emma uses $1\frac{1}{3}$ cups of sugar to make pie filling for one pie. How many cups of sugar will she need to make enough pie filling for four pies?

2. 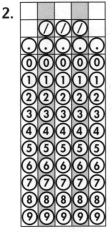 A plastic pipe is $17\frac{1}{2}$ feet in length. If the pipe is cut into four equal pieces, how many feet long will each piece be?

4. At an insurance company, $\frac{3}{8}$ of the employees signed up for a management-training workshop. If the company has 96 employees in all, how many signed up for the workshop?

Unit 3 Review

A. Add, subtract, multiply, or divide the following fractions. Simplify your answers.

1. $\frac{1}{3} + \frac{2}{3}$ $\qquad$ $\frac{3}{5} + \frac{9}{10}$ $\qquad$ $\frac{3}{4} + \frac{7}{8}$ $\qquad$ $\frac{1}{10} + \frac{1}{4}$

2. $\frac{7}{8} - \frac{3}{8}$ $\qquad$ $\frac{4}{5} - \frac{3}{10}$ $\qquad$ $\frac{1}{3} - \frac{1}{4}$ $\qquad$ $\frac{2}{3} - \frac{2}{7}$

3. $\frac{1}{2} \times \frac{1}{3}$ $\qquad$ $\frac{2}{5} \times \frac{3}{4}$ $\qquad$ $\frac{1}{8} \times \frac{1}{10}$ $\qquad$ $\frac{3}{4} \times \frac{4}{5}$

4. $\frac{2}{3} \div \frac{1}{3}$ $\qquad$ $\frac{3}{4} \div \frac{1}{8}$ $\qquad$ $\frac{9}{10} \div \frac{3}{5}$ $\qquad$ $\frac{1}{4} \div \frac{1}{2}$

B. Add, subtract, multiply, or divide the following fractions, whole numbers, and mixed numbers.

5. $2\frac{1}{2} + 5\frac{1}{2}$ $\qquad$ $3\frac{3}{4} + \frac{1}{8}$ $\qquad$ $3\frac{3}{10} + 4\frac{4}{5}$ $\qquad$ $\frac{5}{6} + 3\frac{1}{2}$

6. $5\frac{9}{10} - \frac{1}{5}$ $\qquad$ $2\frac{1}{3} - 1\frac{2}{3}$ $\qquad$ $4\frac{3}{8} - 1\frac{1}{2}$ $\qquad$ $8\frac{1}{4} - 2\frac{3}{5}$

7. $2\frac{1}{2} \times \frac{1}{3}$ $\qquad$ $4\frac{3}{8} \times 1\frac{1}{3}$ $\qquad$ $9\frac{9}{10} \times 1\frac{1}{4}$ $\qquad$ $5\frac{1}{2} \times \frac{3}{5}$

8. $5 \div \frac{1}{3}$ $\qquad$ $3\frac{3}{4} \div 5$ $\qquad$ $2\frac{1}{8} \div 1\frac{1}{4}$ $\qquad$ $10\frac{1}{3} \div 2\frac{1}{2}$

C. Choose the best answer for each problem. Pay careful attention to whether you should add, subtract, multiply, or divide. Also watch out for extra information.

9. How many $1\frac{1}{2}$-centimeter lengths can be cut from a 6-centimeter length?

(1) 9

(2) $7\frac{1}{2}$

(3) 4

10. On three trips, Jen rode $4\frac{1}{2}$ miles, $3\frac{3}{4}$ miles, and $6\frac{3}{4}$ miles. What was her average number of miles?

(1) 5

(2) 10

(3) 15

11. A pharmacist had 8 vials of medicine, each containing $\frac{7}{8}$ ounce of fluid. In all, how many ounces did the vials contain?

(1) $9\frac{1}{7}$

(2) 7

(3) Not enough information is given.

12. James took a $12\frac{1}{2}$-foot-long rubber hose and cut off 2 pieces from it. How many feet were left on the hose?

(1) $10\frac{1}{2}$

(2) $6\frac{1}{4}$

(3) Not enough information is given.

D. Use the drawing to the right to answer the following questions.

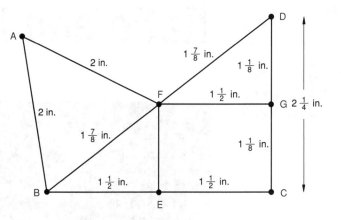

13. How many inches is the distance from A to B to C?

14. Suppose you divided the line between D and F into 3 equal pieces. How long would each piece be?

15. What is $\frac{1}{3}$ of the distance from D to C?

16. How much longer is the distance from C to D than the distance from A to F?

E. Grid in the answer to each problem.

17. 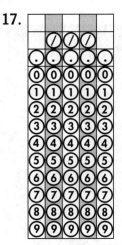 A fence post is $11\frac{1}{4}$ feet long. Max cuts $2\frac{3}{8}$ feet from the top of the post. What is the new length of the post in feet?

18. A stack of plywood is 24 inches high. Each sheet of plywood in the stack is $\frac{3}{4}$ inch thick. How many sheets of plywood are in the stack?

Working Together

Look at the sample fraction cards below. In pairs, come up with answers for the following questions. Compare your answers with others in the class. Then write your own questions about the cards.

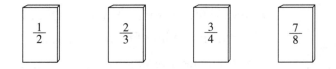

- Adding which two fractions will result in the largest sum? The smallest sum?

- Subtracting which two fractions will result in the largest difference? The smallest difference?

Ratio and Proportion

Skills

Relating fractions to ratios

Writing a ratio

Ratios and patterns

Understanding proportions

Writing proportions

Solving proportion problems

Tools

Calculator

Problem Solver

Making a table

Applications

Unit rates

Scale drawings and maps

Everything you have learned about fractions in the last unit will help you understand **ratio** and **proportion.** In fact, a ratio is just a type of fraction. A proportion is simply a pair of equivalent fractions.

In this unit, you will see how ratio and proportion can help you solve many real-life math problems.

You may want to review these fraction lessons in Unit 1:

• Understanding Fractions............................page 30
• Equivalent Fractions ....page 36

When Do I Use Ratio and Proportion?

Read the following list of situations in which ratios or proportions are used. Check off any that you have encountered in your life:

- ☐ changing the serving quantity in a recipe
- ☐ comparing miles per gallons in two different models of cars
- ☐ computing mileage by measuring inches on a map
- ☐ reading a scale drawing of a building or room
- ☐ determining unit price on a grocery store item
- ☐ changing units of measurement

Now describe some of your thoughts about ratio and proportion on the lines below.

1. Have you ever had to convert one type of measurement into another (for instance, inches to feet)? How did you do it?

   _____

   _____

2. When you shop, do you compare the *cost per unit* of similar items to find the best deal? (For example, have you compared the cost per *one ounce* of two different brands of salad dressing or other product?) Describe what you did.

   _____

   _____

3. Have you ever had to increase a recipe so that it served more people? What did you do?

   _____

   _____

Talk About It

Ratios are forms of comparisons that we make every day. For example, when we talk about rates, we are talking about ratios. An example of rates is when we discuss *miles per gallon*.

In pairs, brainstorm a list of the relationships that use the word *per*. Then compare your list with others in the class. Make one big list for the class as a whole.

Fractions and Ratios

In Unit 1, you learned that fractions express a part of a whole. For example, what fraction represents the shaded part in this rectangle?

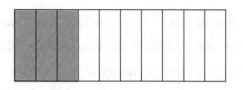

You probably wrote $\frac{3}{10}$, meaning that 3 out of 10 parts are shaded. You can also express what is pictured above as a ratio.

► A **ratio** is a comparison of one number to another. A **fraction** is a specific kind of ratio comparing a part to the whole.

3 shaded parts	3 shaded parts	7 unshaded parts
7 unshaded parts	10 total parts	10 total parts
↑	↑	↑
ratio, not a fraction (It doesn't compare a part to the whole.)	both a ratio and a fraction	both a ratio and a fraction

Ratios can be expressed in three different forms.

Example: Write a ratio of *unshaded parts* to *shaded parts*.

Fraction Form	With a Colon	In Words
$\frac{7}{3}$	7:3	7 to 3

Notice that the order in which the numbers appear is very important. The ratio 7:3 represents the ratio of *unshaded to shaded*. The ratio 3:7 represents *shaded to unshaded*.

Try writing the following ratios based on the picture at right.

• apples to lemons

    ■:■ *or* $\frac{■}{■}$ *or* ■ to ■

• apples to total fruit

    ■:■ *or* $\frac{■}{■}$ *or* ■ to ■

• lemons to apples

    ■:■ *or* $\frac{■}{■}$ *or* ■ to ■

• total fruit to lemons

    ■:■ *or* $\frac{■}{■}$ *or* ■ to ■

You should have written *apples to lemons* as 5:4, $\frac{5}{4}$, and 5 to 4; *lemons to apples* as 4:5, $\frac{4}{5}$, and 4 to 5; *apples to total fruit* as 5:9, $\frac{5}{9}$, and 5 to 9; and *total fruit to lemons* as 9:4, $\frac{9}{4}$, and 9 to 4.

A. **Write ratios based on the figures below. Use any of the three forms you learned on page 136.**

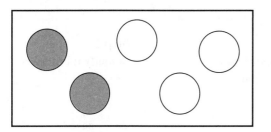
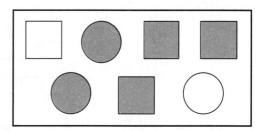

1. shaded circles to unshaded circles _____

2. unshaded circles to all circles _____

3. all circles to shaded circles _____

4. squares to circles _____

5. shaded circles to shaded squares _____

6. all circles to shaded circles _____

B. **Use the figures below to make up your own ratios. Be sure you include labels as in the first one below.**

7. $\dfrac{\text{shaded triangles}}{\$} = \dfrac{1}{4}$

8.

9.

10.

11.

12.

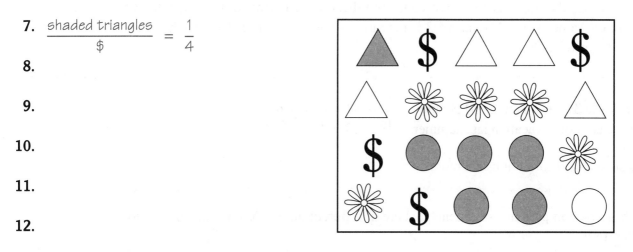

Making Connections: Simplifying Ratios

Like fractions, ratios must be simplified to lowest terms. For example, a ratio of **2:4** should be written as **1:2** or $\frac{1}{2}$. A ratio is *never* written as a whole number. For example, the ratio **6:3** is written as **2:1** or $\frac{2}{1}$, *not* just 2.

Simplify ratios from Part B above, where necessary. Remember—do not simplify to a whole number. Instead, use a denominator of 1 where appropriate.

Writing a Ratio

Many number relationships can be written as ratios. If 2 numbers are being compared, try putting them in ratio form. Remember to simplify a ratio to lowest terms if possible.

Writing a Ratio

	Step 1 Use the first number in the ratio as a numerator. Make the second number the denominator.	**Step 2** Simplify if necessary.
Example 1: Eleanor typed 27 pages in 4 hours. Write a ratio of pages to hours.	$\dfrac{27}{4}$ $\dfrac{\text{pages}}{\text{hours}}$	$\dfrac{27}{4}$ $\dfrac{\text{pages}}{\text{hours}}$
Example 2: The Abelows' rec room is 25 feet long and 15 feet wide. What is the ratio of width to length?	$\dfrac{15}{25}$ $\dfrac{\text{feet wide}}{\text{feet long}}$	$\dfrac{15}{25} = \dfrac{3}{5}$ $\dfrac{\text{feet wide}}{\text{feet long}}$

You can see the importance of putting the numbers in the correct order. The ratio 3:5 is *not* the same as 5:3. The ratio 5:3 is the ratio of *length* to *width*. To keep the ratios in order, use labels.

Example 3: Seven out of 10 people surveyed took a vacation last summer.

$\dfrac{7}{10}$ $\dfrac{\text{summer vacationers}}{\text{people surveyed}}$

Express this information as a ratio.

When you compare measurements that are in different units, convert one unit to the other first.

Converting Units to Write a Ratio

Example: On their last job, Mario worked 2 hours while his brother worked 30 minutes. What is the ratio of time worked by Mario to time worked by his brother?

Step 1 Convert to the same unit of measurement.	**Step 2** Set up a ratio in fraction form.	**Step 3** Simplify if necessary.
2 hours = 120 minutes	$\dfrac{120}{30}$ $\dfrac{\text{minutes}}{\text{minutes}}$	$\dfrac{120}{30} = \dfrac{4}{1}$

Mario worked **4** minutes for each **1** minute his brother worked.

A. **Write ratios for each of the following situations. Be sure to express the ratios in lowest terms.**

In a box of glass figurines shipped this week, there were 4 broken and 14 unbroken ones.

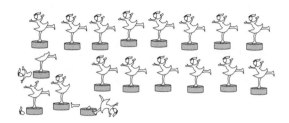

1. Write a ratio of *unbroken* to *broken* figurines.

2. Write a ratio of *broken* figurines to *total* figurines. (*Hint:* To find the *total,* add broken and unbroken together.)

3. Write a ratio of *total* figurines to *unbroken* ones.

Out of a total of 12 free throw attempts during last night's basketball game, the Warriors scored on 9 of them. Warriors player Brad Clayton scored on 6 of the free throws.

4. Write a ratio of *successful* free throws to *total* free throw attempts.

5. Write a ratio of *Clayton's* successful free throws to the *team's* successful free throws.

6. Write a ratio of *Clayton's successful free throws* to the *total attempts made by the team.*

B. **Use the data from the chart below to write ratios for problems 7 through 10. Express the ratios in lowest terms.**

Current Job Positions at SystemSet, Inc.

POSITION	NUMBER OF EMPLOYEES
Support Staff	35
Technical Staff	18
Sales Personnel	20
Sales Manager	5
Brand Manager	8
Director	5
President	1

7. Write a ratio showing the relationship of the number of support staff to the number of directors.

8. What is the ratio of sales managers to sales personnel?

9. What is the ratio of support staff to total SystemSet employees?

10. **Write** Use the chart to write 5 ratios of your own. Label the ratios and express them in lowest terms.

Ratios and Patterns

You know that when you multiply both numerator and denominator of a fraction or ratio by the same number, the result is an equivalent fraction or ratio.

Example: $\frac{1}{2} \times \frac{3}{3} = \frac{3}{6}$

Try to find a pattern in these values. Can you fill in the denominators?

$\frac{1}{2} = \frac{2}{\blacksquare} = \frac{3}{6} = \frac{4}{\blacksquare} = \frac{5}{\blacksquare} = \frac{6}{\blacksquare} = \frac{7}{\blacksquare} = \frac{8}{\blacksquare}$

You should have put a 4 in the first box above because $\frac{1}{2} \times \frac{2}{2} = \frac{2}{4}$

What other patterns do you see in the fractions above?

- The numerators increase by _____.

- The denominators increase by _____.

You can see that as the numerators increase by *1,* the denominators increase by *2.*
Let's look at another pattern.

Example: Out of every $5 that Martha earns, she saves $1. If Martha earns $15, how much will she save?

$ Earned	$5	$10	$15	$20	$25
$ Saved	$1				

Martha will save **$3** because $\frac{\$5}{\$1} = \frac{\$15}{\$3}$

What other patterns do you see in the chart above?

- The dollars earned increase by _____.

- The dollars saved increase by _____.

Can you see that as the dollars earned increase by 5, the dollars saved increase by *1?*
No matter how much Martha earns, her ratio of *earnings to savings* is 5:1 or $\frac{5}{1}$.

A. Find the patterns in the charts below and fill in the blanks.

1. In every pound of chocolates, there are 16 pieces of candy.

Pounds	1	2	3	4	5
Pieces					

2. Out of every $100 spent in its supermarket, Grand Grocery will donate $4 to local schools.

$ Spent	$100	$200			
$ Donated				$16	

3. In every dollar, there are 10 dimes or 20 nickels.

Dollars	1		3		5
Dimes		20			
Nickels				80	

4. The Chandlers' hourly take-home pay is $27.75. In one hour, Mr. Chandler takes home $13.50, and Mrs. Chandler takes home $14.25.

# Hours	1	2	3	4	5
Total Take-home Pay	$27.75	$55.50			
Mr. Chandler		$27.00			$67.50
Mrs. Chandler	$14.25			$57.00	

B. In your own words, describe the patterns in each chart above. The first one is done for you.

5. Chart 1. _As the pounds increase by 1, the pieces increase by 16._

6. Chart 2. _____

7. Chart 3. _____

8. Chart 4. _____

Unit Rates

Rates are ratios that compare different units of measurement. For example, *miles per hour* is a rate; *miles* are compared to *hours*. Rates are often expressed with the word *per*, which means "for each."

Finding Unit Rates

Example: A car traveled 440 miles on 11 gallons of gas. How many miles per gallon does the car get?

Step 1
Write a ratio.

$$\frac{440 \text{ miles}}{11 \text{ gallons}}$$

Step 2
Simplify to get a denominator of 1.

$$\frac{440}{11} \div \frac{11}{11} = \frac{40 \text{ miles}}{1 \text{ gallon}}$$

Step 3
Write the ratio as a rate.

The car gets **40 miles per gallon.**

A. Write the following values as rates. The first one is done for you.

1. The River Bridge raises 2 times an hour to let boats pass.

   2 times per hour

2. The average human heart beats 70 times in 1 minute.

   _____

3. The building manager uses 1 gallon of paint to cover 3 walls.

   _____

4. Rowanda paid $13.50 for a ticket to last night's concert.

   _____

5. In 1 day, Mike's Muffler Shop installs 80 car mufflers.

   _____

B. Find the unit rate.

6. Chana drives 220 miles in 4 hours. How many *miles per hour* does she drive?

7. There are 12 cups in 3 quarts of liquid. How many *cups per quart* are there?

8. Jim drove 80 miles in $2\frac{1}{2}$ hours. How many *miles per hour* did he drive?

9. There are 54 ounces total in 3 boxes of cereal. How many *ounces per box* are there?

Unit Pricing

Another common example of unit rate is **unit pricing.** If you know the cost of several units, you can figure out the cost of one unit. Similarly, if you know the cost of one unit, you can find the cost of several units.

SALE PRICE
3 Quarts
$ 5.00

Finding Unit Price

Example: Suppose you buy 3 pints of strawberries for $5.55. What is the unit price of the berries?

Step 1
Set up a ratio.

$$\frac{\$5.55}{3 \text{ pints}}$$

Step 2
Simplify to get a denominator of 1.

$$\frac{\$5.55}{3} \div \frac{3}{3}$$

Step 3
Find the unit price.

$$\frac{\$5.55}{3} \div \frac{3}{3} = \frac{\$1.85}{1 \text{ pint}}$$

The unit price of the strawberries is **$1.85 per pint.**

If you know the cost of one item, you can use ratios to find the cost of several.

Example: Deana bought 8 scarves that were on sale for $4.50 each. What did she spend in all?

$$\frac{\$4.50}{1} = \frac{?}{8}$$

Since you multiplied the denominator by 8 to get 8, multiply the numerator, $4.50, by 8 as well:

$$\$4.50 \times 8 = \textbf{\$36.00 for 8 scarves}$$

C. Find the costs of the products below by using the chart.

10. What would you pay for 4 pounds of ground sirloin?

11. Suppose you bought a 3-pound bag of potatoes. What did you pay per pound?

12. What is the unit price for beef tips at Sanford Groceries?

13. **a.** A customer bought 3 pounds of onions and 1 pound of beef tips. What did he pay?

   b. A customer paid for the purchases in problem 13a with a $10 bill. What change should he get back?

Sanford Groceries	
ground sirloin	$2.99 per pound
beef tips	$7.98 for a 2-pound pack
potatoes	$2.10 for a 3-pound bag
onions	$.59 per pound
lettuce	$.79 per head
tomatoes	$1.19 per pound

Understanding Proportion

A **proportion** is made up of two equal ratios. When you work with equivalent fractions, you are working with a proportion.

$\frac{2}{3} = \frac{4}{6}$ is a proportion. The two ratios are equal.

▶ Two equal ratios make a proportion. Two ratios are equal if their **cross products** are equal.

Example 1: Is $\frac{3}{4} = \frac{6}{8}$?

Are the cross products equal? $\frac{3}{4} \bowtie \frac{6}{8}$

$3 \times 8 = \mathbf{24}$ and $4 \times 6 = \mathbf{24}$, so *yes,* the ratios are equal.

Example 2: Is $\frac{1}{3} = \frac{2}{5}$?

Are the cross products equal? $\frac{1}{3} \bowtie \frac{2}{5}$

$1 \times 5 = \mathbf{5}$ and $2 \times 3 = \mathbf{6}$, so *no,* the ratios are *not* equal. This is *not* a proportion.

If one number is missing in a proportion, you can use cross products and equations to find out what it is.

Solving Proportions

Example 1: $\frac{2}{3} = \frac{12}{?}$

Step 1
Use a variable for the number you don't know.

$\frac{2}{3} = \frac{12}{p}$

Step 2
Multiply to find the cross products and write an equation.

$\frac{2}{3} \bowtie \frac{12}{p}$

$p \times 2 = 12 \times 3$

Step 3
Solve the equation.

$p \times 2 = 12 \times 3$
$p \times 2 = 36$
$p \times 2 \div 2 = 36 \div 2$
$p = 18$

Since you are dividing by 2 to get the p alone, you can write the third line above as $p = 36 \div 2$.

Step 4
Check your proportion by using cross products.

$\frac{2}{3} = \frac{\mathbf{12}}{\mathbf{18}}$

$2 \times 18 = 3 \times 12$
$36 = 36$

Example 2:
What is g in this proportion: $\frac{1}{8} = \frac{6}{30}$?

$1 \times 30 = g \times 6$
$\frac{30}{6} = \frac{g \times 6}{6}$
$\frac{30}{6} = g$
$\mathbf{5} = g$

Check: $\frac{1}{5} = \frac{6}{30}$
$30 = 30$

A. Use cross products to decide if the following ratios are equal. The first two are done for you.

1. $\frac{3}{4} \overset{?}{=} \frac{6}{8}$ $\frac{1}{6} \overset{?}{=} \frac{12}{2}$ $\frac{3}{10} \overset{?}{=} \frac{12}{15}$ $\frac{1}{3} \overset{?}{=} \frac{12}{36}$

     24 = 24; yes   2 ≠ 72; no

2. $\frac{1}{4} \overset{?}{=} \frac{5}{8}$ $\frac{5}{6} \overset{?}{=} \frac{10}{12}$ $\frac{6}{7} \overset{?}{=} \frac{12}{15}$ $\frac{3}{8} \overset{?}{=} \frac{6}{16}$

3. $\frac{2}{3} \overset{?}{=} \frac{14}{21}$ $\frac{5}{8} \overset{?}{=} \frac{25}{40}$ $\frac{1}{7} \overset{?}{=} \frac{14}{21}$ $\frac{4}{7} \overset{?}{=} \frac{16}{28}$

B. Use cross products and equations to find the missing number in each proportion. The first two are started for you.

4. **a.** $\frac{1}{5} = \frac{r}{40}$ **b.** $\frac{7}{8} = \frac{a}{40}$ **c.** $\frac{4}{9} = \frac{12}{15}$ **d.** $\frac{x}{3} = \frac{12}{18}$

     $1 \times 40 = 5 \times r$ $7 \times 40 = 8 \times a$

5. **a.** $\frac{w}{6} = \frac{30}{36}$ **b.** $\frac{5}{9} = \frac{s}{27}$ **c.** $\frac{d}{8} = \frac{12}{16}$ **d.** $\frac{2}{9} = \frac{8}{x}$

6. **a.** $\frac{2}{5} = \frac{r}{20}$ **b.** $\frac{1}{8} = \frac{a}{200}$ **c.** $\frac{6}{9} = \frac{30}{15}$ **d.** $\frac{x}{7} = \frac{12}{21}$

7. **a.** $\frac{w}{10} = \frac{40}{100}$ **b.** $\frac{2}{9} = \frac{s}{45}$ **c.** $\frac{d}{6} = \frac{12}{18}$ **d.** $\frac{7}{8} = \frac{35}{x}$

8. **a.** $\frac{r}{5} = \frac{60}{100}$ **b.** $\frac{3}{7} = \frac{s}{49}$ **c.** $\frac{s}{5} = \frac{18}{90}$ **d.** $\frac{9}{10} = \frac{45}{x}$

Making Connections: Understanding Similar Figures

When two figures are in proportion, they are said to be **similar figures.** Suppose you have a photograph that is 4 inches wide and 5 inches long. If the photo is enlarged, it will have different dimensions, but the same *proportions*. The two photos are similar figures.

The proportion below represents the figures on the right:

$$\frac{4 \text{ inches wide } (\times 2)}{5 \text{ inches long } (\times 2)} = \frac{8 \text{ inches wide}}{10 \text{ inches long}}$$

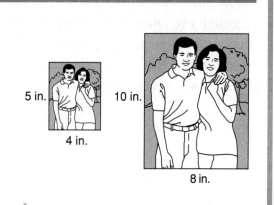

5 in.   10 in.

4 in.

8 in.

Making a Table

As you know, it can be difficult to decide what to do with all the numbers in a math problem. By making a chart or table, you can often tell whether a proportion can be used to solve a problem.

Example 1: Mary Lou can complete 48 circuit boards during an 8-hour shift. How many boards can she complete in 6 hours?

Can a proportion be used to solve this problem? Make a table to find out. Use the labels that go with the numbers to set it up.

Circuit Boards	48	n
Hours	8	6

If you can make a table that compares two units (such as *circuit boards* and *hours*), and if you can fill in 3 of the 4 values, you can write a proportion.

$$\frac{48 \text{ boards}}{8 \text{ hours}} = \frac{n \text{ boards}}{6 \text{ hours}}$$

$$48 \times 6 = 8 \times n$$

$$\frac{48 \times 6}{8} = \frac{8 \times n}{8}$$

$$\frac{288}{8} = n$$

$$\mathbf{36 = \textit{n}}$$

There are some situations in which a proportion *won't* help you.

Example 2: Of the 48 circuit boards that Mary Lou completed on her shift, 46 were ready to be shipped. How many boards were *not* ready for shipping?

Can you make a proportion for this problem?

Circuit Boards	48
Ready for Shipping	46

Although two numbers are being compared in this problem, you cannot set up a proportion. To write a proportion, you need to be able to write two equal ratios. To solve this problem, simply subtract 48 − 46, and you get an answer of **2 boards.**

A. Put the correct numbers in the tables below. Then use the tables to help you write a proportion. Solve for the unknown.

1. The Cantin family drove 320 miles in an 8-hour trip. At this rate, how many miles could they drive in 10 hours?

Miles		
Hours		

2. It takes 2.5 gallons of paint to cover 6 walls at Garden Apartments. How many gallons are needed to cover 12 walls?

Walls		
Gallons		

3. There are 2.54 centimeters in 1 inch. How many inches are there in 101.6 centimeters?

Centimeters		
Inches		

4. One yard is equal to 36 inches. How many inches are there in $2\frac{1}{2}$ yards?

Yards		
Inches		

B. Some of the problems below can be solved using a proportion. Some cannot. Make a table for each problem and use it to decide whether you can write a proportion. Then solve each problem.

Can I use a proportion?

5. A farmer planted corn in 2.5 of his 18 acres of fields. How many acres are *not* used for corn?   Yes   No

6. Jeffrey paid $11 for a 4-pound roast. At this same rate, how much would a 3-pound roast cost?   Yes   No

7. Out of every 1,000 newspapers that come off the press, 12 of them are usually defective. How many papers would be defective out of a daily run of 40,000 newspapers?   Yes   No

8. A square has a side that measures $3\frac{1}{2}$ inches. What is the perimeter (distance around) the square?   Yes   No

9. Ramon bought a sandwich for $4.35 and a soda for $.75. How much did he spend before sales tax?   Yes   No

10. The Aces usually are successful in 3 of every 4 foul shots they attempt. How many attempts did they make if they scored on 15 foul shots?   Yes   No

Solving Problems with Proportions

You can use proportions to solve many kinds of problems. First you must know how to write a proportion.

Example 1: If 5 boxes of matches cost $1.25, then 3 boxes of matches would cost $.75. Write this relationship as a proportion.

$$\frac{5 \text{ boxes}}{\$1.25} = \frac{3 \text{ boxes}}{\$.75}$$

Can you see that the first ratio compares boxes to dollars, and that the second ratio uses the same order? This is a correct proportion. What is wrong with the proportion below?

$$\frac{5 \text{ boxes}}{\$1.25} = \frac{\$.75}{3 \text{ boxes}}$$

The two ratios do not compare the same unit in their numerators or the same unit in their denominators. This is *not* a true proportion.

▶ When you write a proportion, be sure that the two ratios have corresponding units on top and corresponding units on the bottom.

Writing a Proportion

Example 2: At Floyd's Market, 2 pounds of greens cost $1.40. At this rate, how much would 3 pounds cost?

Step 1
Write a ratio with two numbers in the problem. Include labels.

$$\frac{2 \text{ pounds}}{\$1.40}$$

Step 2
Write a proportion, using a variable for the number you do not know.

$$\frac{2 \text{ pounds}}{\$1.40} = \frac{3 \text{ pounds}}{\$p}$$

Step 3
Multiply to find the cross products and find the unknown.

$2 \times p = 1.40 \times 3$
$2 \times p = 4.20$
$p = 4.20 \div 2$
$\boldsymbol{p = \$2.10}$

Step 4
Check your proportion by using cross products.

$$\frac{2}{1.40} = \frac{3}{\mathbf{2.10}}$$

$2 \times 2.10 = 1.40 \times 3$
$4.20 = 4.20$

The cost of 3 pounds of greens is **$2.10.**

Here is another way to set up a proportion for this problem: $\dfrac{\$1.40}{2 \text{ pounds}} = \dfrac{\$p}{3 \text{ pounds}}$

Can you see that it does not matter which number goes on top or bottom in the *first* ratio? What *does* matter is that the second ratio has the *same* units on top and bottom as the first ratio.

A. **Choose *two* correct proportions that could be used to solve each problem below. (Be sure there are corresponding units on the top and corresponding units on the bottom.) Do not solve.**

1. Tom drove 80 miles in 3.5 hours. At this same rate, how far could he drive in 4.5 hours?

   (1) $\frac{80}{x} = \frac{3.5}{4.5}$ **(2)** $\frac{80}{3.5} = \frac{4.5}{x}$ **(3)** $\frac{3.5}{80} = \frac{4.5}{x}$ **(4)** $\frac{80}{3.5} = \frac{x}{4.5}$

2. If 5 yards of silk cost $21.00, how much would 6 yards cost?

   (1) $\frac{5}{21} = \frac{6}{c}$ **(2)** $\frac{5}{6} = \frac{21}{c}$ **(3)** $\frac{21}{5} = \frac{c}{6}$ **(4)** $\frac{6}{5} = \frac{21}{c}$

3. For every 3 women in the town of Milton, there are 2 men. If there are 2,400 women in all of Milton, how many men are there?

   (1) $\frac{3}{m} = \frac{2,400}{2}$ **(2)** $\frac{3}{2} = \frac{2,400}{m}$ **(3)** $\frac{2}{3} = \frac{m}{2,400}$ **(4)** $\frac{2,400}{2} = \frac{m}{3}$

4. In 6 square yards of her garden, Mrs. Tanaka can produce about 80 pounds of squash. How many square yards would it take to produce 100 pounds?

   (1) $\frac{6}{p} = \frac{80}{100}$ **(2)** $\frac{80}{6} = \frac{100}{p}$ **(3)** $\frac{6}{80} = \frac{p}{100}$ **(4)** $\frac{100}{80} = \frac{6}{p}$

B. **Write a proportion and solve for the unknown in each problem below.**

5. Ricardo can travel 250 miles on 10 gallons of gas. At this rate, how many gallons does he need to travel 300 miles?

6. Carol picked 8 quarts of strawberries and paid $10.00 for them. How much did she pay per quart?

7. A recipe calls for $1\frac{1}{2}$ cups of sugar to make 24 brownies. How much sugar is needed for 36 brownies?

8. A survey stated that 2 out of 3 residents were against the addition of a fast-food restaurant in their town. If 3,240 people were against the restaurant, how many people were surveyed in all?

9. If $2\frac{1}{2}$ pints of bonemeal is enough to fertilize 10 square feet of soil, how many square feet can 10 pints fertilize?

10. **Multiple Solutions** Write two correct proportions for this problem, then solve: At a rate of $15.00 per dozen, how much will 30 roses cost?

Gridding in Ratio and Proportion Answers

As you know, there are three ways to write a ratio. You can write a ratio using the word *to* or with a colon. You can also write a ratio using a fraction. Use the fraction form (/) to enter a ratio in the five-column grid. The grid to the right shows the ratio 5/2, 5 to 2, or 5:2.

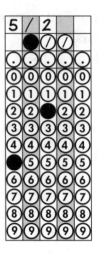

The answer to a proportion problem may be a whole number, a mixed number, a fraction, or a decimal. Review these basic rules for entering answers in a grid.

- You may start in any column as long as your answer fits within the five columns. Write your answer in the row of boxes at the top of the grid. Write only one number or symbol in each box. Do not use commas.

- Always enter mixed numbers as improper fractions.

- Do not leave blank spaces within your answer. There may be blank spaces at the beginning or end of your answer.

As you work with grid-in items, keep in mind that the test-scoring machine will accept either the fraction or decimal forms of a number. If you are working a problem on a calculator, you may want to enter the answer as a decimal. Choose the form that will take the least amount of time to find.

Filling in the Grid

Example: At a bakery, Brenda used 20 cups of rye flour and 16 cups of cornmeal flour to make 8 loaves of bread. In lowest terms, what is the ratio of cornmeal flour to rye flour?

Step 1
Write the ratio in the order stated in the problem. Then simplify to lowest terms.

$$\frac{\text{cornmeal}}{\text{rye}} \quad \frac{16}{20} = \frac{16}{20} \div \frac{4}{4} = \frac{4}{5}$$

Step 2
Write your answer in the top row of boxes. Use the slash for the fraction bar.

Step 3
Fill in the correct circles on the grid. Use the digits in the top row as a guide.

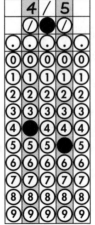

150

Solve the following problems. Record your answers in the grids.

1. A traffic counter records 60 vehicles in 15 minutes. At the same rate, how many vehicles will pass the counter in 120 minutes?

2. A basketball team's record is shown below.

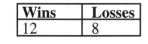

Wins	Losses
12	8

In lowest terms, what is the ratio of losses to games played?

3. An inspector finds 15 defective radios in a shipment of 300 radios. In lowest terms, what is the ratio of defective radios to radios in the shipment?

4.  At a company, 4 out of 7 employees changed health insurance plans. If there are 112 employees at the company, how many changed health insurance plans?

5. A school store earns a profit of $0.65 on every two ballpoint pens it sells. If the school made a profit of $12.35 on pen sales one day, how many pens did they sell?

6. At one point in the season, a professional baseball team had 40 players on its roster. If 12 of the players were pitchers, what is the ratio of non-pitchers to pitchers on the team? Write your answer in lowest terms.

Calculators and Proportion Problems

Once you have set up a proportion, a calculator can make it easy to solve for the unknown. The important step is to set up the proportion with corresponding units in the correct places. *A calculator will not help you set up a proportion; it can only help you solve it.*

Example: Nine out of 10 children in South Elementary School ride a bus. There are 180 children who ride a bus. How many students attend South Elementary in all?

First, set up a proportion:
$$\frac{9 \text{ bus riders}}{10 \text{ students}} = \frac{180 \text{ bus riders}}{s \text{ (students)}}$$

Next, use your calculator to solve the proportion. You need to multiply to find one cross product, then divide by the third amount to find the unknown amount:

$$\frac{9 \text{ bus riders}}{10 \text{ students}} \diagdown\!\!\!\!\diagup \frac{180 \text{ bus riders}}{s}$$

$(180 \times 10) \div 9 = \textbf{200 students in all}$

> **For another look**
> at the scientific calculator, see pages 239–240.

Key in:	Your display reads:
1 0	10.
×	10.
1 8 0	180.
÷	1800.
9	9.
=	200.

A. Use your calculator to solve the following proportions. Multiply to find one cross product, then divide by the third known amount to find the unknown amount.

1. $\frac{w}{12} = \frac{10}{60}$ $\frac{3}{9} = \frac{s}{18}$ $\frac{d}{10} = \frac{12}{40}$ $\frac{2}{7} = \frac{8}{x}$

2. $\frac{4}{5} = \frac{r}{100}$ $\frac{1}{4} = \frac{a}{200}$ $\frac{3}{q} = \frac{30}{150}$ $\frac{x}{7} = \frac{12}{28}$

3. $\frac{w}{1} = \frac{40}{5}$ $\frac{3}{9} = \frac{s}{54}$ $\frac{d}{6} = \frac{8}{48}$ $\frac{7}{8} = \frac{42}{x}$

4. $\frac{r}{5} = \frac{60}{100}$ $\frac{2}{7} = \frac{s}{49}$ $\frac{s}{5} = \frac{36}{90}$ $\frac{9}{11} = \frac{45}{x}$

B. Use a calculator to solve these problems. Before you key any numbers in, be sure you have set up your proportion correctly.

5. To get color #327, a hardware store clerk mixes 2 parts yellow paint and 3 parts gray paint. How many pints of yellow paint should he add to 12 pints of gray to get #327?

6. A marathon runner can run 2 miles in 12.3 minutes. At this same rate, how long will it take her to run 6 miles?

7. Four pounds of shrimp costs $35. How much will 3 pounds cost?

8. A tailor uses 4.75 yards of fabric to make 2 skirts. How many skirts can he make with 19 yards?

9. Gwyn drove 236 miles in 4 hours. At this rate, how many miles can she drive in 5 hours?

10. Out of every 20 pie shells a baker makes, she discards 1. How many did she make on Wednesday if she discarded 6 that day?

Making Connections: Changing Recipe Quantities

Use proportions to change the recipe to make only 20 cookies

1. _____ cup flour

2. _____ eggs

3. _____ cup walnuts

4. _____ cup minichips

Fudge Brownie Cookies

(Makes 30 cookies)

$1\frac{1}{2}$ boxes standard brownie mix

$1\frac{1}{3}$ cups flour

3 eggs

$\frac{3}{4}$ cup walnuts

$1\frac{1}{2}$ cups minichips

Scale Drawings and Maps

A **scale drawing** such as a floor plan uses proportions to compare values in the drawing to actual values. For example, if a floor plan shows that a room's length is twice its width, then the actual room will be twice as long as it is wide.

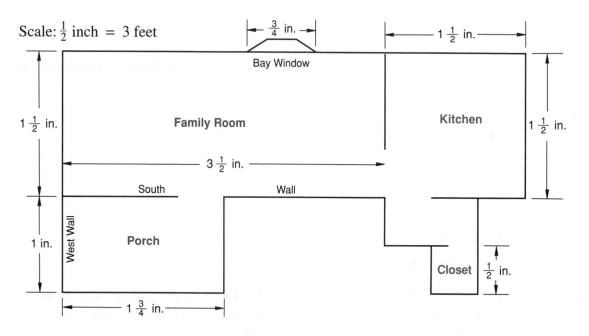

The scale above tells you that every $\frac{1}{2}$ inch on this drawing represents 3 feet on the real floor. This ratio—inches in the drawing to feet in the building—helps you determine the size of all the rooms by letting you set up a proportion.

Setting Up a Proportion for a Scale Drawing

Example: The window in the drawing measures $\frac{3}{4}$ inch. How many feet across will the bay window be?

Step 1
Set up a proportion.

$$\frac{\frac{1}{2} \text{ inch}}{3 \text{ feet}} = \frac{\frac{3}{4} \text{ inch}}{n \text{ feet}}$$

Step 2
Multiply to find the cross products and find the unknown.

$$\frac{1}{2} \times n = \frac{3}{4} \times 3$$
$$\frac{1}{2} \times n = 2\frac{1}{4}$$
$$\boldsymbol{n = 4\frac{1}{2} \textbf{ feet}}$$

Step 3
Check your proportion by using cross products.

$$\frac{\frac{1}{2}}{3} = \frac{\frac{3}{4}}{4\frac{1}{2}}$$
$$\frac{1}{2} \times 4\frac{1}{2} = 3 \times \frac{3}{4}$$
$$2\frac{1}{4} = 2\frac{1}{4}$$

A. Use proportions and the drawing above to find the following measurements.

1. closet wall

2. west wall of porch

3. south wall of family room

4. square footage of kitchen
   (*Hint:* Multiply length by width.)

Maps

Maps are also a common place to find ratios. Where distances are measured in miles, a map is usually accompanied by a **scale of miles.** This scale, or ratio, tells you how many miles are indicated by an inch, part of an inch, or more than 1 inch. For example, what is the ratio of inches to miles in the map on the right?

You are correct if you said *1 inch = 200 miles,* or *1:200.*

You can use proportions to find mileage between two points on a map.

Finding Distances on a Map

Example: Approximately how many miles is it from Dallas to Houston?

Step 1
Use a ruler to find the number of inches, or the fraction of an inch, between the two cities.

The distance measured on the map is about $1\frac{1}{4}$ inches.

Step 2
Using the ratio given in the scale of miles, set up a proportion.

$$\frac{1 \text{ inch}}{200 \text{ miles}} = \frac{1\frac{1}{4} \text{ inch}}{m \text{ miles}}$$

Step 3
Solve for the unknown by using cross products.

$$1 \times m = 1\frac{1}{4} \times 200$$

$$m = 250 \text{ miles}$$

The distance between Dallas and Houston is about **250 miles.**

B. **Use the map above, a ruler, and your understanding of proportions to find the following *approximate* distances.**

5. Lubbock to Houston   **6.** Dallas to Austin   **7.** Laredo to Corpus Christi

Unit 4 Review

A. Write a ratio for each relationship below.

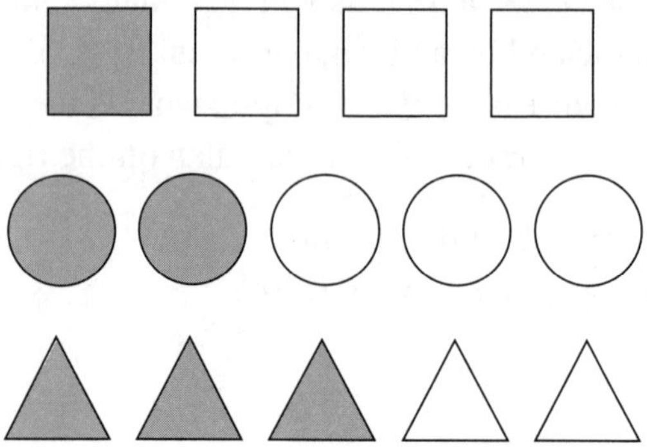

1. circles to squares

2. shaded circles to all circles

3. unshaded circles to shaded circles

4. triangles to all figures

5. shaded triangles to shaded squares

6. unshaded squares to unshaded triangles

B. Use the chart below to choose the correct ratios.

Tritown City Council	Men	Women
Democrats	14	15
Republicans	10	5
Independents	0	2

7. What is the ratio of Republicans to Democrats on the Tritown City Council?
   (1) 15:14   **(2)** 5:7   **(3)** 1:3   **(4)** 15:29   **(5)** 15:31

8. What is the ratio of women to men on the Tritown City Council?
   (1) 15:14   **(2)** 10:12   **(3)** 11:12   **(4)** 1:2   **(5)** 2:1

9. What is the ratio of Independents to all city council members?
   (1) 1:23   **(2)** 1:22   **(3)** 1:10   **(4)** 2:0   **(5)** 23:1

10. What is the ratio of women Republicans to all Republicans?
    (1) 1:2   **(2)** 2:1   **(3)** 1:15   **(4)** 1:3   **(5)** 3:1

C. Use the chart above to write your own ratios. Be sure you include labels, and simplify each ratio.

11.

12.

D. Find the missing term in each proportion below.

13. $\frac{w}{10} = \frac{30}{60}$ $\frac{3}{5} = \frac{s}{75}$ $\frac{d}{4} = \frac{5}{20}$ $\frac{5}{8} = \frac{35}{x}$

14. $\frac{r}{4} = \frac{75}{100}$ $\frac{5}{7} = \frac{s}{49}$ $\frac{s}{5} = \frac{120}{300}$ $\frac{9}{10} = \frac{45}{x}$

E. Use proportions to solve the following problems.

15. A recipe calls for $1\frac{1}{2}$ pounds of beef for 4 servings. How many pounds of beef are needed for 6 servings?

16. The Recycling Center gives $.05 for every 2 twelve-ounce cans returned. How many cans did the Earley family return if they received $1.75?

17. How long will it take the Zapatas to travel 228 miles if they drive at a rate of 57 miles per hour?

18. Out of the 25 students in Mrs. McDonough's class, 15 are female. If this ratio is true for the entire school, how many of the school's 175 students are female?

F. Grid in the answer to each problem.

19. 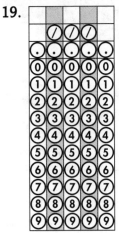 A basketball player made 36 out of 50 shots taken. In lowest terms, what is the ratio of shots made to shots taken?

20. 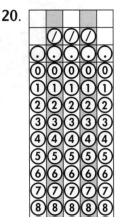 A sign in a store window says:

> **T-shirts**
> **4 for $9.00**

Not including sales tax, Leo spent $20.25 on T-shirts at the store. At the rate advertised, how many T-shirts did he buy?

Working Together

Break into small groups. Gather comparative information about your classmates—for example, male/female, brown eyes/blue eyes, and so on. Then write ratios to represent the comparisons—for example, *blue eyes to all eyes* or *blue eyes to brown eyes*. See which group can come up with the most ratios.

Unit 5

Percents

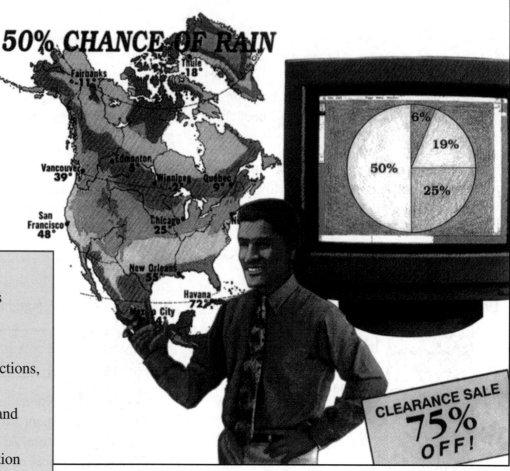

Skills

Understanding percents

Estimating the size of percents

Changing decimals, fractions, and percents

The percent statement and equation

Solving a percent equation

Two-step percent problems

Percent of increase and decrease

Tools

Calculator

Problem Solver

Does the answer make sense?

Applications

Statistics and percent

Discounts

Like a fraction or a decimal, a **percent** expresses a part of a whole. With a fraction or a decimal, the whole can be divided into different numbers of parts—for instance, tenths, thirds, or halves. With percents, the whole is *always divided into hundredths*.

For example, if you read that 85% of Americans like ice cream, you know that *not all* Americans like ice cream. Rather, 85 out of every 100 Americans like ice cream.

You may want to review this percents lesson in Unit 1:
• Understanding Percent ....page 42

When Do I Use Percents?

Read the following list of situations in which percents are used. Check off any that you have encountered in your life.

- ☐ a newspaper headline that gives a numerical fact, or statistic, in the form of a percent *(10% unemployment rate)*
- ☐ a percent used at a store sale or in an advertisement *(25% off)*
- ☐ a percent expressing probability, or the chance that something may happen *(30% chance of rain)*
- ☐ a percent used to represent a part of a group *(50% of the people)*
- ☐ a percent used to express part of a whole *(80% of the day)*
- ☐ percents used in banking or loans *(14.9% interest rate on a credit card)*

Now describe some of your experiences with percents.

1. Write about something you've read or heard in the news that contains a percent statistic. What was the statistic? What do you think it means?

   _____

   _____

2. Describe a store sale that advertised a "percent off" discount. What was the percent off, and what did you buy? Was the discount large or small?

   _____

   _____

3. Think of the last time you left or received a tip at a restaurant. How do you figure out whether the tip is actually 15% of the total bill?

   _____

   _____

Talk About It

You want to buy a new winter coat. At a local store, you see a sale advertised: 25% off all coats.

Come up with three questions that would help you decide whether this is a good deal. Compare your questions with others. With the group, choose the three best questions.

Understanding Percents

A **percent** represents a part of a whole that is divided into 100 parts.

Can you think what 100% means? Suppose a classroom teacher reported 100% attendance one day. This means that out of 30 students, all 30 were present.

In fact, 100% represents the *whole amount.* $100\% = 1$

25% of the box on the right is shaded. What percent is *not* shaded?

Think of the *whole* box as 100%.
$100\% - 25\% = \mathbf{75\%}$

Fractions, Decimals, and Percents

Any percent can be written in decimal or fraction form without any change in value. Each number represents the same part of a whole.

Example 1: What is 57% written as a fraction?

Because 57% means 57 parts out of 100 parts, write 57 as the numerator and 100 as the denominator.

$$\frac{57}{100} \quad \begin{array}{l} \text{parts} \\ \text{total parts} \end{array}$$

Example 2: Write 57% as a decimal.

As you know, percent means *per hundred* or *hundredths.* To write 57 hundredths as a decimal, write 57, then place a decimal point so that the 7 in 57 is in the hundredths place.

.57

⎯ hundredths place

To remember the value of percent, think of it in this way:

$$57\% = \frac{57}{100} = .57$$

2 zeros   2 decimal places

A. Fill in the blanks of the chart. When you are finished, each number will be expressed as a percent, a decimal, and a fraction.

Part of Whole	Percent	Fraction	Decimal
23 out of 100	23%	$\frac{23}{100}$	.23
7 out of 100			.07
		$\frac{93}{100}$	
	39%		
33 out of 100			.33
9 out of 100			

For another look at common decimal, fraction, and percent equivalencies, turn to page 237.

B. Answer the following questions. Some will take more than one step to solve. Express fraction answers in lowest terms.

1. A tire company discarded 6% of the tires produced on the evening shift last Friday. What *fraction* of the tires from that shift did it *not* discard?

2. A customer got a 25% discount on an item that originally cost $1. Express this discount as a decimal.

3. In a recent election, 35 out of 100 voters voted for Komuro. What *percent* of voters did *not* vote for Komuro?

4. What part of the figure below is *not* shaded? Express your answer as a decimal.

5. What percent of the figure in problem 4 *is* shaded?

6. A meter is 100 centimeters. What fraction of a meter is 67 centimeters?

7. For every $100 of take-home pay, Ann Lih *saves* $15. What percent of her take-home pay does she *spend?*

8. A building contractor estimates that 30% of a job has been completed. What *fraction* of the job is *not* completed?

9. The shaded part of the bar below represents the part of a computer disk that is filled with data. What fraction is *not filled?*

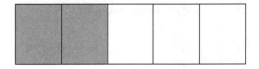

10. **Draw** Make a box with 100 squares. Shade in the number of squares that represents 25%.

Estimating the Size of Percents

A report states that 99% of the flooring in a warehouse is covered with lead paint. Is 99% a large part of the whole floor or a small part?

Think visually:

Shade the part of the floor with lead paint.

Think numerically:

99% means 99 parts out of a total of 100 parts.

Did you shade a large part of the floor?

Is 99 a large part of 100?

You can see that 99% *is* a large part of a whole.

Suppose that 2% of the hamburgers at Joe's are served plain. Is 2% a large or small part of the whole number of hamburgers served?

Think visually:

Write *P* over each plain hamburger below.

○ ○ ○ ○ ○ ○ ○ ○ ○ ○ ○ ○ ○ ○ ○ ○ ○ ○ ○ ○

○ ○ ○ ○ ○ ○ ○ ○ ○ ○ ○ ○ ○ ○ ○ ○ ○ ○ ○ ○

○ ○ ○ ○ ○ ○ ○ ○ ○ ○ ○ ○ ○ ○ ○ ○ ○ ○ ○ ○

○ ○ ○ ○ ○ ○ ○ ○ ○ ○ ○ ○ ○ ○ ○ ○ ○ ○ ○ ○

○ ○ ○ ○ ○ ○ ○ ○ ○ ○ ○ ○ ○ ○ ○ ○ ○ ○ ○ ○

Did you write *P* over a large part of the total?

Think numerically:

2% means 2 parts out of a total of 100 parts.

Is 2 a large part of 100?

You can see that 2% is *not* a large part of the whole.

Percents Close to $\frac{1}{2}$

Shade 50 of the 100 squares below.

You have shaded in exactly $\frac{1}{2}$ of the whole figure. 50% is the same as $\frac{1}{2}$.

Shade 48 or 51 squares below.

Do you see that 51% and 48% are very close to $\frac{1}{2}$?

Percents Greater than 100%

If 100% is equal to 1 whole, then what does 200% mean? Think of this percent as a fraction:

parts
total parts $\qquad \frac{200}{100} \div \frac{100}{100} = \frac{2}{1} = 2$ $\qquad\qquad$ 200% of something is the same as 2 times something.

Remember that a percent greater than 100% is a number greater than 1. On a number line, percents would look like this:

0%	50%	100%	150%	200%
0	$\frac{1}{2}$	1 whole	$1\frac{1}{2}$	2

Read the percent in each situation below. Choose the answer that best describes the size of the percent.

1. A total of 5% of Newtown residents voted in favor of a tax hike.

   (1) more than 1 whole

   (2) a large part

   (3) close to $\frac{1}{2}$

   (4) a small part

2. Of all the cameras made by Vonic Inc., 85% are made in the United States.

   (1) more than 1 whole

   (2) a large part

   (3) close to $\frac{1}{2}$

   (4) a small part

3. A homeless shelter reported a 140% increase in the number of its clients last winter.

   (1) more than 1 whole

   (2) a large part

   (3) close to $\frac{1}{2}$

   (4) a small part

Problems 4 and 5 refer to the chart below.

Adult Education Program Students

Age	Percent of Students
18–25	53%
26–40	27%
41–60	19%
61–80	1%

4. How much of the adult ed program is ages 18–25?

   (1) more than 1 whole

   (2) a large part

   (3) close to $\frac{1}{2}$

   (4) a small part

5. How much of the adult ed program is ages 61–80?

   (1) more than 1 whole

   (2) a large part

   (3) close to $\frac{1}{2}$

   (4) a small part

Changing Decimals and Percents

To change percents into decimals and decimals into percents, remember the connections between these different parts of a whole.

Writing a Percent as a Decimal

Example: Write 30% as a decimal.

Step 1
Drop the percent sign, and move the decimal point 2 places *to the left*.

30% = .30. = .30

Step 2
Drop any unnecessary zeros.
.30 = **.3**

└── unnecessary zero

Percent	Move Decimal Point 2 Places to Left	Decimal
67%	67.	.67
11.5%	11.5	.115
125%	125.	1.25
9%	.09.	.09

Add a zero to hold the 9 in the hundredths place.

Percents over 100% convert to a whole or mixed number.

Tip
All numbers have a written decimal point or an understood decimal point. If there is no written decimal point in a number, it is understood to be *to the right* of the last digit.

50   3%

└── understood decimal point ──┘

Writing a Decimal as a Percent

Example: What is .4 expressed as a percent?

Step 1
Move the decimal point 2 places *to the right*, adding any necessary zeros.

.40

Add a zero to move the decimal point 2 places.

Step 2
Add a percent sign.

.40 = **40%**

Decimal	Move Decimal Point 2 Places to Right	Percent
.28	.28	28%
.1	.10 ← Add a zero here.	10%
3.5	3.50	350%
.06	.06	6%

└── Drop this unnecessary zero.

A. Change the percents below into decimals or whole or mixed numbers.

1. 7% _____

2. 25% _____

3. 9.9% _____

4. 80% _____

5. 165% _____

6. 12.5% _____

7. 500% _____

8. 5% _____

9. 50% _____

10. .5% _____

B. Change the following decimals, whole numbers, and mixed numbers into percents.

11. .5 _____

12. .50 _____

13. 5.5 _____

14. .05 _____

15. 5 _____

16. 120 _____

17. 10.9 _____

18. .65 _____

19. .2 _____

20. .02 _____

Making Connections: Moving the Decimal Point

When changing the form of a decimal or a percent, remember this rule:

$$D \longleftarrow P$$

> Remember: D is to the left of P because it is to the left of (or before) P in the alphabet.

If you are changing
- a decimal to a percent, the decimal point moves *to the right:* $D \longrightarrow P$
- a percent to a decimal, the decimal point moves *to the left:* $D \longleftarrow P$

Use this hint to decide if each problem below is solved correctly. If it is not, correct it.

1. $7\% \overset{?}{=} 700$ $.05 \overset{?}{=} 5\%$ $25\% \overset{?}{=} .25$ $3.3 \overset{?}{=} 33\%$

2. $21\% \overset{?}{=} .21$ $.2 \overset{?}{=} 2\%$ $13\% \overset{?}{=} 1300$ $1.09 \overset{?}{=} 109\%$

Changing Fractions and Percents

You've already had some practice changing the form of fractions and percents. See how much you remember.

Writing a Percent as a Fraction

Example: Luisa completed 75% of her typing test. What fraction of the test did she complete?

Step 1
Drop the percent sign, and write the number with a denominator of 100.

$$75\% = \frac{75}{100}$$

Step 2
Simplify the fraction if necessary.

$$\frac{75}{100} \div \frac{25}{25} = \frac{3}{4}$$

Louisa completed $\frac{3}{4}$ of her typing test.

Writing a Fraction as a Percent

Example: A town reports that $\frac{1}{4}$ of its residents do not have renters or homeowners insurance. What percent of town residents is this?

Step 1
Divide the denominator into the numerator.

$$\begin{array}{r} .25 \\ 4\overline{)1.0} \\ \underline{8} \\ 20 \end{array}$$

Step 2
Change the decimal answer into a percent by moving the decimal point 2 places to the right.

.25

Step 3
Add a percent sign.

.25 = **25%**

25% of town residents do not have renters or homeowners insurance.

A. Change the following percents into fractions, whole numbers, or mixed numbers. Remember to simplify if necessary.

1. 30%   13%   125%   9%   90%

2. 100%   50%   20%   300%   65%

B. Change the following fractions into percents. Use a calculator if you'd like.

3. $\frac{1}{5}$ $\frac{3}{100}$ $\frac{5}{8}$ $\frac{1}{8}$ $\frac{1}{2}$

4. $\frac{3}{5}$ $\frac{1}{10}$ $\frac{7}{20}$ $\frac{9}{10}$ $\frac{15}{100}$

Common Fractional Percents

Two common fractions, $\frac{1}{3}$ and $\frac{2}{3}$, do not divide evenly when changed into percents. Try to *memorize* their percent values:

► $\frac{1}{3} = 33\frac{1}{3}\%$ $\frac{2}{3} = 66\frac{2}{3}\%$

C. Solve the following problems.

5. Common Contractors quit a construction project when it was $\frac{4}{5}$ completed. What *percent* of the job did they finish?

6. Miguel's salary has risen an impressive $33\frac{1}{3}\%$ since he began working at Floyd's Corner Market. By what fraction has his salary increased?

7. **a.** Nine-tenths of the Porters' land is forest. What percent is this?

   b. What percent is *not* forested?

8. Mrs. Feng estimates that $\frac{2}{3}$ of her time is spent taking care of her mother. What percent of Mrs. Feng's day does this represent?

9. Sales of luxury cars at Woody's Auto amount to about 5% of total sales. What fraction of total sales are luxury cars?

10. **a.** What percent of the rectangle is shaded?

   b. What percent is *not shaded?*

Making Connections: Commonly Used Fractions, Decimals, and Percents

For another look at decimal, fraction, and percent equivalencies, turn to page 237.

Fill in the blanks on these charts. Then memorize as much as you can. This information will be useful to you in this book and in everyday life.

Decimal	Fraction	Percent
.1	$\frac{1}{10}$	
	$\frac{2}{10} = \frac{1}{5}$	
		25%
.3		
	$\frac{1}{3}$	
		40%
	$\frac{5}{10} = \frac{1}{2}$	

Decimal	Fraction	Percent
.6		
	$\frac{2}{3}$	
		70%
.75		
	$\frac{8}{10} = \frac{4}{5}$	
		90%
	$\frac{10}{10}$	

The Percent Statement

► A *percent* of the *whole* is equal to the *part*.

The **percent statement** above will help you with percent problems.
Study how the situations below are written as percent statements.

Claudia saved $20 on a dress originally priced at $80. She saved 25%.	<u>25%</u> of <u>$80</u> is equal to <u>$20</u>. percent whole part
A typist completed 90% of a 200-page report. In other words, he typed 180 pages.	<u>90%</u> of <u>200</u> is equal to <u>180</u>. percent whole part
About 22% of all voters, or 11,000 citizens, submitted ballots. There are 50,000 total voters.	<u>22%</u> of <u>50,000</u> is equal to <u>11,000</u>. percent whole part

A. Fill in the blanks to write a percent statement for each situation below. Then reread the statement.

1. On Monday, a baker made 40% of his cheesecakes low-fat.
   He made 6 of his total 15 cheesecakes low-fat.

   _____ of _____ is equal to _____.
   percent   whole   part

2. Seven hours, or 70%, of Delmar's 10-hour day is spent on the road.

   _____ of _____ is equal to _____.
   percent   whole   part

3. Julio received a $1,540 raise, or 7% of his $22,000 salary.

   _____ of _____ is equal to _____.
   percent   whole   part

4. A 5% sales tax, or $1.50, is added to the cost of a $30 watch.

   _____ of _____ is equal to _____.
   percent   whole   part

5. Of Esther's 60 weekly customers, 25% are local. She has 15 local customers.

   _____ of _____ is equal to _____.
   percent   whole   part

The Percent Problem

In all percent problems, either the *part,* the *percent,* or the *whole* is missing. To find which element is missing, plug known values into the percent statement.

Example 1: Ming paid a $55 deposit for a new stereo. This was 20% of the total cost. How much did the stereo cost?

> **Tip**
>
> In percent problems, the value following the word *of* represents the whole.

Plug in values you know:

<u>20%</u> of _____ is equal to <u>$55</u>.   A deposit is *part* of the whole.
percent   whole   part

The value you do not know is the *whole.*

Example 2: In 2000, about 51% of the U.S. population was female. The U.S. population was about 280 million. How many people in the United States were female?

Plug in values you know:

<u>51%</u> of <u>280 million</u> is equal to _____.
percent   whole   part

the *part* of the population that is female

The value you do not know is the *part.*

Example 3: Out of a total of 40 questions, Shatara got 28 correct. What percent did she get right?

Plug in values you know:

_____ of <u>40</u> is equal to <u>28</u>.
percent   whole   part

The value you do not know is the *percent.*

B. Choose the value that is missing in each problem below. Do not solve the problems.

6. Marta paid $34 for shoes. What percent of the original $50 price did she pay?
   Missing value: Part   Percent   Whole

7. Fifteen is 18% of what number?
   Missing value: Part   Percent   Whole

8. Marcella has filed 50% of her 220 reports. How many reports has she filed?
   Missing value: Part   Percent   Whole

9. Jay got 1,200 votes—9% of all votes cast. How many votes were cast in all?
   Missing value: Part   Percent   Whole

10. The 6% sales tax on a purchase was $3.40. What was the price of the item?
    Missing value: Part   Percent   Whole

11. What is 35% of $9,000?
    Missing value: Part   Percent   Whole

Does the Answer Make Sense?

When solving problems, be sure that your answer makes sense. Your own experiences and common sense will help you. Read this example:

A nurse gave a patient $\frac{1}{2}$ of the 3 liters of medicine prescribed. How many liters has she given the patient?

Jerome's answer: $3 \div \frac{1}{2} = 3 \times \frac{2}{1} =$ **6 liters**

Does Jerome's answer make sense? Would the patient receive 6 liters when only 3 liters were prescribed? No. One-half is *smaller* than the original amount. Jerome should have *multiplied* 3 by $\frac{1}{2}$, not *divided*:

$3 \times \frac{1}{2} = \frac{3}{2}$ or **$1\frac{1}{2}$ liters.**   This is a sensible answer.

If you use the wrong operation to solve a problem, you can usually find the error by *checking to be sure your answer makes sense.*

A. **Do not solve the problems below. Instead, look at the two answer choices given and choose the one that is sensible. The operation used to solve each is identified.**

1. A report stated that $\frac{3}{4}$ of the 1,200 handgun accidents involved children. How many involved children?

   (1) multiplication: 900

   (2) division: 1,600

2. Ricky had $348 in his account. He withdrew $50. What is his balance now?

   (1) addition: $398

   (2) subtraction: $298

3. Saja withdrew $115 from her account, leaving $780. What was her balance before the withdrawal?

   (1) addition: $895

   (2) subtraction: $565

4. Denise pays $.20 per foot for contact paper. She spent $12 in all for contact paper. How many feet did she buy?

   (1) multiplication: 2.4 feet

   (2) division: 60 feet

5. A garden measures 14 feet long and 8 feet wide. How many square feet is it?

   (1) multiplication: 112 square feet

   (2) division: $1\frac{3}{4}$ square feet

6. A club has 120 members. Of them, 76 are female. How many are male?

   (1) addition: 196

   (2) subtraction: 44

Sensible Percent Problem Answers

When solving percent problems, always check your answers.

Example: Mrs. Smith wanted to know how much tax she would pay on a $150 purchase. The tax rate in her state is 5%. She figured out that she would pay $3,000 in tax.

Does Mrs. Smith's answer make sense? No. Mrs. Smith mistook the *whole* for the *part*. By checking her answer, however, she could rethink her solution and find that her tax would be $7.50—a much more *sensible* answer.

To find a sensible answer, use these hints:

- If the percent is less than 100%, the **part** is smaller than the **whole.**
  (5% of $150 is $7.50.)

- If the word *of* appears in a problem, the value following is the **whole.**
  (5% of $150 is $7.50.)
  whole

B. Read each problem and decide whether the *part, percent,* or *whole* is missing.
Choose the sensible answer.

7. The Saunders pay 6.5% interest on a loan. The interest payment comes to $130. How much was the loan amount?
   - **(1)** part: $8.45
   - **(2)** whole: $2,000

8. What percent of 400 church members attended a fair if 320 went?
   - **(1)** part: 128,000
   - **(2)** percent: 80%

9. At least 75% of Telcot's 560,000 cans of shaving cream are sold in Europe. How many cans are sold in Europe?
   - **(1)** part: 420,000
   - **(2)** whole: 746,000

10. Sock sets are on sale for $10.50, down $3.50 from their original price. What percent savings is this?
    - **(1)** whole: $14.00
    - **(2)** percent: 25%

11. Elton spends 50% of his 9-hour day supervising. How many hours is this?
    - **(1)** part: 4.5
    - **(2)** whole: 18

12. Cynthia saved $345 last month—15% of her monthly earnings. How much money did she make that month?
    - **(1)** part: $51.75
    - **(2)** whole: $2,300

> **For another look**
> at the five-step problem-solving plan, turn to page 235.

Answers start on page 224.

The Percent Equation

A percent statement can easily be changed into a **percent equation.**

Example 1: Anton delivered 40% of his 220 newspapers. How many did he deliver?

Percent statement: ⌐ part

40% of 220 is equal to p.

Changing a Percent Statement to an Equation

Example: 40% of 220 is equal to _____.

Step 1
Represent the unknown with a variable.

40% of 220 is p.

Step 2
Change the percent, if there is one, to a decimal.

40% = .40. = .40

.40 of 220 is p.

Step 3
Replace the word *of* with a × and the word *is* with an =.

.40 of 220 is p.

.40 × 220 = p

Example 2: Nate wrote a check for $50, which was 25% of his pledged amount to a charity. How much had Nate pledged?

Percent statement:

25% of _____ is equal to $50.

Step 1
Represent the unknown with a variable.

25% of w is equal to $50.

Step 2
Change the percent, if there is one, to a decimal.

.25 of w is equal to $50.

Step 3
Replace the word *of* with a × and the words *is equal to* with an =.

.25 × w = $50

A. Change the following percent statements into equations. Use p to represent the part, w to represent the whole, and n% to represent the percent.

1. 80% of _____ is 6,800.

2. _____ of 125 is 12.5.

3. 6% of $140 is _____.

4. _____ of 2,345 is 908.

5. 55% of _____ is 15.

6. 100% of 1,237 is _____.

7. 78% of _____ is 45.

8. _____ of 54 is 52.

B. For each problem below, write a percent statement. Then write a percent equation.

9. Brad spent 30% of his paycheck on new tires. The tires cost $216. How much was Brad's paycheck?

   _____ of _____ is equal to _____.

   Equation: _____

10. A customer paid $1.35 tax on a $27 item. What percent tax did he pay?

    _____ of _____ is equal to _____.

    Equation: _____

11. If 90% of all Americans have a telephone, and there are 280,000,000 Americans, how many have a telephone?

    _____ of _____ is equal to _____.

    Equation: _____

Problems 12 and 13 refer to the circle graph below. Remember that the whole circle represents 100% of employees.

Allied Business Systems Employees

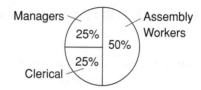

12. If there are 325 employees at Allied Business, how many of them are managers?

    _____ of _____ is equal to _____.

    Equation: _____

13. Of the total 325 employees, how many are assembly workers?

    _____ of _____ is equal to _____.

    Equation: _____

Making Connections: Circle Graphs

Circle graphs show a whole (the circle) and its parts (each wedge).

Example: Of their $740 weekly income, the Santiagos spend $207.20 each week on rent. Write a percent statement using information from the graph.

**Santiago Weekly Budget
$740 weekly income**

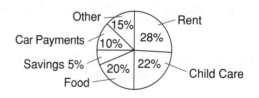

<u>28%</u> of <u>$740</u> is <u>$207.20</u>.
percent   whole   part

Equation: .28 × 740 = 207.20

Write a percent statement and equation for each of the following.

1. $148 for food
2. $37 for savings
3. $74 for car payments
4. $162.80 for child care

Solving a Percent Equation

Solving a percent equation is like solving other equations: your goal is to get the unknown on one side of the equal sign. In a percent equation, this will always involve multiplying or dividing.

Example 1: Mr. and Mrs. Torres put down a deposit of $5,000 on a house in Warren. The deposit was 10% of the total cost of the home. What was the price of the house?

Percent statement: 10% of w is equal to $5,000.
    percent whole   part

Percent equation: $.10 \times w = \$5,000$

Divide both
sides by .10 so
that *w* is alone.

$$\frac{.10 \times w}{.10} = \frac{\$5,000}{.10}$$

$$w = \$5,000 \div .10 = \mathbf{\$50,000}$$

The price of the house was **$50,000.**

▶ To find the *whole,* divide the part by the percent:

$$W = \frac{P}{\%}$$

Example 2: Of 120 people attending a meeting, 84 were men. What percent were men?

Percent statement: m% of 120 is equal to 84.
    percent whole   part

Percent equation: $m \times 120 = 84$

Divide both
sides by 120 so
that *m* is alone.

$$\frac{m \times 120}{120} = \frac{84}{120}$$

$$m = 84 \div 120 = .70 = \mathbf{70\%}$$

70% of the people at the meeting were men.

▶ To find the *percent,* divide the part by the whole:

$$\% = \frac{P}{W}$$

Example 3: A forest ranger estimated that 25% of a state park was damaged in a forest fire. If the park has 700 acres of land, about how many acres were damaged?

Percent statement: 25% of 700 is equal to a.
    percent whole   part

Percent equation: $.25 \times 700 = a$

$$175 = a$$

▶ To find the *part,* multiply the percent by the whole:

$$P = \% \times W$$

About **175 acres** were damaged.

A. Write and solve percent equations for each statement below.

1. 30% of _____ is 2,700.

2. _____% of 20 is 15.

3. 95% of 150 is _____.

4. 65% of 1,800 is _____.

5. _____% of 48 is 96.

6. _____% of 350 is 84.

7. 10% of _____ is 200.

8. 8% of 160 is _____.

9. 27% of 13 is _____.

10. 35% of _____ is 140.

B. Solve the following percent problems.

11. When Chih bought his car, he made a 20% down payment of $2,400. What was the purchase price of Chih's car?

12. What is the tax rate if a customer pays $15.60 on a $240 purchase?

13. Seventy percent of the flooring in Dawn's 2,000-square-foot house is hardwood. How many square feet of hardwood are there in Dawn's house?

14. Twelve hours, or 20%, of Ricardo's workweek is spent making service calls to current customers. How many hours is Ricardo's workweek?

15. Naia earns 15% commission on each sale she makes. Last month she received an $840 commission check. What was her total sales amount last month?

16. If there were 17 grandchildren at a recent family reunion of 34 people, what percent of the total was made up of grandchildren?

17. In 1994, there were 12,000 residents in Fanson. An additional 300 people moved to town in 1995. By what percent did the town's population grow?

18. Yolanda drove 50 miles of her 80-mile trip. What percent did she complete?

Problems 19 and 20 refer to this graph.

Opinion Poll

Question: Do you think the current president is doing a good job in office?

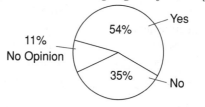

19. If 3,000 people were surveyed for this poll, how many think the president is doing a good job?

20. **Describe** Write a paragraph that describes the data shown on the graph.

Gridding in Percent Answers

Tools

$x - 7 = 3$

The five-column grid does not include a percent symbol, so it isn't possible to grid in a percent. However, you know that a percent is one way to express a fractional part of something. Percents have both decimal and fraction equivalencies. For example, 50% is equal to 0.5 and $\frac{1}{2}$.

Read a problem carefully for special instructions on the form the answer should take. You may want to review the common decimal, fraction, and percent equivalencies in the Tool Kit on page 237.

Many percent problems ask you to solve for either the part or the whole. These answers may be whole numbers, fractions, or decimals. Follow these basic rules for entering answers in a grid.

- You may start in any column as long as your answer fits within the five columns. Write your answer in the row of boxes at the top of the grid.

- Write only one number or symbol in each box. Do not use commas.

- Do not leave blank spaces within your answer. There may be blank spaces at the beginning or end of your answer.

Filling in the Grid

Example: A neighborhood association has 260 members. Recently, 65% of the members signed a petition to change the zip code in their area. How many of the members signed the petition?

Step 1
Solve for the part using the equation: P = % × W.

$0.65 \times 260 = 169$

A total of **169 members** signed the petition.

Step 2
Write your answer in the top row of boxes. Remember, you can begin in any column as long as your answer fits.

Step 3
Fill in the correct circles on the grid. Use the digits in the top row as a guide.

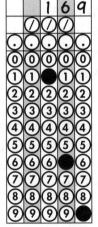

Solve the following problems. Record your answers in the grids.

1.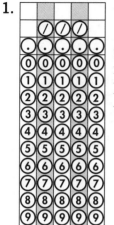
Cynthia estimates that she spends 15% of her net income on food. What fraction of her net income is spent on food? Express your answer in lowest terms.

4.
Zebra Electronics has 200 employees. Of these, 130 work part-time. What percent of its employees work part-time?

(*Hint:* Enter your answer in the percent form, not as a decimal.)

2.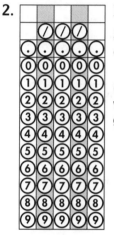
Ed earns $350 per week. If he gets a 12% raise, how many dollars will he earn per week?

(*Hint:* Enter the amount as a whole number. You cannot grid in a dollar sign.)

5.
A store has the following sign in its window:

Z-500 Digital Camera Now Only $260!

The sale price of the Z-500 camera is 20% less than the original price. What was the original price in dollars?

3.
On a test, Monica received a score of 80% because she answered 32 questions correctly. How many questions were on the test?

6.
In an election, only 76% voted for Proposition C. If 3,400 people voted in the election, how many voted for Proposition C?

Statistics and Percents

What do the following percents mean?

65% of all breast cancers were originally discovered through self-examination.

Women make up 51% of the world's population.

National defense takes up 16% of the U.S. budget.

The 2000 U.S. Census reports that 12% of the population is African American.

These percents are called statistics. **Statistics** are numerical figures that have been collected, organized, and interpreted to give us information about the world around us.

When you read or hear statistics, you should have an idea of what they mean and where they came from.

You know that 12% means 12 out of 100, or $\frac{12}{100}$. So what does it mean when we say that 12% of Americans are African American?

$$\frac{12 \text{ African Americans}}{100 \text{ total Americans}}$$

This statistic means that out of every 100 Americans, 12 are African American. Of course, there are many, many more than 100 Americans, just as there are many, many more than 12 African Americans. 12%, or $\frac{12}{100}$, is simply a **ratio** that shows the relationship between these two groups.

What do these other statistics mean? Fill in the blanks below.

16% of budget	$\dfrac{16 \quad \text{defense dollars}}{100 \quad \text{total dollars in budget}}$	Out of every ___100___ dollars in the budget, _____ dollars are spent on defense.
65% of breast cancers	$\dfrac{\rule{1cm}{0.4pt} \quad \text{detected by self-exam}}{100 \quad \text{total breast cancers reported}}$	Out of every _____ breast cancers reported, _____ are detected by self-exam.
51% of world population	$\dfrac{\rule{1cm}{0.4pt} \quad \text{women}}{100 \quad \text{total people in the world}}$	Out of every _____ people in the world, _____ are women.

You are correct if you completed column 3 as follows: 100 dollars, 16 dollars; 100 cancers reported, 65 detected by self-exam; 100 people, 51 women.

Percents are used so often in statistics because they are the results of comparing *two* numbers. One value is compared to another value.

For example, suppose a candidate receives 9,000 votes in an election. That might sound pretty good. But what if there were 60,000 votes cast in all? By using *both* numbers, you can see that although 9,000 votes seems like a lot of votes, it actually represents only 15% of all votes cast.

Use the information below to find the missing statistics and to write newspaper headlines.

1. _____% VOTE FOR MATHERSON

   . . . 1,500 of the 20,000 citizens voting in last week's mayoral election voted for Matherson, whom many had considered the most likely winner. . . .

2. _____% of contestants finish race in under 4 hours

   Of the 850 contestants in last Tuesday's race, 527 finished in under 4 hours, breaking last year's record by . . .

3. _____% of Gray County 3- and 4-year-olds enrolled in school

   In 1995, 300 of the 750 three- and four-year-old children in Gray County were enrolled in school. . . .

4. _____% of women surveyed prefer female doctor, study shows

   Of the 4,200 women surveyed by *Health Choice* magazine, an overwhelming 3,780 said that they preferred to see a female doctor. . . .

Making Connections: Draw a Circle Graph

Using the data below, determine percentages and label the circle graph at right.

In 1994, there were 170 students enrolled in the Learning Center. Of those, 85 were women who were planning to return to the workforce, 51 were men currently unemployed, and 34 were teenage mothers.

1994 Learning Center Population

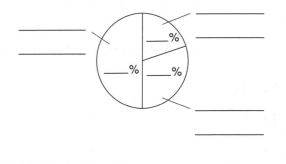

Mixed Review

A. Find the following decimal, fraction, and percent values on the number line below. Some letters may be used more than once.

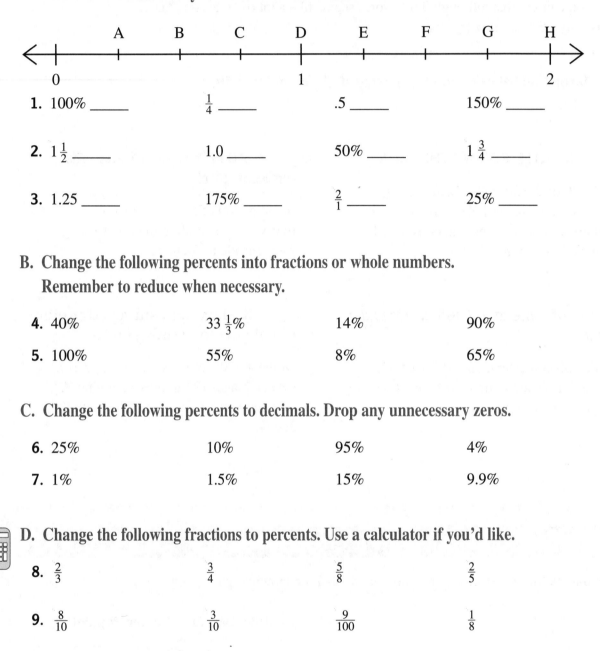

1. 100% _____ $\frac{1}{4}$ _____   .5 _____   150% _____

2. $1\frac{1}{2}$ _____   1.0 _____   50% _____ $1\frac{3}{4}$ _____

3. 1.25 _____   175% _____ $\frac{2}{1}$ _____   25% _____

B. Change the following percents into fractions or whole numbers. Remember to reduce when necessary.

4. 40% $33\frac{1}{3}$%   14%   90%

5. 100%   55%   8%   65%

C. Change the following percents to decimals. Drop any unnecessary zeros.

6. 25%   10%   95%   4%

7. 1%   1.5%   15%   9.9%

D. Change the following fractions to percents. Use a calculator if you'd like.

8. $\frac{2}{3}$ $\frac{3}{4}$ $\frac{5}{8}$ $\frac{2}{5}$

9. $\frac{8}{10}$ $\frac{3}{10}$ $\frac{9}{100}$ $\frac{1}{8}$

E. Change the following decimals to percents.

10. .08   .8   .18   .45

11. 1.3   .09   .50   .1

F. Write a percent statement for each situation below.

12. Betsy spends 15% of her income on her rent, which is $660 per month. Her monthly income is $4,400.

_____ of _____ is equal to _____.
percent   whole   part

13. Seventy percent of Dalemore residents are over the age of 80. A total of 35 of the 50 residents are over 80.

_____ of _____ is equal to _____.
percent   whole   part

G. Solve the percent equations below. Use a calculator if you'd like.

14. 80% of $h = 140$

15. What percent of 125 is 15?

16. 95% of $w = 1,900$

17. What percent of 300 is 75?

18. 68% of $40 = p$

19. 12% of $250 = b$

H. Write a percent equation and solve these word problems.

20. Matthias completed 60% of his 15 foul shots on Sunday. How many shots did he complete?

  (1) 25   **(3)** .04

  (2) 9

21. When he passed the 13-mile mark, Ed knew he had completed 50% of the Boston Marathon. About how long is this marathon?

  (1) 6.5 miles   **(3)** 260 miles

  (2) 26 miles

22. The Recreation Club added 120 new members to its 750-member roster. By what percent did its membership increase?

  (1) 16%

  (2) 6.25%

  (3) 1.6%

23. In a state with a 6.5% sales tax, how much tax did Felicia pay on a $68 coat?

  (1) $4.42

  (2) $10.46

  (3) $442

I. Grid in the answer to each problem.

24. 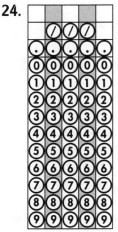 A company ordered 28 cartons of copier paper. A clerk puts 75% of the cartons in a supply room. How many cartons did the clerk put in the supply room?

25. 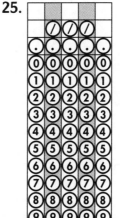 In a survey, 45% of those polled, or 108 people, said that they buy at least three brands of cereal each week. How many people were surveyed?

Using a Calculator with Percents

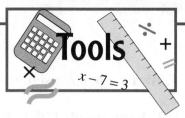

A calculator is a very useful tool for working with percents.

Finding the Part

Example: Mrs. Gutierrez wants to leave a 15% tip on her lunch bill of $10.80. How can she use her calculator to find the tip?

▶ $P = \% \times W$

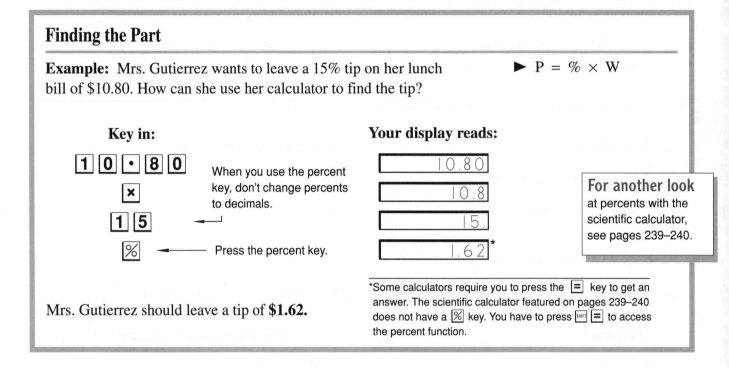

Key in:

[1] [0] [·] [8] [0]

When you use the percent key, don't change percents to decimals.

[×]

[1] [5]

[%] ◀—— Press the percent key.

Your display reads:

| 10.80 |
| 10.8 |
| 15. |
| 1.62* |

For another look at percents with the scientific calculator, see pages 239–240.

*Some calculators require you to press the [=] key to get an answer. The scientific calculator featured on pages 239–240 does not have a [%] key. You have to press [SHIFT] [=] to access the percent function.

Mrs. Gutierrez should leave a tip of **$1.62.**

With pencil-and-paper multiplication, you can multiply the two numbers in any order. However, calculators require you to **key in the percent value *last*.** Try reversing the order of the problem above. What happens?

Finding the Percent

Example: Out of her $420 paycheck, Lana's employer withholds $37.80. What percent of her pay is withheld?

▶ $\% = \dfrac{P}{W}$

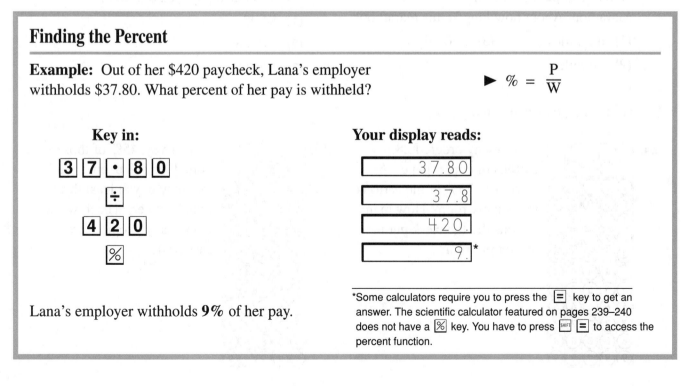

Key in:

[3] [7] [·] [8] [0]

[÷]

[4] [2] [0]

[%]

Your display reads:

| 37.80 |
| 37.8 |
| 420. |
| 9.* |

*Some calculators require you to press the [=] key to get an answer. The scientific calculator featured on pages 239–240 does not have a [%] key. You have to press [SHIFT] [=] to access the percent function.

Lana's employer withholds **9%** of her pay.

Finding the Whole

Example: Theodore completed 80% of the service calls scheduled for today. If he made 16 service calls, how many were scheduled?

$$\blacktriangleright\ W = \frac{P}{\%}$$

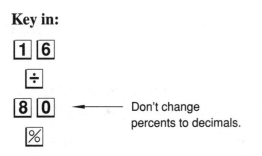

Key in:

| 1 | 6 |

÷

| 8 | 0 | ← Don't change percents to decimals.

%

Your display reads:

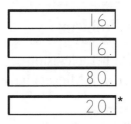

```
16.
16.
80.
20.*
```

There were **20** service calls scheduled for today.

*Some calculators require you to press the = key to get an answer. The scientific calculator featured on pages 239–240 does not have a % key. You have to press SHIFT = to access the percent function.

Use your calculator to solve the following percent problems. Remember to key the numbers in the correct order.

1. What is 45% of 160?

2. 50 is what percent of 400?

3. 20 is 10% of what number?

4. How much should Sally leave for a tip on a $48 dinner bill if she usually leaves 15%?

5. What percent interest is a customer charged if he pays $66.60 in interest on a balance of $360?

6. Ronald planted 45 trees this week, which represented 90% of the trees the nursery had in stock. How many trees did the nursery have in stock?

7. Wayne received an $8 tip from a group that spent $47 on dinner. What percent of the bill does this tip represent?

8. The Walkers want to save $5,000. They have saved 40% of this goal. How much money have they saved?

9. What is 22% of 15?

10. 18 is what percent of 360?

11. 35 is 80% of what number?

12. What is 20% of $50?

Problems 13 and 14 refer to the following chart.

Municipal Sales Tax

Alameda	4%
Twin Oaks	4.5%
Mendon	6%
Parker City	6.25%
Roanoke Township	7%

13. What would a person pay in sales tax on a $345 purchase in Mendon?

14. If sales tax came to $12.40 on a purchase made in Parker City, what was the cost of the item?

Two-Step Percent Problems

In this unit, you've practiced finding the part, the percent, and the whole. In many real-life situations and math problems, you must solve a percent equation, *then* use the information to find another answer.

Solving Two-Step Percent Problems

Example 1: When she bought her television set, Micaela made a 10% down payment. If the set cost $440, how much will Micaela have left to pay after the down payment?

Step 1	**Step 2**	**Step 3**	**Step 4**
Set up the percent equation. Let d = down payment.	Solve for the unknown.	Decide what operation is needed for the second step.	Solve.
10% of 440 is ___.	$.10 \times 440 = d$	*Subtract the down payment from the total cost to find what is left to pay.*	$440 - $44 = $**396**
$.10 \times 440 = d$	$44 = d$		cost down payment

Micaela has **$396** left to pay.

In the example above, once you found the *part,* your next step was to *subtract* to find the final answer. What steps will you need to take to solve the next example?

Example 2: Each month, Kim sends 5% of his take-home pay, or $100, to his mother in New York. What is Kim's *yearly* take-home pay?

Step 1	**Step 2**	**Step 3**	**Step 4**
Set up the percent equation. Let t = take-home pay.	Solve for the unknown.	Decide what operation is needed for the second step.	Solve.
5% of _____ is $100.	$.05 \times t = 100$	*Now you know that Kim takes home $2,000 per month. If you multiply this amount by 12 months in a year, you'll get his yearly take-home pay.*	$2,000 \times 12 = $**24,000**
$.05 \times t = 100$	$t = 100 \div .05$		per months per
	$t = $2,000$		month year

Kim's yearly take-home pay is **$24,000.**

A. Solve the following two-step percent problems. First write and solve a percent equation. Then decide whether to add, subtract, multiply, or divide to find your final answer.

1. Mary paid 4.5% sales tax on her purchase of a set of towels priced at $16. What total amount did she pay, including the tax?

2. A customer put a 20% deposit on a car priced at $12,400. What is the balance left to pay on the car?

3. Every week Kyra puts aside $50, or 8% of her weekly pay, for her vacation fund. If she is paid for 52 weeks per year, how much money does Kyra make each year?

4. A salesperson completed 70% of her 30 projected calls this week. If she worked 7 days, what was her average number of calls per day?

5. David withdrew 50% of the money in his savings account and put a down payment on a used Chevrolet selling for $1,245. If he started with $890 in his bank account, how much money did he have left to pay on the Chevrolet?

B. Using the tax table below, determine the total cost, including tax, of the items pictured below. Use a calculator if you'd like.

Municipal Sales Tax	
Grant's Island	3%
River Crossings	4%
Collins	5%
Mendota	6%
Stockton	6.5%
Mineral Junction	5%
Oscaloola	4.5%
Judith Gap	6.25%
Beaverton	3.5%

6.

$17.50 in River Crossings

8.

$375 in Mendota

10.

$16,400 in Beaverton

7.

$42 in Mineral Junction

9.

$25,000 in Oscaloola

11.
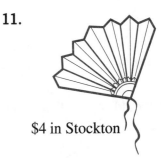
$4 in Stockton

Discounts

 **25% off all merchandise!!**

DISCOUNT
Save 10% on all sale items!!!

LOW PRICES!
Deduct 20% at the register!

When you see a discount advertised, what does it mean? How can you figure out how much you'll save and the actual price you'll pay?

When a store advertises "25% off on all merchandise," you will be charged the regular price *minus* 25% of the regular price. Let's look at an example of this two-step problem.

Finding a Discount Price

Example 1: At a 25%-off sale, Marian bought a tool set originally priced at $55. How much did she pay for the tool set?

Step 1
Set up an equation to find the *part,* or the *discount* on the item.

25% of $55 is *d.*

$.25 \times \$55 = d$

Step 2
Solve the equation to determine the amount of discount.

$.25 \times \$55 = d$

$\$13.75 = d$

Step 3
Subtract the discount from the original price.

$\$55 - \$13.75 = \mathbf{\$41.25}$
original   discount
price

Marian will pay **$41.25** for a tool set that was originally priced at $55.

When a store uses a percent discount, the higher the price of the item, the more you save off the original price. Look at an example.

Example 2: At a 25%-off sale, how much would Marian save on a tool set originally priced at $80? How much would she spend?

Step 1
Set up an equation to find the *part,* or the *discount* on the item.

25% of $80 is *d.*

$.25 \times \$80 = d$

Step 2
Solve the equation to determine the amount of discount.

$.25 \times \$80 = d$

$\$20 = d$

Step 3
Subtract the discount from the original price.

$\$80 - \$20 = \mathbf{\$60}$
original   discount
price

Marian would save **$20,** and she would pay **$60.**

Another Way to Look at Discounts

It is possible to find discounted prices in a slightly easier way—if you remember one important fact:

▶ 100% − % of Discount = % Paid

This means that if a store is offering a 20% discount, you will pay 100% − 20%, or 80%, of the original price. Let's see how this fact would help us with Marian's purchases.

Example: Marian is buying a $55 tool set at a 25% discount.

This means that she is paying 100% − 25%, or 75%, of the original price:

75% of $55 is d.
.75 × $55 = **$41.25**

Notice that subtracting the discount percent from 100% gives you the same result as the two-step process on the previous page.

Use the sales advertised below to determine the total cost of the items on Mrs. Shen's shopping list. Use either method shown in this lesson.

SHOPPING LIST

Item	Original Price	Discounted Pretax Price
1 potted geranium	$4.60	$ _____
2 boxes envelopes	$3.28 each	$ _____
1 tropical fish	$5.20	$ _____
20 pounds fertilizer	$10.80 each bag	$ _____
	Total Pretax Cost:	$ _____

Percent of Increase/Decrease

Two common types of percent problems require you to find

- the percent by which a number has gone up (**percent of increase**)

- the percent by which a number has gone down (**percent of decrease**)

Let's compare a regular percent problem with a problem that asks you to find a percent of increase.

Example 1

Dan has paid $350 of his $1,000 loan. What percent of the loan has he paid?

Example 2

The cost of a magazine subscription has gone up from $25 per year to $30 per year. By what percent was the price raised?

Example 1 asks you to find a percent. Example 2 asks you to find the *percent of increase*. If a problem asks for percent of increase or decrease, remember that

- the *part* is the *change* in value
- the *whole* is the *original* value

Finding Percent of Increase or Decrease

Example 3: What is the percent of increase if a price is raised from $25 to $30?

Step 1	**Step 2**	**Step 3**
Find the change in value by subtracting.	Using the *change in value* as the *part* and the *original value* as the *whole*, write a percent equation.	Solve the equation to find the percent of increase or decrease.

Step 1

$30 − $25 = $5
new   original   change

Step 2

____% of $25 is $5.

$n \times 25 = 5$

Step 3

$n \times 25 = 5$
$n = 5 \div 25$
n = .20 or 20%

The subscription price went up by **20%**.

Example 4: In a special offer, another magazine has lowered its rate from $30 to $25. What percent has the price decreased?

Step 1
Find the change in value.

Step 2
Using the *change in value* as the *part* and the *original value* as the *whole*, write a percent equation.

Step 3
Solve.

$30 − $25 = $5
original   new   change

____% of $30 is $5.

$n \times 30 = 5$

$n \times 30 = 5$
$n = 5 \div 30$
n = .16666 or $16\frac{2}{3}$%

The price has decreased **$16\frac{2}{3}$%**.

A. For each problem below, write what the change in value *(part)* and the original amount *(whole)* are. Then write a percent equation and solve it. Use a calculator if you'd like.

1. Danielle's hourly wage went up from $5.80 to $6.38. By what percent did her hourly wage go up?

   Change: _____ Original amount: _____

   Equation: _____

   Answer: _____

2. A car that Mr. Yun bought for $5,000 last year is worth only $3,600 this year. What percent decrease is this?

   Change: _____ Original amount: _____

   Equation: _____

   Answer: _____

3. The Hair Fair increased the price of a permanent from $50 to $55. By what percent did the price go up?

   Change: _____ Original amount: _____

   Equation: _____

   Answer: _____

4. La Choza charges $.90 for a side order of sour cream on its dinner menu, and $.60 for the same thing on the lunch menu. What percent decrease does the price on the lunch menu represent?

   Change: _____ Original amount: _____

   Equation: _____

   Answer: _____

B. Read the problems below. First decide whether you need to find a percent or a percent of change. Then solve.

5. Out of an expected 350 guests, only 245 showed up at the fund-raiser. What percent of the expected guests came?

6. Last year, Mitchell Milk had 520 customers on its morning route. This year, the number of customers went down to 494. By what percent did Mitchell Milk customers decrease?

7. When Bruce took over as math instructor, attendance went up from 10 students per night to 20 students. What is the percent increase?

Problems 8 and 9 refer to this graph.

Monthly Rental Price for Two-Bedroom Apartment in Dixon County

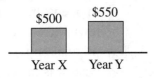

8. If Joe's income in Year X was $2,000 per month and he rented a two-bedroom apartment in Dixon County, what percent of his income would he be paying toward rent?

9. **Write** Describe the data in this graph by completing this sentence:
   Monthly rental prices in Dixon County rose _____% from Year X to Year Y.

Unit 5 Review

A. Change the decimals below into percents and the percents below into decimals. Be sure to drop any unnecessary zeros.

1. 30% = _____   .06 = _____   .8 = _____

2. 67% = _____   1.5 = _____   9% = _____

B. Change the fractions below into percents and the percents below into fractions. Reduce fractions to lowest terms.

3. $\frac{1}{5}$ = _____   24% = _____   18% = _____

4. $\frac{1}{3}$ = _____ $66\frac{2}{3}\%$ = _____ $\frac{3}{8}$ = _____

5. $\frac{8}{10}$ = _____   90% = _____ $\frac{1}{4}$ = _____

C. Solve the following percent statements.

6. What percent of 45 is 9?   **9.** What percent of 74 is 23.68?

7. 15% of what number is 90?   **10.** 25% of what number is 420?

8. 95% of 450 is what?   **11.** 40% of 560 is what?

D. Grid in the answer to each problem. You <u>may</u> use a calculator.

12. 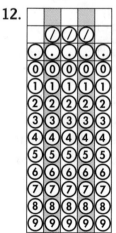 In one year, the population of a town increased by 4%. If the original population was 8,650, what was the population after the increase?

13.  A paint job is expected to take 36 hours. Of this time, only 30% will be spent painting. The rest of the time will be spent on preparation and cleanup. How many hours will be spent on preparation and cleanup?

E. Solve the following word problems. First decide whether you are finding the part, the percent, or the whole. Be sure your answer makes sense.

14. Seventeen of the students in Clara's adult ed class have been out of school for more than 5 years. If there are 20 students in the class, what percent have been out of school more than 5 years?

15. Tina left a $3.60 tip on an $18 lunch bill. What percent tip did she leave?

16. Sal's Deli raised the price of a tuna melt from $2.80 to $3.50. What percent increase does this new price reflect?

17. What total amount did Gail pay for a $48.50 toaster oven if she paid a 7% sales tax on top of the purchase price?

18. Paul plans to buy a suit at the Jordan Men's Clothing 25%-off sale. If the regular price of the suit is $220, how much will Paul pay, not including sales tax?

F. José knows the model of personal computer he would like to buy. The advertisements below describe sales on this computer. Study the information, then answer the question that follows.

CompuData of New Hampshire	New England Best Computer	NEW YORK WHOLESALE COMPUTERS
NO SALES TAX	$1200 base price	$1250 base price
$1300 base price	5% sales tax	7% sales tax
10% discount on cash-and-carry purchases	8% cash-and-carry discount	5% cash-and-carry discount

19. How much would José pay for the computer at each store if he took advantage of the cash-and-carry discount? (*Note:* Amount of tax is always determined *after* discount.)

Working Together

Find the advertisements in your local newspaper. (The Sunday paper is a good choice.) Look for an ad that gives a percent discount. Then write out a "fantasy" shopping list of five items that you'd like to purchase. Give the ad and your list to a classmate. Ask him or her to figure out how much you'd save by shopping at this sale instead of buying at regular prices.

Posttest

Part I

Solve the following problems. You <u>may</u> use a calculator.

1. At the start of a trip, the Alvarezes' car odometer read 34,290.7. At the end of the trip, it read 34,908.9. How many miles did the car travel on this trip?
   - **(1)** 69,199.6
   - **(2)** 9,102.1
   - **(3)** 1,518.2
   - **(4)** 618.2
   - **(5)** 520.1

2. How many $2\frac{1}{2}$-cup bread molds can be filled with $12\frac{1}{2}$ cups of dough?
   - **(1)** 31.25
   - **(2)** 31
   - **(3)** 10
   - **(4)** 5
   - **(5)** $2\frac{1}{2}$

3. There are 1.6 kilometers in a mile. How many miles are there in 48 kilometers?
   - **(1)** .03
   - **(2)** 3
   - **(3)** 30
   - **(4)** 76.8
   - **(5)** 768

4. Gerald lives in a state with no sales tax. He had $32 in his wallet. He bought a $4.50 magazine and a $.95 soda at the corner market. He paid with a $10 bill. How much change should he get back?
   - **(1)** $26.55
   - **(2)** $22.00
   - **(3)** $16.55
   - **(4)** $4.55
   - **(5)** $5.45

5. Winnie left her apartment at 9:00 A.M. and arrived at her mother's house at about 1:00 P.M. She had driven 3.75 hours at 55 miles per hour. How many miles did she cover?
   - **(1)** 14.6
   - **(2)** 51.25
   - **(3)** 165
   - **(4)** 206.25
   - **(5)** 220

6. Marcella speed-walked $2\frac{1}{2}$ miles Monday, $4\frac{3}{4}$ miles on Wednesday, $1\frac{1}{4}$ miles on Friday, and 5 miles on Sunday. What was the average number of miles she speed-walked per day over this time period?
   - **(1)** $13\frac{1}{2}$
   - **(2)** $3\frac{3}{8}$
   - **(3)** 3
   - **(4)** $2\frac{1}{4}$
   - **(5)** Not enough information is given.

7. Of the residents of Harbor Housing Project, 340 voted for Thompson for city council and 272 voted for Gladon. What percent of all residents voted for Gladon?
   - **(1)** 80%
   - **(2)** 61.2%
   - **(3)** 44%
   - **(4)** 34%
   - **(5)** Not enough information is given.

8. In a large box of Centro Theater popcorn, there are 80 grams of fat. Fifty of those grams are saturated fat. What percent is saturated fat?

(1) 1.6%
(2) 16%
(3) 30%
(4) 40%
(5) 62.5%

9. For every 3 apartments Nikki cleans, she earns $85. At this rate, how much did she earn in 4 days, cleaning 15 apartments?

(1) $1,275
(2) $425
(3) $340
(4) $28.33
(5) $17

10. Glenda's daughter weighed 35 pounds at age 3. At age 4, she weighed 42 pounds. What percent increase does this weight gain represent?

(1) 7%
(2) 20%
(3) 77%
(4) 83%
(5) Not enough information given.

Problems 11–13 refer to the following information.

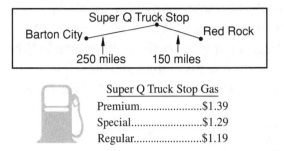

Super Q Truck Stop Gas
Premium......................$1.39
Special........................$1.29
Regular.......................$1.19

11. The Mardsons drove from Super Q Truck Stop to Red Rock at 50 miles per hour. If they left at 4:00 P.M. and drove straight through without stopping, at what time did they arrive in Red Rock?

(1) 1:30 P.M.
(2) 6:00 P.M.
(3) 7:00 P.M.
(4) 8:30 P.M.
(5) Not enough information is given.

12. Enrique drove from Super Q Truck Stop to Barton City in a car that gets 25 miles per gallon of gas. Before leaving, his gas tank was empty, so he filled it with premium. How much did he pay for all the gas he used on this trip?

(1) $1.39
(2) $13.90
(3) $103.90
(4) $347.50
(5) Not enough information is given.

13. A cyclist completed 75% of the trip from Barton City to Red Rock. How many miles did the cyclist cover?

(1) 533
(2) 475
(3) 400
(4) 300
(5) 112

14. At the beginning of a trip, Calvin's car odometer read 8736.7. After driving 199.5 miles, he stopped to fill up his gas tank. When he arrived at his destination, the odometer read 9251.1. How many miles did Calvin drive in all?

(1) 314.9   **(4)** 17,987.8

(2) 514.4   **(5)** 18,187.3

(3) 713.9

15. John needs to ship three items in the same box. The items weigh $1\frac{1}{2}$, $\frac{7}{10}$, and $2\frac{3}{5}$ pounds. What is the total weight of the shipment in pounds?

(1) $3\frac{1}{2}$ **(4)** $4\frac{1}{2}$

(2) $3\frac{11}{20}$ **(5)** $4\frac{4}{5}$

(3) $3\frac{4}{5}$

16. The scale on a map says that $\frac{3}{4}$ inch equals 60 miles. How many miles is it between cities that are 4 inches apart on the map?

(1) 180   **(4)** 320

(2) 240   **(5)** 340

(3) 280

17. A town council conducts a survey to see whether its citizens are in favor of a new shopping mall. The results of the survey are shown below.

Shopping Mall Survey

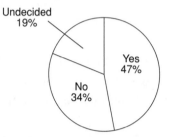

If 700 people were surveyed, how many said "Yes"?

(1) 133   **(4)** 371

(2) 238   **(5)** 462

(3) 329

18. Of the 65 workers at Green Landscaping, 25 are women. In lowest terms, what is the ratio of <u>men to women</u> workers at the landscaping company?

Mark your answer in the grid.

19. 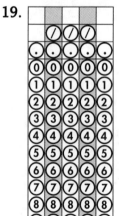 A piece of fabric is 7.2 meters in length. Hannah cuts the piece of fabric into three equal pieces. How many meters long is each piece of fabric?

Mark your answer in the grid.

Part II

Solve the following problems. You <u>may not</u> use a calculator.

20. The regular price of a drill is $89.99. Which of the following expressions represents the cost of the drill at a 30%-off sale?

    (1) .30 × 89.99

    (2) (.30 × 89.99) − 89.99

    (3) 89.99 − (.30 × 89.99)

    (4) 89.99 − .30

    (5) 89.99 − (30 ÷ 89.99)

21. A 9-square-foot plot yielded 12 quarts of beans. If 12 square feet of beans are planted next year, how many quarts of beans would the the plot yield at this rate?

    (1) 1.3   **(4)** 21

    (2) 3   **(5)** 108

    (3) 16

22. Which expression shows the number of inches the molding is after .625 inch is cut off each end?

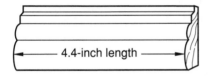

    4.4-inch length

    (1) 4.4 − .625

    (2) 4.4 + .625 + .625

    (3) 4.4 ÷ (.625 × 2)

    (4) (.625 + .625) − 4.4

    (5) 4.4 − (.625 × 2)

23. A chef bought $3\frac{3}{4}$ pounds of greens at $.60 per pound. What did he pay in all?

    (1) $.16   **(4)** $2.25

    (2) $1.80   **(5)** Not enough

    (3) $2.04   information is given.

24. Two-year-old Shatilla is 70 centimeters tall. How many meters tall is she?

    (1) 700

    (2) 10

    (3) 7

    (4) .7

    (5) .07

Problems 25 and 26 refer to the following information.

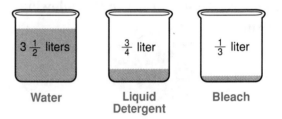

    $3\frac{1}{2}$ liters $\frac{3}{4}$ liter $\frac{1}{3}$ liter

    Water   Liquid Detergent   Bleach

25. If you poured together all the liquid pictured above, how many liters would you have?

    (1) $4\frac{7}{12}$

    (2) $2\frac{3}{4}$

    (3) $3\frac{1}{2}$

    (4) $3\frac{5}{12}$

    (5) $4\frac{2}{3}$

26. One-half of the water above is deionized. Which of the following expressions represents the number of liters that are deionized?

    (1) $3\frac{1}{2} \times 2$

    (2) $3\frac{1}{2} \times \frac{1}{2}$

    (3) $3\frac{1}{2} \div \frac{1}{2}$

    (4) $\frac{1}{2} \div 3\frac{1}{2}$

    (5) $3\frac{1}{2} - \frac{1}{2}$

27. 59% of people surveyed watch the 11:00 P.M. news. If the total number of people surveyed was 12,000, *approximately* how many said they watched the 11:00 P.M. news?

(1) about 1,000

(2) about 1,200

(3) about 2,800

(4) about 7,200

(5) about 20,000

Problems 28 and 29 refer to the following drawing.

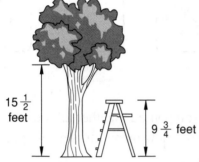

$15\frac{1}{2}$ feet

$9\frac{3}{4}$ feet

28. How many feet shorter is the ladder than the tree trunk?

(1) $3\frac{1}{2}$

(2) $4\frac{1}{4}$

(3) $5\frac{3}{4}$

(4) $6\frac{1}{2}$

(5) $25\frac{1}{4}$

29. A bird-feeder is hung from a branch that is $\frac{2}{3}$ of the way up the tree trunk. How high is the branch?

(1) $9\frac{1}{6}$ feet

(2) $10\frac{1}{3}$ feet

(3) $15\frac{5}{6}$ feet

(4) $23\frac{1}{4}$ feet

(5) Not enough information is given.

Problems 30–32 refer to the following chart.

Myriad Laboratories, Inc.
Experimental Tests
Week of 5/2

Lab Team	Failed Tests	Successful Tests
#31	18	102
#32	40	80
#34	20	100
#35	4	116
#36	8	112

30. What is the ratio of successful tests to failed tests for Lab Team #34?

(1) 1 to 5

(2) 5 to 1

(3) 1 to 6

(4) 6 to 1

(5) 1 to 2

31. What percent of *all tests taken* by Lab Team #32 failed?

(1) .5%

(2) 5%

(3) $33\frac{1}{3}\%$

(4) 50%

(5) 100%

32. On every test that failed, Lab Team #36 let the lab cultures sit $\frac{1}{2}$ hour too long. How much total time too long did Lab Team #36 let the cultures sit?

(1) 16 hours

(2) 8 hours

(3) $7\frac{1}{2}$ hours

(4) 4 hours

(5) 2 hours

33. Rex rides his bicycle $2\frac{1}{2}$ miles to work each day. He stays on a bike path for $\frac{2}{3}$ of the ride. Then he rides the rest of the way in the street. For how many miles does he ride in the street?

(1) $\frac{5}{6}$

(2) $1\frac{1}{3}$

(3) $1\frac{2}{3}$

(4) $1\frac{5}{6}$

(5) Not enough information is given.

34. Last year, 50 girls tried out for the high school softball team. This year, 120 girls tried out for the team. What is the percent of increase in the number of girls who tried out from last year to this year?

(1) 58%

(2) 70%

(3) 140%

(4) 170%

(5) 240%

35. Tickets to a community play are $6.75 each. Leslie buys five tickets. If she pays for them with two $20 bills, how much change will she receive?

(1) $5.75

(2) $6.25

(3) $12.75

(4) $13.25

(5) $33.75

36. A library collection has 1,530 books of fiction. If the number of fiction books is 30% of the collection, how many books are in the entire collection?

(1) 2,600

(2) 3,900

(3) 5,100

(4) 10,470

(5) 11,600

37. Kim uses a copy machine to increase the size of a drawing from $5\frac{3}{4}$ inches in height to $7\frac{5}{8}$ inches. How many inches longer is the height of the enlargement than the original drawing?

Mark your answer in the grid.

38. A recipe calls for 9 ounces of chocolate chips to make a dessert that serves 6 people. How many ounces of chocolate chips would you need to make 20 servings of the dessert?

Mark your answer in the grid.

1. **(4) 618.2**

   $34{,}908.9 - 34{,}290.7 = 618.2$

2. **(4) 5**

   $12\frac{1}{2} \div 2\frac{1}{2} = 5$

3. **(3) 30**

   $$\frac{1.6 \text{ kilometers}}{1 \text{ mile}} = \frac{48 \text{ kilometers}}{m \text{ miles}}$$

   $1.6 \times m = 48$

   $m = 48 \div 1.6$

   $m = 30$

4. **(4) $4.55**

   $\$10 - (\$4.50 + \$.95) =$

   $\$10 - \$5.45 = \$4.55$

5. **(4) 206.25**

   $3.75 \text{ hours} \times 55 \text{ miles per hour} = 206.25 \text{ miles}$

6. **(2) $3\frac{3}{8}$ miles**

   $2\frac{1}{2} + 4\frac{3}{4} + 1\frac{1}{4} + 5 = 13\frac{1}{2}$ total miles

   $13\frac{1}{2}$ miles $\div 4 = 3\frac{3}{8}$

7. **(5) Not enough information is given.**

   You do not know the *total* number of residents.

8. **(5) 62.5%**

   $n\% \times 80 = 50$

   $n\% = 50 \div 80$

   $n\% = .625$ or 62.5%

9. **(2) $425**

   $$\frac{3 \text{ apartments}}{\$85} = \frac{15 \text{ apartments}}{a}$$

   $3 \times a = 15 \times 85$

   $3 \times a = 1{,}275$

   $a = 1{,}275 \div 3$

   $a = 425$

10. **(2) 20%**

    $42 - 35 = 7$ pounds (change)

    $n\% \times 35 = 7$

    $n\% = 7 \div 35$

    $n\% = .20$ or 20%

11. **(3) 7:00 P.M.**

    $150 \text{ miles} \div 50 \text{ miles per hour} = 3 \text{ hours}$

    4:00 P.M. $+ 3$ hours $= 7:00$ P.M.

12. **(2) $13.90**

    $250 \text{ miles} \div 25 \text{ miles per gallon} = 10 \text{ gallons}$

    $10 \times \$1.39 \text{ per gallon} = \$13.90$

13. **(4) 300**

    $.75 \times (250 + 150) = p$

    $.75 \times 400 = p$

    $300 = p$

14. **(2) 514.4**

    Subtract: $9251.1 - 8736.7 = 514.4$

    The 199.5 miles is not needed to solve the problem.

15. **(5) $4\frac{4}{5}$**

    Add: $1\frac{1}{2} + \frac{7}{10} + 2\frac{3}{5} =$

    $1\frac{5}{10} + \frac{7}{10} + 2\frac{6}{10} =$

    $3\frac{18}{10} = 4\frac{8}{10} = 4\frac{4}{5}$

16. **(4) 320**

    Set up a proportion and solve. You may want to use the decimal 0.75 for $\frac{3}{4}$.

    $$\frac{0.75 \text{ inches}}{60 \text{ miles}} = \frac{4 \text{ inches}}{x \text{ miles}}$$

    $0.75 \times x = 60 \times 4$

    $0.75 \times x = 240$

    $x = 240 \div 0.75$

    $x = 320$ miles

17. **(3) 329**

    47% of 700 is x

    $0.47 \times 700 = x$

    $x = 329$

18. $\frac{8}{5}$

    Subtract to find the number of men:

    65 workers $-$ 25 women $= 40$ men.

    Write a ratio as a fraction and simplify in lowest terms.

    $$\frac{40 \text{ men}}{25 \text{ women}} \quad \frac{40}{25} \div \frac{5}{5} = \frac{8}{5}$$

19. 2.4

    Divide: $7.2 \div 3 = 2.4$ meters.

20. **(3) $89.99 - (.30 \times 89.99)$**

    regular price $-$ discount

21. (3) 16

$$\frac{9 \text{ square feet}}{12 \text{ quarts}} = \frac{12 \text{ square feet}}{q \text{ quarts}}$$

$9 \times q = 12 \times 12$

$9 \times q = 144$

$q = 144 \div 9 = 16$

22. (5) 4.4 − (.625 × 2)

whole width − (2 times length trimmed each side)

23. (4) \$2.25

$3.75 \times .60 = 2.25$

24. (4) .7

70 centimeters $\div$ 100 = .7 meter

25. (1) $4\frac{7}{12}$

$3\frac{1}{2} + \frac{3}{4} + \frac{1}{3} = 4\frac{7}{12}$

26. (2) $3\frac{1}{2} \times \frac{1}{2}$

$\frac{1}{2}$ of $3\frac{1}{2}$ means $\frac{1}{2} \times 3\frac{1}{2}$

27. (4) about 7,200

$59\% \approx 60\%$

$.60 \times 12,000 = p$

$7,200 = p$

28. (3) $5\frac{3}{4}$

$15\frac{1}{2} - 9\frac{3}{4} = 5\frac{3}{4}$

29. (2) $10\frac{1}{3}$ feet

$\frac{2}{3} \times 15\frac{1}{2} = \frac{31}{3} = 10\frac{1}{3}$ feet high

30. (2) 5 to 1

$\frac{100}{20} = \frac{5}{1}$

31. (3) $33\frac{1}{3}\%$

$40 + 80 = 120$ total tests taken

$n\% \times 120 = 40$

$n\% = 40 \div 120$

$n\% = .3333333$

32. (4) 4 hours

8 tests failed $\times \frac{1}{2}$ hour = $\frac{8}{2}$ or 4 hours

33. (1) $\frac{5}{6}$

If he rides $\frac{2}{3}$ of the way on the bike path, then he rides $\frac{1}{3}$ of the distance in the street.

Multiply: $2\frac{1}{2} \times \frac{1}{3} = \frac{5}{2} \times \frac{1}{3} = \frac{5}{6}$

34. (3) 140%

Subtract to find the amount of increase, then divide by the original number.

$120 - 50 = 70$, and $70 \div 50 = 1.4 = 140\%$

35. (2) \$6.25

Multiply: $\$6.75 \times 5 = \$33.75$

Two \$20 bills equal \$40.

Subtract: $\$40 - \$33.75 = \$6.25$

36. (3) 5,100

There are 1,530 fiction books.

30% of the total collection (c) is 1,530.

$0.3 \times c = 1,530$

$c = 1,530 \div 0.3$

$c = 5,100$ books

37. $\frac{15}{8}$

Subtract:

$7\frac{5}{8} - 5\frac{3}{4} =$

$7\frac{5}{8} - 5\frac{6}{8} =$

$6\frac{13}{8} - 5\frac{6}{8} = 1\frac{7}{8} = \frac{15}{8}$

Remember to enter mixed numbers as improper fractions in the grid.

38. 30

Write a proportion and solve:

$$\frac{9 \text{ ounces}}{6 \text{ servings}} = \frac{x \text{ ounces}}{20 \text{ servings}}$$

$9 \times 20 = 6 \times x$

$180 = 6 \times x$

$x = 180 \div 6$

$x = 30$ ounces

Posttest Evaluation Chart

Make note of any problems that you answered incorrectly. Review the skill area for each of those problems, using the unit number given.

Problem Number	Skill Area	Unit
1, 3, 4, 5, 11, 12, 14, 19, 22, 24, 35	Decimals	2
2, 6, 15, 23, 25, 26, 28, 29, 32, 33, 37	Fractions and mixed numbers	3
9, 16, 18, 21, 30, 38	Ratio and proportion	4
7, 8, 10, 13, 17, 20, 27, 31, 34, 36	Percents	5

Answer Key

Unit 1

Understanding Decimals pp. 14–15

Part A

1. <u>4 3</u> . <u>8 7 5</u>

2. **a.** tens place: 9
   b. tenths place: 2
   c. hundredths place: 5
   d. ones place: 0

3. **a.** tens place: 5
   b. tenths place: 2
   c. hundredths place: 9
   d. ones place: 6

Part B

4. b
5. a
6. c

Making Connections: Decimals and Money p. 15

1. 100 wholes, 9 hundredths
2. 100 wholes, 90 hundredths
3. 21 wholes, 50 hundredths
4. 21 wholes, 5 hundredths

Reading Decimals pp. 16–17

Part A

1. thirty-five hundredths
2. nine and one tenth
3. four and one thousandth
4. twenty-five thousandths
5. ninety and twenty-five hundredths
6. twenty-five and nine tenths

Part B

7. **(3)** one hundred twenty and two thousandths
8. **(2)** forty-two thousandths
9. **(2)** $33.05
10. **(1)** Two hundred fifty dollars and fifty cents
11. **(3)** five and nine hundredths
12. **(1)** 0.25 and **(2)** .25

Part C

13. seventy-five and nine hundred thirty-three thousandths miles per hour
14. 1925
15. 1991
16. Your answer should read something like this: The more decimal places used, the more precise the measurements.

Writing Decimals pp. 18–19

Part A

1. 0.17
2. 2.3
3. 140.7
4. 29.070
5. 2,000.75
6. 1.80
7. 0.040
8. 40.004
9. 721.4
10. 8.08

Part B

11. **(2)** $1.53
12. **(3)** 0.8
13. **(1)** 6.25%
14. **(2)** 3.125

Part C

15. 2.03
16. 0.125
17. 1.025
18. 0.2
19. 2.015
20. 0.255

Making Connections: Reading Decimals Out Loud p. 19

15. two point zero-three
16. zero point one-two-five
17. one point zero-two-five
18. zero point two
19. two point zero-one-five
20. zero point two-five-five

Comparing Decimals pp. 20–21

Part A

1. 9.55
2. 0.9
3. 49.9
4. 10.75
5. 5.6
6. 4.3

Part B

7. 4.75
   4.8
   5.75
   5.9
8. 10.625
   10.67
   10.85
   10.9

9. 20.4
21.04
21.12
21.2

10. 75.07
75.5
75.55
75.7

Part C

11. (2) 1.1 millimeters

12. (3) .22, .221, 2.12, 2.21

13. The box with 1.1 ounces has the largest lump of gold.

14. largest: 2.7
2.625
2.10
2.01
smallest: 2.009

Making Connections: Comparing Numbers p. 21

1. <

6. >

2. >

7. <

3. <

8. <

4. >

9. <

5. >

Reading Digital Measurements pp. 22–23

Part A

1. a. 55 thousand 478 and 9 tenths miles

b. 99 thousand 318 and 4 tenths miles

c. 65 thousand 630 and 8 tenths miles

2. Car A and Car C

Part B

3. Yes

4. a. Lower

b. Yes

5. Yes. The child's temperature is 99.8°, which is higher than 99.5°. The doctor recommends medicine for temperatures over 99.5°.

Part C

6. Incorrect; should be 2.5

7. Incorrect; should be 0.25

8. Correct

Using Your Calculator pp. 24–25

1. 437.8	1,620	605.33333	8,755
2. 5.4	43,022	1,334.5	2,215.1
3. 73	574	590.1	4,802

4. 92 trees
$150 - 22 - 36 = 92$

5. $3,850
$11,550 \div 3 = \$3,850$

Writing Expressions pp. 26–27

1. (2) $g \div 5$

2. (3) $\$912 - b$

3. (1) $60 \times h$

4. (1) $s + 5$

5. $p + 4$ $4 + p$

Solving Word Problems pp. 28–29

Your wording may vary, but answers should contain the following information.

1. a. Question: After she charged $52, what is Janelle's new credit card balance?

b. Information: $346 balance, $52 charge

c. Strategy: To solve, add $52 to $346.

d. Estimate: $346 ≈ $350; $52 ≈ $50
$350 + $50 = $400

e. Solve and Check: $346 + $52 = $398. This answer is close to the estimate.

2. a. Question: How many eggs are needed?

b. Information: 2 dozen eggs, 6 eggs, 8 eggs

c. Strategy: To solve, multiply 2 × 12 (12 eggs in a dozen), then add 6, then add 8.

d. Estimate: 25 + 5 + 10 = 40

e. Solve and Check: 24 + 6 + 8 = 38. This answer is close to the estimate.

3. a. Question: How much did each woman spend on groceries?

b. Information: $122 total, split between 2 women

c. Strategy: To solve, divide $122 by 2.

d. Estimate: $120 ÷ 2 = $60

e. Solve and Check: $122 ÷ 2 = $61. This answer is close to the estimate.

4. a. Question: How much did he spend on 5 gallons of paint?

b. Information: $14 per gallon, 5 new gallons

c. Strategy: To solve, multiply $14 × 5.

d. Estimate: 15 × $5 = $75

e. Solve and Check: $14 × 5 = $70. This answer is close to the estimate.

Understanding Fractions pp. 30–31

Part A

1. a. $\frac{1}{4}$
   b. $\frac{5}{8}$
   c. $\frac{7}{12}$

2. a. $\frac{2}{3}$
   b. $\frac{2}{6}$
   c. $\frac{1}{10}$

Part B

3. $\frac{12}{27}$

   $\dfrac{12 \text{ women}}{27 \text{ people}}$

4. $\frac{7}{12}$

   $\dfrac{7 \text{ inches}}{12 \text{ inches}}$

5. $\frac{45}{212}$

   $\dfrac{\$45}{\$212}$

6. $\frac{2{,}003}{2{,}180}$

   $\dfrac{2{,}003 \text{ excellent parts}}{2{,}180 \text{ total parts}}$

7. $\frac{6}{7}$

   $\dfrac{6 \text{ days working}}{7 \text{ days in a week}}$

8. $\frac{1}{8}$

   $\dfrac{1 \text{ hour on phone}}{8 \text{ hours working}}$

Making Connections: Fractions and Decimals p. 31

1. a. $\frac{275}{1{,}000}$
      $\frac{32}{100}$
      $\frac{9}{10}$
   b. $\frac{1}{10}$
      $\frac{1}{100}$
      $\frac{1}{1{,}000}$

2. a. .3
      .21
      .875
   b. .007
      .07
      .7

The Size of Fractions pp. 32–33

Part A

1.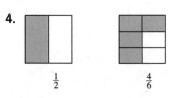

   $\frac{1}{4}$ $\frac{1}{8}$

   $\frac{1}{4}$ is larger than $\frac{1}{8}$.

2.

   $\frac{3}{4}$ $\frac{5}{8}$

   $\frac{3}{4}$ is larger than $\frac{5}{8}$.

3.

   $\frac{2}{3}$ $\frac{3}{4}$

   $\frac{3}{4}$ is larger than $\frac{2}{3}$.

4.

   $\frac{1}{2}$ $\frac{4}{6}$

   $\frac{4}{6}$ is larger than $\frac{1}{2}$.

Part B

5. Less than $\frac{1}{2}$
6. More than $\frac{1}{2}$
7. More than $\frac{1}{2}$
8. Equal to $\frac{1}{2}$
9. More than $\frac{1}{2}$
10. Equal to $\frac{1}{2}$

Part C

11. A
    $\frac{3}{8} < \frac{1}{2}$
12. B
    $\frac{8}{16} = \frac{1}{2}$
13. C
    $\frac{2}{3} > \frac{1}{2}$
14. C
    $\frac{5}{8} > \frac{1}{2}$
15. C
    $\frac{3}{4} > \frac{1}{2}$
16. B
    $\frac{2}{4} = \frac{1}{2}$

Forms of Fractions pp. 34–35

Part A

1. $2\frac{1}{3}$
   $1\frac{1}{2}$
   $4\frac{1}{2}$
   $2\frac{2}{3}$

2. $1\frac{1}{3}$
   $1\frac{3}{4}$
   $1\frac{2}{7}$
   $1\frac{4}{5}$

Part B

3. $\frac{7}{2}$
   $\frac{21}{5}$
   $\frac{7}{3}$
   $\frac{17}{8}$

4. $\frac{9}{2}$
   $\frac{13}{4}$
   $\frac{8}{5}$
   $\frac{13}{8}$

Making Connections: Expressing Fractions as Decimals p. 35

1. 0.8
2. 0.25
3. 0.5
4. 0.375
5. 0.4
6. 0.625

Equivalent Fractions pp. 36–37

Part A

Your answers may be different from these. Be sure you multiplied both the numerator and denominator of a fraction by the *same* number.

1. $\frac{2}{7} \times \frac{4}{4} = \frac{8}{28}$

$\frac{3}{5} \times \frac{4}{4} = \frac{12}{20}$

$\frac{1}{8} \times \frac{4}{4} = \frac{4}{32}$

$\frac{3}{4} \times \frac{4}{4} = \frac{12}{16}$

2. $\frac{3}{8} \times \frac{2}{2} = \frac{6}{16}$

$\frac{1}{4} \times \frac{2}{2} = \frac{2}{8}$

$\frac{2}{3} \times \frac{2}{2} = \frac{4}{6}$

$\frac{1}{5} \times \frac{2}{2} = \frac{2}{10}$

Part B

3. $\frac{4}{6} \div \frac{2}{2} = \frac{2}{3}$

$\frac{6}{8} \div \frac{2}{2} = \frac{3}{4}$

$\frac{2}{6} \div \frac{2}{2} = \frac{1}{3}$

$\frac{6}{10} \div \frac{2}{2} = \frac{3}{5}$

4. $\frac{15}{21} \div \frac{3}{3} = \frac{5}{7}$

$\frac{3}{9} \div \frac{3}{3} = \frac{1}{3}$

$\frac{12}{15} \div \frac{3}{3} = \frac{4}{5}$

$\frac{3}{18} \div \frac{3}{3} = \frac{1}{6}$

Part C

5. Yes

$\frac{2}{3}$

Yes

Yes

6. $\frac{1}{3}$

$\frac{1}{2}$

Yes

$\frac{1}{4}$

Making Connections: Equivalent Fractions and Decimals p. 37

1. $.40 = \frac{40}{100}$

$\frac{40}{100} \times \frac{100}{100} = \frac{4,000}{10.000}$ or .4000

2. $.9 = \frac{9}{10}$

$\frac{9}{10} \times \frac{100}{100} = \frac{900}{1,000}$ or .900

3. $.80 = \frac{80}{100}$

$\frac{80}{100} \times \frac{10}{10} = \frac{800}{1,000}$ or .800

4.

$\frac{5}{10} \times \frac{10}{10} = \frac{50}{100}$ or .50

Filling in a Grid pp. 38–39

1. $\frac{9}{16}$

There are 16 boxes, and 9 are shaded.

2. .6

Divide: $3 \div 5 = 0.6$.

3. $\frac{6}{25}$

Twenty-four cents is $\frac{24}{100}$ of a dollar. In lowest terms: $\frac{24}{100} = \frac{24}{100} \div \frac{4}{4} = \frac{6}{25}$

4. 1.012

The third decimal place value column is the thousandths place. Make sure the final decimal digit is in this place.

Reading Fraction Measurements pp. 40–41

Part A

1. >

2. <

3. Belle's

$\frac{3}{4} > \frac{2}{3}$

4. >

5. <

6. Too little

$\frac{1}{2} < \frac{2}{3}$

Part B

7. 1 inch

8. $1\frac{3}{4}$ inches

9. $3\frac{1}{2}$ inches

Understanding Percent pp. 42–43

Part A

1. Shaded 55%

Unshaded 45%

2. Shaded 20%

Unshaded 80%

3. Shaded 90%

Unshaded 10%

4. Shaded 35%

Unshaded 65%

Part B

5. (3) **72%**

   $(100 - 28 = 72)$

6. (3) **60%**

   $(100 - 13 - 27 = 60)$

7. (2) **75%**

   $(100 - 25 = 75)$

8. (2) **97%**

   $(100 - 3 = 97)$

Making Connections: Relating Parts of a Whole p. 43

1. $43\% = \frac{43}{100} = 0.43$

2. $\frac{21}{100} = 21\% = 0.21$

3. $.99 = \frac{99}{100} = 99\%$

4. $33\% = \frac{33}{100} = 0.33$

5. $\frac{67}{100} = 0.67 = 67\%$

6. $0.13 = \frac{13}{100} = 13\%$

Solving Multistep Problems pp. 44–45

1. a. Multistep

   b. First multiply $2 \times 4 = 8$.

   Subtract $10 - 8 = 2$.

   c. 2 cars

2. a. Single-step

   b. Multiply 4 cups $\times$ 5 = 20 cups for 5 loaves.

   c. No, he does not have enough flour for 5 loaves.

3. a. Multistep

   b. First add all phone books delivered by Shift A and by Shift B. Then subtract the smaller number from the larger: 567 books $-$ 558 books.

   c. 9 books

4. a. Multistep

   b. Multiply 20 students $\times$ 6 trips = 120. Then multiply that total by \$5 per trip: $120 \times \$5$.

   c. \$600

Unit 1 Review pp. 46–47

Part A

1. 0.025

2. 10.5

3. 0.89

4. 0.2

5. 1.044

6. 0.57

Part B

7. $13.05 < 14.1$

8. $10.3 > 10.21$

9. $5.15 > 5.099$

10. $120.1 = 120.100$

11. $3.5 < 3.6$

12. $0.20 = .200$

Part C

13. $\frac{321}{1,000}$

   $\frac{87}{100}$

   $\frac{3}{100}$

   $\frac{1}{1,000}$

   $\frac{7}{10}$

Part D

14. $\frac{4}{7}$

15. $\frac{2}{10} = \frac{1}{5}$

16. $\frac{13}{39} = \frac{1}{3}$

17. $\frac{50}{350} = \frac{1}{7}$

Part E

18. $20\% = \frac{20}{100}$ or $\frac{1}{5} = 0.20$ or 0.2

19. $\frac{45}{100} = 0.45 = 45\%$

20. $.50 = \frac{50}{100}$ or $\frac{1}{2} = 50\%$

21. $.09 = \frac{9}{100} = 9\%$

Part F

22. $\frac{3}{5}$

   They had completed $\frac{60}{100}$ of their trip.

   In lowest terms: $\frac{60}{100} = \frac{60}{100} \div \frac{20}{20} = \frac{3}{5}$

23. .08

   $8\% = \frac{8}{100} = 0.08$

Part G

24. $\frac{40}{100} = \frac{2}{5}$

25. $\frac{35}{100} = 0.35$

26. a. 15%

   b. $\frac{15}{100} = \frac{3}{20}$

27. $\frac{117}{300} = \frac{39}{100}$

   Excellent: $40 + 35 + 42 = 117$

   Total: $100 + 100 + 100 = 300$

28. $\frac{22}{300} = \frac{11}{150}$

   Rejected: $5 + 2 + 15 = 22$

   Total: $100 + 100 + 100 = 300$

Working Together

Answers will vary.

Unit 2

Rounding and Estimating Decimals pp. 50–51

Part A

1. **a.** 11   2   4   **b.** 5   2   3
2. **a.** 901   900   13   **b.** 12   42   42

Part B

3. **a.** 1.9   2.0   4.1   **b.** 4.9   2.1   2.5
4. **a.** 0.8   0.8   11.0   **b.** 10.9   0.1   0.2

Part C

5. **a.** Regular: $1.22   6. **a.** Regular: $1.23
   b. Super: $1.24   **b.** Super: $1.44
   c. Supreme: $1.29   **c.** Supreme: $1.50

Understanding the Question pp. 52–53

Part A

Your answers may be worded differently from these.

1. I need to find the total bill, including tax.
2. total sum of purchases plus tax
3. the difference between $40 and the total cost of purchases plus tax
4. whether the correct change from $40 is more than $13.53

Part B

5. **b.** $24 - 12 = 12$ miles
6. **d.** $24 + 40 = 64$ square miles
7. **c.** $12 \div 24 = .5$ hour or 30 minutes
8. **a.**

   | ⊢——— 24 miles ———⊣ |
   | Station 1 | Station 2 | Station 3 | Station 4 |

   Four evenly spaced gas stations divide the road into 3 equal lengths. $24 \div 3 = 8$ miles. No, the distance between neighboring stations cannot be more than 10 miles.

Part C

Questions and answers will vary.

Adding Decimals pp. 54–55

Part A

1. 11.81   33.25   60.655   96.65
2. 17.25   15.8   12.47   4.08

Part B

3. **6 inches**

   $1.5 + 1.5 + 1.5 + 1.5 = 6$
4. **13.6 miles**

   $4.3 + 4.3 + 5 = 13.6$
5. **$8.39**

   $\$5 + \$2.99 + \$.40 = \$8.39$
6. **Yes**

   $1.3 + .3 + .6 = 2.2$ miles in 1 hour

   (From 9:00 to 10:00 is one hour.)

Making Connections: Grouping to Solve Problems p. 55

You may have used techniques different from the ones used in these examples.

1. **23**

   $4.5 + 8.5 + 10$

   Group halves: you know that $.5 + .5 = 1$, so

   $1 + 4 + 8 + 10 = 23$
2. **22**

   $9.1 + 5.5 + 4.9 + 2.5$

   Group the friendly numbers: $.1 + .9 = 1$, $.5 + .5 = 1$, so

   $1 + 1 + 9 + 5 + 4 + 2 = 22$
3. **100**

   $42.6 + 38.4 + 19$

   Group the friendly numbers: $.6 + .4 = 1$, so

   $1 + 42 + 38 + 19 = 100$

Subtracting Decimals pp. 56–57

Part A

1. 1.989   0.6   2.425   0.925
2. 8.775   3.5   3.185   1.39
3. 2.1   2.3   6.3   12.8

Part B

4. 2.0   95.1   8.375   1.2
5. 7.2   0.123   1.7   71

Part C

Estimates will vary.

6. **2.25 feet**

   $10.5 - 8.25 = 2.25$

7. **180.7 miles**

$42{,}771.5 - 42{,}590.8 = 180.7$

8. **Patient A**

$101.9° - 99.5° = 2.4°$ drop

$100° - 98.6° = 1.4°$ drop

$2.4 > 1.4$

9. **No**

$\$3.95 + \$.95 + \$.95 = \$5.85$ for lunch

$\$6.50 - \$5.85 = \$.65$ left for ride home

$\$.65 < \$1.20$ for bus fare

Making Connections: Changing Fractions to Decimals p. 57

1. $3 \div 5 = .6$

   $1 \div 4 = .25$

   $.6 - .25 = .35$

   $.35 = \frac{35}{100} = \frac{7}{20}$

2. $1 \div 4 = .25$

   $1 \div 2 = .5$

   $.25 + .5 = .75$

   $.75 = \frac{75}{100} = \frac{3}{4}$

3. $1 \div 5 = .2$

   $1 \div 4 = .25$

   $.2 + .25 = .45$

   $.45 = \frac{45}{100} = \frac{9}{20}$

4. $1 \div 2 = .5$

   $2 \div 5 = .4$

   $.5 - .4 = .1$

   $.1 = \frac{1}{10}$

5. $4 \div 5 = .8$

   $3 \div 4 = .75$

   $.8 - .75 = .05$

   $.05 = \frac{5}{100} = \frac{1}{20}$

Addition and Subtraction Equations pp. 58–59

Part A

1. **(1)** $x - 41 = \$298$
2. **(1)** $\$41 + y = \$298$
3. **(2)** $45 + 35 = m$
4. **(2)** $45 - 35 = t$
5. **(1)** $215 - 207 = g$

Part B

You may have written any of the four equations given for problems 6–9.

6. Let x = original length of molding

   $x - 1.625 = 11.5$

   $x - 11.5 = 1.625$

   $1.625 + 11.5 = x$

   $11.5 + 1.625 = x$

7. Let x = original number of liters in bowl

   $3.5 + x = 5.75$

   $x + 3.5 = 5.75$

   $5.75 - 3.5 = x$

   $5.75 - x = 3.5$

8. Let x = miles from Point A to Point B

   $x + 100 = 305.5$

   $100 + x = 305.5$

   $305.5 - 100 = x$

   $305.5 - x = 100$

9. Let x = number of books added to the collection

   $135 - 112 = x$

   $135 - x = 112$

   $x + 112 = 135$

   $112 + x = 135$

Solving Addition and Subtraction Equations pp. 60–61

Part A

1. $x - 3.5 = 2.5$

   $x - 3.5 + 3.5 = 2.5 + 3.5$

   $\mathbf{x = 6}$

2. $250 + h = 375$

   $250 + h - 250 = 375 - 250$

   $\mathbf{h = 125}$

3. $y + 4.2 = 6.2$

   $y + 4.2 - 4.2 = 6.2 - 4.2$

   $\mathbf{y = 2}$

4. $x - .90 = 1.10$

   $x - .90 + .90 = 1.10 + .90$

   $\mathbf{x = 2}$

5. $1.5 + z = 3$

   $1.5 + z - 1.5 = 3 - 1.5$

   $\mathbf{z = 1.5}$

6. $x - 10.5 = 3.1$

   $x - 10.5 + 10.5 = 3.1 + 10.5$

   $\mathbf{x = 13.6}$

7. $10.6 - 3.6 = b$

   $\mathbf{7 = b}$

8. $15 + 20.4 = h$

   $\mathbf{35.4 = h}$

9. $p + 80 = 120$

   $p + 80 - 80 = 120 - 80$

   $\mathbf{p = 40}$

10. $r + 12.5 = 12.8$

$r + 12.5 - 12.5 = 12.8 - 12.5$

$r = 0.3$

Part B

You may have written any of the four equations given for problems 11–14.

11. Let x = miles Nina walked before weekend.

$x + 6.5 = 21.7$

$x = 21.7 - 6.5$

$21.7 - x = 6.5$

$6.5 + x = 21.7$

$x = 15.2$ miles

12. Let x = total weight of lamb.

$x - 1.5 = 3.75$

$x - 3.75 = 1.5$

$3.75 + 1.5 = x$

$1.5 + 3.75 = x$

$x = 5.25$ pounds

13. Let x = grams of fat consumed before diet.

$x - 10 = 25$

$x = 25 + 10$

$25 + 10 = x$

$x - 25 = 10$

$x = 35$ grams

14. Let x = number of hours less.

$12.5 - 10.5 = x$

$12.5 - x = 10.5$

$x + 10.5 = 12.5$

$10.5 + x = 12.5$

$x = 2$ hours

Balancing a Checkbook pp. 62–63

Part A

CHECK NUMBER	DATE	DESCRIPTION OF TRANSACTION	AMOUNT OF WITHDRAWAL	FEE (IF ANY)	✓ T	AMOUNT OF DEPOSIT	NEW BALANCE
		RECORD ALL CHARGES OR CREDITS THAT AFFECT YOUR ACCOUNT					$832.40
#121	9/1	Peterson Rental Agency	$320				$512.40
#122	9/5	Giant Groceries	$32.89				$479.51
	9/8	paycheck deposit				$458.75	$938.26
#123	9/10	Townwide Savings Bank	$300				$638.26
#124	9/10	Corner Market	$25				$613.26
	9/17	child support check				$155	$768.26
#125	9/17	Giant	$64.90				$703.36
#126	9/20	Bell Telephone	$22.67				$680.69
#127	9/20	East Electric	$12.73				$667.96
#128	9/20	Continental Cable	$34.95				$633.01

Part B

Answers will vary.

Multiplying Decimals pp. 64–65

Part A

1. 57.75   18.9   .0036   .0045   .05

Part B

2. 44.1   8.75   41   15.375   0.036

3. 4.5   27.72   1.5625   311.5   6.15

Part C

Estimates will vary.

4. $2.25

$15 \times \$.15 = \$2.25$

5. 4.95 grams

$1.65 \times 3 = 4.95$

6. 47.52 gallons

$2.64 \times 18 = 47.52$

7. Yes

$10 \times .07 = .7$

$.7 < 1$

Part D

8. 480   12.25   75   350   620

9. 2,050   1,690   125   355   82,000

Gridding in Decimal Answers pp. 66–67

1. **1.875**

Multiply: $0.125 \times 15 = 1.875$ kilograms

2. **2.25**

Subtract: $10 - 7.75 = 2.25$ hours

3. **4.3**

Add: $0.8 + 1.4 + 2.1 = 4.3$ miles

4.

.5

Multiply: 0.0125 × 40 = 0.5 meter. *Note:* If you multiply using paper and pencil, your product will be written 0.5000. To fit the answer in the grid, drop the zeros to the right of the 5.

Mixed Review pp. 68–69

Part A

1. 6   101   101   99   9   **2.** 3   2   87   88   1

Part B

3. 5.5   82.91   12.3

Part C

4. 15.4   19.25   90.125   **6.** 50.9   92.5275   20.15

5. 116.7   165.6   5   **7.** 255.65   150   174.995

Part D

8. a. 0.67 **b.** 0.8 **c.** 0.13 **d.** 0.9 **e.** 0.7 **f.** 0.75 **g.** 0.83

Part E

9. $.5 + .75 = 1.25 = 1\frac{1}{4}$

$.8 + .25 = 1.05 = 1\frac{1}{20}$

$.4 + .5 = .9 = \frac{9}{10}$

10. $.5 \times .25 = .125 = \frac{1}{8}$

$.9 - .6 = .3 = \frac{3}{10}$

$.3 \times .75 = .225 = \frac{9}{40}$

Part F

11. 245

$p + 250 = 495$

$p + 250 - 250 = 495 - 250$

$p = 245$

70

$x - 26 = 44$

$x - 26 + 26 = 44 + 26$

$x = 70$

$18.00

$\$1.99 + d = \$19.99$

$\$1.99 + d - \$1.99 = \$19.99 - \$1.99$

$d = \$18.00$

12. $10.50

$\$12.50 - \$2.00 = p$

$\$10.50 = p$

24.8

$g - 14.7 = 10.1$

$g - 14.7 + 14.7 = 10.1 + 14.7$

$g = 24.8$

250

$750 + m = 1,000$

$750 + m - 750 = 1,000 - 750$

$m = 250$

Part G

13. 7.7 centimeters

$2.5 + 3.8 + 1.4 = 7.7$

14. $816.76

$\$760.40 - \$43.55 - \$100.09 = \$616.76$

$\$616.76 + \$200 = \$816.76$

15. 502.5 square inches

$12.5 \times 40.2 = 502.5$

16. No, she did not receive the correct change. You know this because:

$\$16.00 - \$3.86 = \$12.14$

She was given $1 too little.

Part H

17. .65

Subtract: 1.5 − 0.85 = 0.65 liter

18. .05

Add: 1.4 + 2.85 = 4.25 centimeters

Subtract: 4.25 − 4.2 = 0.05 centimeter

Part I

		RECORD ALL CHARGES OR CREDITS THAT AFFECT YOUR ACCOUNT					
CHECK NUMBER	DATE	DESCRIPTION OF TRANSACTION	AMOUNT OF WITHDRAWAL	FEE (IF ANY)	✓ T	AMOUNT OF DEPOSIT	NEW BALANCE $629.43
1415	5/10	Super-K Foods	$63.93				$565.50
1416	5/13	Bank of the States (car payment)	$282.88				$282.62
	5/15	deposit (paycheck)				$795.85	$1,078.47
1417	5/15	Bette's Boutique	$82.14				$996.33
1418	5/17	Citizen's Gas	$49				$947.33
	5/20	deposit				$250.00	$1,197.33

Dividing a Decimal by a Whole Number pp. 70–71

Part A

1. 1.125   4.46   1.51   0.19
2. 2.25   0.07   25.5   18.07

Part B

Estimates will vary.

3. **35.03 pounds**

   $26.5 + 50.4 + 25.25 + 30.1 + 42.9 = 175.15$

   $175.15 \div 5 = 35.03$

4. **7.8 hours**

   $4.5 + 8.25 + 8.5 + 10.25 + 7.5 = 39$

   $39 \div 5 = 7.8$

5. **Yes**

   $8.5 \div 4 = 2.125$

   $2.125 < 2.2$

6. **$4.01**

   $\$16.04 \div 4 = \$4.01$

7. Segment A   3.5 feet

   Segment B   3.5 feet

   Segment C   3.5 feet

Part C

8. 1 place to the left
9. 2 places to the left
10. 3 places to the left

Part D

11. 3.45   0.20356   0.015

Dividing by a Decimal pp. 72–73

Part A

1. 200   2   2   0.2
2. 3.7   370   37   0.37
3. 2.1   21.3   21.3   213

Part B

4. 2   20   20   200   2
5. 0.0002   2   0.02   2   0.02

Part C

6. **$2.07**

   $\$7.24 \div 3.5 = \$2.06857 \approx \$2.07$

7. **1.895 seconds**

   $2.25 + 2.05 + 2.5 + 1.175 + 1.5 = 9.475$

   $9.475 \div 5 = 1.895$

8. **10 servings**

   $12 \div 1.2 = 10$

9. **4.56 inches**

   $3.65 + 4.5 + 3.25 = 11.4$

   $11.4 \div 2.5 = 4.56$

10. **3.75 pounds**

    $22.5 \div 6 = 3.75$

11. **7 weeks**

    $\$351.75 \div \$50.25 = 7$

12. **12 napkin rings**

    First subtract the cost of the tablecloths from the total price paid:

    $\$126.35 - \$114.95 = \$11.40$

    $11.40 is the amount spent on napkin rings. Divide $11.40 by $.95 (the cost of each napkin ring):

    $\$11.40 \div \$.95 = 12$

    She bought 12 napkin rings.

Metric Measurement pp. 74–75

Part A

1. 2.5 liters
2. 1,400 grams
3. 9,000 centimeters
4. 8,200 milliliters
5. 0.05 kilograms
6. 0.9 meter

Part B

7. **20 lengths**

   6 meters = 600 centimeters

   $600 \div 30 = 20$

8. **174.5 centimeters**

   2 meters = 200 centimeters

   $200 - 25.5 = 174.5$

Estimating with Friendly Numbers pp. 76–77

Part A

1. 1.4 and 2.8
2. 11 and 33
3. 2.0 and 40
4. 1.8 and 36

Part B

5. **(1) $1.94**

   Use friendly numbers: $4.7 \approx 5$ and $\$9.12 \approx \$10$

   $\$10 \div 5 = \$2$

   The closest answer to $2 is $1.94.

6. (1) 20.35

Use friendly numbers: $519 \approx 500$
and $25.5 \approx 25$

$500 \div 25 = 20$

The closest answer to 20 is 20.35.

7. (2) $10.30

Round off: $\$1.98 \approx \$2$ and $5.2 \approx 5$

$\$2 \times 5 = \$10$

The closest answer to $10 is $10.30.

8. (1) about 20

Use friendly numbers: $2.54 \approx 2.5$ and $51.2 \approx 50$

$50 \div 2.5 = 20$

Making Connections: Estimating with 10s p. 77

1. 81   **3.** 8

2. 750   **4.** 0.125

Order of Operations pp. 78–79

Part A

1. 967	**4.** 20	**7.** 114
2. 86	**5.** 64.8	**8.** 114
3. 200	**6.** 60	**9.** 5

Part B

10. $(3 \times \$5.95) + \$3.85 + (4 \times \$.70)$

11. $\$10 - \$2.25 - (2 \times \$.85)$

Part C

12. (3) $\$4.99 + \$13 + \$2.01$ **14. (1)** $(60 \div .6) \times 2$

13. (3) $(6.8 + 3.5) \div 2$ **15. (2)** $16 \times (3 + .5)$

Calculators and Decimal Answers pp. 80–81

Part A

1. 0.8333   **2.** 6.8181   **3.** 1.3444

Part B

4. $231.67

$\$695 \div 3 = \$231.66666 \approx \$231.67$

5. 1.5

$124 \div 82 = 1.5121951219 \approx 1.5$

6. 2.333

$7 \div 3 = 2.3333333 \approx 2.333$

7. $159.67

$\$958 \div 6 = \$159.6666 \approx \$159.67$

8. Estimates will vary, but should be between $30 and $33.

$\$300 \div 9 = \$33.33333 \approx \$33.33$

Mileage and Miles per Gallon pp. 82–83

Part A

1. 37.9 miles	**4.** 4,790.5 miles
2. 3,156.2 miles	**5.** 688.4 miles
3. 1,070.6 miles	

Part B

6. a. 340 miles

$35,121.1 - 34,781.1 = 340$

b. 27 miles per gallon

$340 \div 12.5 = 27.2 \approx 27$

c. $16.24

$12.5 - \$1.299 = \$16.2375 \approx \$16.24$

Unit 2 Review pp. 84–85

Part A

1. 2.24	110.6	4.05
2. 5	55.875	22.315
3. 4.375	33.3	165.845
4. 4	0.5225	1,004
5. 792	18.05	41.4

Part B

6. (2) $1.24

$\$2.48 \div 2 = \$1.24$

7. (5) C, E, A, B, D

C. 1.250 meters

E. 0.750 meter

A. 0.425 meter

B. 0.420 meter

D. 0.075 meter

8. (4) $21.76

$\$108.79 \div 5 = \$21.758 \approx \$21.76$

9. (4) $(.25 \times 3) + 8.5$

$(.25 \times 3) + 8.5$

track   run

miles   miles

Part C

10. **.425**

Subtract: $2.5 - 2.075 = 0.425$ inches

11.  **37**

Divide: $50 ÷ $1.35 = 37 with a remainder.

Henry can buy 37 enlargements. Ignore the remainder.

Part D

12. **$34.80**

Round $0.076781 to $0.08.
435 × $0.08 = $34.80

13. **$13.05**

Round $0.034198 to $0.03.
435 × $0.03 = $13.05

14. **$52.16**

$4.31 + $34.80 + $13.05 = $52.16

15. **$203.58**

$151.42 + $52.16 = $203.58

Working Together

Shopping lists will vary.

Unit 3

Estimating the Size of Fractions pp. 88–89

Part A

There is more than one correct answer for each. Your fractions should be close to, or equal to, the ones below.

1. $\frac{8}{16}$ $\frac{3}{6}$ $\frac{11}{22}$ $\frac{7}{14}$ $\frac{34}{68}$
2. $\frac{7}{15}$ $\frac{3}{7}$ $\frac{2}{4}$ $\frac{6}{12}$ $\frac{10}{21}$
3. $\frac{5}{10}$ $\frac{4}{8}$ $\frac{7}{14}$ $\frac{6}{13}$ $\frac{1}{2}$

Part B

There is more than one correct answer for each. Your fractions should be close to, or equal to, the ones below.

4. $\frac{5}{6}$ $\frac{20}{21}$ $\frac{17}{18}$ $\frac{7}{8}$ $\frac{34}{35}$
5. $\frac{11}{12}$ $\frac{6}{7}$ $\frac{3}{4}$ $\frac{8}{9}$ $\frac{23}{24}$
6. $\frac{9}{10}$ $\frac{3}{4}$ $\frac{4}{5}$ $\frac{4}{5}$ $\frac{39}{40}$

Part C

7. **(1)** much less than a centimeter
8. **(3)** close to 1 second
9. **(2)** about $\frac{1}{2}$ the members
10. **(3)** close to 1 foot

Adding and Subtracting Like Fractions pp. 90–91

Part A

1. $\frac{3}{5}$ $\frac{2}{11}$ $\frac{1}{3}$ $\frac{1}{4}$
2. $\frac{4}{7}$ 1 $1\frac{1}{2}$ $1\frac{1}{3}$

Part B

3. **(2)** $\frac{1}{2}$ inch

$\frac{1}{8} + \frac{3}{8} = \frac{4}{8} = \frac{1}{2}$

4. **(3)** 1 hour

$\frac{1}{4} + \frac{3}{4} = \frac{4}{4} = 1$

5. **(3)** $\frac{5}{16}$ inch

$\frac{12}{16} - \frac{7}{16} = \frac{5}{16}$

6. **(3)** $\frac{3}{10}$ second

$\frac{7}{10} - \frac{4}{10} = \frac{3}{10}$

7. **(2)** $\frac{10}{21}$

$\frac{20}{21} - \frac{10}{21} = \frac{10}{21}$

8. **(1)** $1\frac{1}{2}$ cups

$\frac{7}{8} + \frac{5}{8} = \frac{12}{8} = 1\frac{4}{8} = 1\frac{1}{2}$

Part C

9. 10:00   10. 3:00

Choosing Necessary Information pp. 92–93

Part A

1. Necessary information: $\frac{7}{8}$ mile, $\frac{3}{8}$ mile

Answer: $\frac{4}{8} = \frac{1}{2}$ **mile**

2. Necessary information: $\frac{7}{8}$ mile, $\frac{1}{2}$ mile

Answer: **more than $\frac{1}{2}$ mile**

3. Necessary information: $\frac{3}{8}$ mile, $\frac{5}{8}$ mile

Answer: $\frac{8}{8} = 1$ **mile**

4. Necessary information: $\frac{5}{8}$ mile, $\frac{3}{8}$ mile

Answer: $\frac{2}{8} = \frac{1}{4}$ **mile**

Part B

5. $\frac{1}{2}$ **hour**

$\frac{1}{4} + \frac{1}{4} = \frac{2}{4} = \frac{1}{2}$

The amount of time shopping is not necessary information.

6. $\frac{1}{2}$ **yard**

$\frac{7}{8} - \frac{3}{8} = \frac{4}{8} = \frac{1}{2}$

The cost of the cloth is not necessary information.

7. $\frac{1}{4}$ **inch**

$\frac{7}{16} - \frac{3}{16} = \frac{4}{16} = \frac{1}{4}$

The width of the rack is not necessary information.

8. **Not enough information is given.**

You are not told how many cups of mixture would make how many cookies.

Making Connections: Adding Measurements p. 93

1. 21 inches $= \frac{21}{12}$ feet *or* $1\frac{3}{4}$ feet
2. 11 inches $= \frac{11}{12}$ foot
3. 18 inches $= \frac{18}{12}$ feet *or* $1\frac{1}{2}$ feet

Writing Equivalent Fractions pp. 94–95

Part A

1. $\frac{9}{12}$ $\frac{8}{10}$ $\frac{3}{21}$ $\frac{28}{32}$ $\frac{20}{30}$

2. $\frac{3}{18}$ $\frac{16}{40}$ $\frac{4}{36}$ $\frac{24}{28}$ $\frac{90}{100}$

3. $\frac{10}{20}$ $\frac{30}{80}$ $\frac{8}{18}$ $\frac{42}{63}$ $\frac{40}{100}$

Part B

4. 4: 4, 8, 12, 16, (20)
   5: 5, 10, 15, (20), 25
   2: 2, 4, (6), 8, 10
   6: (6), 12, 18, 24, 30
   7: 7, 14, (21), 28, 35
   3: 3, 6, 9, 12, 15, 18, (21)

5. 3: 3, 6, 9, 12, (15)
   5: 5, 10, (15), 20, 25
   4: 4, 8, 12, 16, 20, 24, (28)
   7: 7, 14, 21, (28), 35
   6: 6, 12, (18), 24, 30
   9: 9, (18), 27, 36, 45

6. 9: 9, 18, 27, 36, (45)
   5: 5, 10, 15, 20, 25, 30, 35, 40, (45)
   10: 10, (20), 30, 40, 50
   4: 4, 8, 12, 16, (20)
   3: 3, 6, 9, (12), 15
   4: 4, 8, (12), 16, 20

Part C

7. $\frac{5}{10}$ and $\frac{6}{10}$ $\frac{9}{12}$ and $\frac{1}{12}$ $\frac{14}{63}$ and $\frac{27}{63}$ $\frac{3}{24}$ and $\frac{8}{24}$

8. $\frac{5}{20}$ and $\frac{8}{20}$ $\frac{9}{30}$ and $\frac{25}{30}$ $\frac{3}{30}$ and $\frac{10}{30}$ $\frac{8}{12}$ and $\frac{9}{12}$

9. $\frac{12}{15}$ and $\frac{5}{15}$ $\frac{35}{40}$ and $\frac{8}{40}$ $\frac{8}{9}$ and $\frac{3}{9}$ $\frac{20}{24}$ and $\frac{3}{24}$

Adding Unlike Fractions pp. 96–97

Part A

1. $1\frac{1}{6}$ $1\frac{1}{15}$ $\frac{7}{8}$ $1\frac{23}{35}$

2. $\frac{13}{40}$ $\frac{24}{35}$ $1\frac{1}{9}$ $\frac{5}{14}$

3. $1\frac{7}{40}$ $\frac{7}{12}$ $\frac{13}{14}$ $\frac{7}{8}$

4. $\frac{23}{30}$ $1\frac{13}{20}$ $\frac{11}{24}$ $1\frac{7}{10}$

5. $\frac{3}{4}$ $1\frac{1}{2}$ $\frac{2}{3}$ $\frac{8}{9}$

6. $1\frac{1}{10}$ $\frac{7}{12}$ $1\frac{1}{8}$ $\frac{8}{9}$

Part B

7. **$1\frac{1}{4}$ hours**

$$\frac{3}{4} + \frac{1}{2} = \frac{3}{4} + \frac{2}{4} = \frac{5}{4} = 1\frac{1}{4}$$

8. **$1\frac{1}{8}$ inches**

$$\frac{3}{8} + \frac{3}{4} = \frac{3}{8} + \frac{6}{8} = \frac{9}{8} = 1\frac{1}{8}$$

9. **$1\frac{3}{20}$ pounds**

$$\frac{9}{10} + \frac{1}{4} = \frac{18}{20} + \frac{5}{20} = \frac{23}{20} = 1\frac{3}{20}$$

10. **$1\frac{13}{24}$ inches**

$$\frac{5}{8} + \frac{1}{4} + \frac{2}{3} = \frac{15}{24} + \frac{6}{24} + \frac{16}{24} = \frac{37}{24} = 1\frac{13}{24}$$

11. **$1\frac{5}{8}$ pounds**

$$\frac{7}{8} + \frac{3}{4} = \frac{7}{8} + \frac{6}{8} = \frac{13}{8} = 1\frac{5}{8}$$

Part C

Wording will vary, but paragraphs should contain the following information:

12. To solve this problem, you need to add $\frac{3}{8}$ fluid ounce (the contents of Test Tube A) to $\frac{1}{4}$ fluid ounce (the contents of Test Tube B). To add these fractions, first multiply $\frac{1}{4}$ by $\frac{2}{2}$ to get a common denominator of 8 for the two fractions. Finally, add the fractions to find the answer of $\frac{5}{8}$ fluid ounces.

$$\frac{3}{8} + \frac{1}{4} = \frac{3}{8} + \frac{2}{8} = \frac{5}{8}$$

13. To find the new amount of liquid in Beaker B, add $\frac{7}{8}$ fluid ounce (the amount in Flask A) to $\frac{3}{4}$ fluid ounce (the amount in originally in Beaker B). Multiply $\frac{3}{4}$ by $\frac{2}{2}$ to get a common denominator of 8 for the two fractions. Add $\frac{7}{8}$ plus $\frac{6}{8}$ to find the answer of $\frac{13}{8}$. Finally, divide 13 by 8 to change the improper fraction to a mixed number: $1\frac{5}{8}$ fluid ounces.

$$\frac{7}{8} + \frac{3}{4} = \frac{7}{8} + \frac{6}{8} = \frac{13}{8} = 1\frac{5}{8}$$

14. You must add the four liquid amounts, $\frac{7}{8}$, $\frac{3}{8}$, $\frac{1}{4}$, and $\frac{3}{4}$. First, to find a common denominator for the four fractions, multiply $\frac{1}{4}$ and $\frac{3}{4}$ by $\frac{2}{2}$. Now add $\frac{7}{8}$, $\frac{3}{8}$, $\frac{2}{8}$, and $\frac{6}{8}$ to find an answer of $\frac{18}{8}$. Divide 18 by 8 to change the improper fraction to a mixed number: $2\frac{2}{8}$ or $2\frac{1}{4}$ fluid ounces.

$$\frac{7}{8} + \frac{3}{8} + \frac{1}{4} + \frac{3}{4} = \frac{7}{8} + \frac{3}{8} + \frac{2}{8} + \frac{6}{8} = \frac{18}{8} = 2\frac{2}{8} = 2\frac{1}{4}$$

Subtracting Unlike Fractions pp. 98–99

Part A

1. $\frac{19}{40}$ $\frac{5}{48}$ $\frac{1}{6}$ $\frac{1}{6}$

2. $\frac{13}{35}$ $\frac{11}{40}$ $\frac{1}{2}$ $\frac{13}{16}$

3. $\frac{13}{20}$ $\frac{1}{4}$ $\frac{13}{30}$ $\frac{5}{9}$

4. $\frac{9}{16}$ $\frac{5}{8}$ $\frac{7}{15}$ $\frac{1}{12}$

5. $\frac{7}{10}$ $\frac{5}{36}$ $\frac{1}{16}$ $\frac{3}{8}$

6. $\frac{1}{2}$ $\frac{5}{14}$ $\frac{13}{16}$ $\frac{7}{45}$

Part B

7. **$\frac{1}{2}$ of the group**

Write the whole group as 1 or $\frac{10}{10}$.

$$\frac{10}{10} - \frac{2}{5} - \frac{1}{10} = \frac{10}{10} - \frac{4}{10} - \frac{1}{10} = \frac{5}{10} = \frac{1}{2}$$

8. **$\frac{11}{16}$ inch**

$$\frac{7}{8} - \frac{3}{16} = \frac{14}{16} - \frac{3}{16} = \frac{11}{16}$$

9. **$\frac{3}{8}$ inch**

$$\frac{7}{8} - \frac{1}{2} = \frac{7}{8} - \frac{4}{8} = \frac{3}{8}$$

10. **$\frac{11}{16}$ mile**

$$\frac{15}{16} - \frac{1}{4} = \frac{15}{16} - \frac{4}{16} = \frac{11}{16}$$

Making Connections: Number Sense with Fractions p. 99

Estimates will vary.

1. a little more than $\frac{1}{2}$
2. about $1\frac{1}{2}$
3. about $\frac{1}{2}$
4. about 2
5. about $1\frac{1}{2}$
6. about $\frac{1}{2}$
7. about 1
8. a little more than 1

Adding Mixed Numbers pp. 100–101

Part A

1. $4\frac{5}{6}$ $20\frac{45}{56}$ $9\frac{1}{2}$ $37\frac{9}{14}$ $6\frac{11}{12}$
2. $205\frac{1}{20}$ $7\frac{7}{24}$ $13\frac{5}{12}$

Part B

3. **$24\frac{7}{8}$ inches**

   $19\frac{3}{8} + 5\frac{1}{2} = 24\frac{7}{8}$

4. **$15\frac{1}{4}$ feet**

   $4\frac{1}{2} + 10\frac{3}{4} = 15\frac{1}{4}$

5. **$2\frac{1}{12}$ cups**

   $\frac{1}{3} + 1\frac{3}{4} = 2\frac{1}{12}$

6. **$1\frac{3}{4}$ inches**

   $\frac{1}{4} + \frac{1}{2} + \frac{1}{8} + \frac{3}{4} + \frac{1}{8} = 1\frac{3}{4}$

7. Estimates will vary, but should be between 3 and 4 inches.

   $3\frac{1}{8}$ inches

   $\frac{1}{4} + \frac{1}{2} + \frac{1}{8} + \frac{3}{4} + \frac{1}{8} + 1\frac{1}{8} + \frac{1}{4} = 3\frac{1}{8}$

Part C

Answers will vary.

Subtracting Mixed Numbers pp. 102–103

Part A

1. $1\frac{2}{3}$ $7\frac{4}{7}$ $\frac{1}{2}$

Part B

2. $\frac{4}{5}$ $6\frac{5}{8}$ $1\frac{1}{3}$ $2\frac{1}{4}$
3. $\frac{3}{4}$ $\frac{1}{4}$ 12 1
4. $1\frac{3}{4}$ $1\frac{1}{14}$ $5\frac{1}{2}$ $2\frac{7}{8}$

Making Connections: Estimating with Mixed Numbers p. 103

Estimates will vary. Answers should be similar to the ones below.

1. **78**
   $57\frac{1}{8} \approx 57$
   $20\frac{4}{5} \approx 21$
   $57 + 21 = 78$

   10
   $12\frac{1}{2} = 12\frac{1}{2}$
   $2\frac{1}{3} \approx 2\frac{1}{2}$
   $12\frac{1}{2} - 2\frac{1}{2} = 10$

   8
   $3\frac{5}{12} \approx 3$
   $4\frac{7}{8} \approx 5$
   $3 + 5 = 8$

2. **$11\frac{1}{2}$**
   $17\frac{5}{8} \approx 17\frac{1}{2}$
   $5\frac{5}{6} \approx 6$
   $17\frac{1}{2} - 6 = 11\frac{1}{2}$

   8
   $4\frac{3}{4} \approx 5$
   $3\frac{4}{9} \approx 3$
   $5 + 3 = 8$

   9
   $9\frac{9}{10} \approx 10$
   $1\frac{1}{3} \approx 1$
   $10 - 1 = 9$

Working with Distances pp. 104–105

Part A

1. **home to Mary's Market to school to library**

   $3\frac{1}{2} + 1\frac{3}{8} = 4\frac{7}{8}$ (home to train to library)

   $1\frac{3}{4} + 1\frac{1}{8} + 1\frac{1}{2} = 4\frac{3}{8}$ (home to Mary's Market to school to library)

   $4\frac{3}{8} < 4\frac{7}{8}$

2. **$3\frac{1}{8}$ miles**

   $2\frac{1}{2} + \frac{5}{8} = 3\frac{1}{8}$

3. **$\frac{7}{8}$ mile**

   $2\frac{5}{8} - 1\frac{3}{4} = \frac{7}{8}$

4. **$1\frac{3}{4}$ miles**

   $\frac{5}{8} + 1\frac{1}{8} = 1\frac{3}{4}$

Part B

Answers will vary.

Mixed Review pp. 106–107

Part A

1. close to 1
2. less than $\frac{1}{2}$
3. close to $\frac{1}{2}$
4. greater than 1

Part B

5. $\frac{1}{2}$ 1 $\frac{7}{12}$ $\frac{3}{5}$
6. $1\frac{2}{5}$ $\frac{1}{2}$ $\frac{7}{8}$ $\frac{3}{7}$

Part C

7. $1\frac{1}{2}$ $1\frac{11}{12}$ $\frac{2}{3}$
8. $2\frac{1}{3}$ $\frac{5}{8}$
9. $2\frac{1}{3}$ 2

Part D

10. $\frac{8}{12}$ $\frac{15}{21}$ $\frac{6}{8}$ $\frac{28}{32}$
11. $\frac{10}{14}$ $\frac{90}{100}$ $\frac{18}{30}$ $\frac{10}{45}$

Part E

12. $1\frac{1}{2}$ $1\frac{1}{2}$ $1\frac{1}{8}$ $\frac{7}{8}$
13. $\frac{11}{21}$ $\frac{1}{2}$ $\frac{2}{15}$ $\frac{1}{10}$
14. $\frac{13}{40}$ $\frac{11}{12}$ $\frac{7}{12}$ $1\frac{11}{24}$

Part F

15. $15\frac{5}{6}$ $15\frac{27}{40}$ $7\frac{17}{20}$
16. $\frac{23}{28}$ $4\frac{1}{2}$ $1\frac{1}{10}$

Part G

17.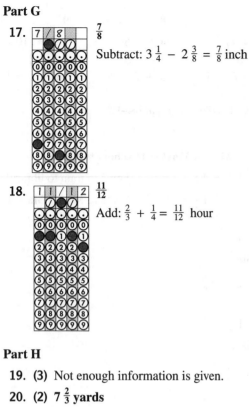
$\frac{7}{8}$

Subtract: $3\frac{1}{4} - 2\frac{3}{8} = \frac{7}{8}$ inch

18. $\frac{11}{12}$

Add: $\frac{2}{3} + \frac{1}{4} = \frac{11}{12}$ hour

Part H

19. **(3)** Not enough information is given.
20. **(2) $7\frac{2}{3}$ yards**

$5\frac{1}{3} + 2\frac{1}{3} = 7\frac{2}{3}$

21. **(2) about 53**
22. **(1) $3\frac{2}{5}$**

$9\frac{9}{10} - 6\frac{1}{2} = 3\frac{2}{5}$

Multiplying Whole Numbers and Fractions
pp. 108–109

Part A

1. $16 \div 4 = 4$ 3. $20 \div 5 = 4$
2. $64 \div 8 = 8$ 4. $96 \div 6 = 16$

Part B

5. $16 \div 8 = 2, 2 \times 7 = 14$
6. $15 \div 5 = 3, 3 \times 3 = 9$
7. $27 \div 9 = 3, 3 \times 7 = 21$
8. $21 \div 3 = 7, 7 \times 2 = 14$

Part C

9. **855 labels**

$\frac{9}{10} \times 950, 950 \div 10 = 95, 95 \times 9 = 855$

10. **9 inches**

$\frac{3}{8} \times 24, 24 \div 8 = 3, 3 \times 3 = 9$

11. **55 miles**

$220 \times \frac{1}{4}$ (part remaining)
$220 \div 4 = 55$

12. **45 members**

$\frac{3}{5} \times 75, 75 \div 5 = 15, 15 \times 3 = 45$

13. **16 people**

$\frac{2}{3} \times 24, 24 \div 3 = 8, 8 \times 2 = 16$

14. **44 pages**

Strategy 1
$\frac{1}{3} \times 66 = 22$ pages typed
$66 - 22 = 44$ pages to be typed

Strategy 2

$\begin{array}{r} 22 \\ 3\overline{)66} \end{array}$ pages typed

$66 - 22 = 44$ pages to be typed

Multiplying Fractions pp. 110–111

Part A

1. $\frac{3}{8}$ $\frac{3}{40}$ $\frac{6}{35}$ $\frac{3}{40}$
2. $\frac{5}{12}$ $\frac{21}{32}$ $\frac{3}{32}$ $\frac{27}{40}$
3. $\frac{2}{5}$ $\frac{3}{10}$ $\frac{2}{15}$ $\frac{1}{24}$
4. $\frac{7}{12}$ $\frac{1}{21}$ $\frac{4}{45}$ $\frac{9}{13}$

Part B

5. $\frac{3}{4}$ $\frac{1}{4}$ $\frac{4}{11}$ $\frac{5}{8}$
6. $\frac{3}{25}$ $\frac{1}{6}$ $\frac{2}{5}$ $\frac{1}{3}$
7. $\frac{5}{14}$ $\frac{2}{9}$ $\frac{6}{25}$ $\frac{27}{50}$

Part C

8. **$\frac{3}{8}$ acre**   9. **$\frac{3}{5}$ yard**   10. **$\frac{3}{8}$ pie**

$\frac{1}{2} \times \frac{3}{4} = \frac{3}{8}$ $\frac{2}{3} \times \frac{9}{10} = \frac{3}{5}$ $\frac{3}{4} \times \frac{1}{2} = \frac{3}{8}$

Multiplying Whole Numbers and Mixed Numbers
pp. 112–113

Part A

1. $3\frac{1}{3}$ $2\frac{1}{4}$ $3\frac{1}{2}$ $\frac{1}{2}$
2. 3 2 $1\frac{1}{3}$ $\frac{2}{3}$
3. 1 $\frac{12}{35}$ 9 $3\frac{1}{3}$

Part B

4. $\frac{32}{3} = 10\frac{2}{3}$ $\frac{15}{8} = 1\frac{7}{8}$ $\frac{70}{3} = 23\frac{1}{3}$ $\frac{80}{9} = 8\frac{8}{9}$
5. $\frac{17}{12} = 1\frac{5}{12}$ $\frac{13}{8} = 1\frac{5}{8}$ $\frac{9}{4} = 2\frac{1}{4}$ $\frac{44}{1} = 44$
6. $\frac{75}{4} = 18\frac{3}{4}$ $\frac{33}{50}$ $\frac{33}{16} = 2\frac{1}{16}$ $\frac{27}{8} = 3\frac{3}{8}$

Part C

7. **12 miles**

$\frac{3}{4} \times 16 = 12$

8. **$\frac{3}{4}$ hour**

$\frac{1}{2} \times 1\frac{1}{2} = \frac{1}{2} \times \frac{3}{2} = \frac{3}{4}$

9. **$3\frac{3}{8}$ feet**

$\frac{3}{4} \times 4\frac{1}{2} = \frac{3}{4} \times \frac{9}{2} =$
$\frac{27}{8} = 3\frac{3}{8}$

10. **25 inches**

$\frac{5}{8} \times 40 = 25$

Drawing a Picture pp. 114–115

Pictures will vary.

1. **$11\frac{3}{8}$ miles**

   $22\frac{3}{4} \times \frac{1}{2} = \frac{91}{4} \times \frac{1}{2} = \frac{91}{8} = 11\frac{3}{8}$

2. **$3.02**

   $27.18 \div 9 = \$3.02$

3. **42 meters**

   $\frac{3}{4} \times 56 = 42$

Dividing Fractions pp. 116–117

Part A

1. a. $\frac{4}{1}$ $\frac{1}{10}$ $\frac{3}{2}$ $\frac{7}{4}$ b. $\frac{4}{3}$ $\frac{10}{9}$ $\frac{100}{7}$ $\frac{1}{11}$ $\frac{1}{15}$

Part B

2. $1\frac{1}{3}$ $\frac{1}{8}$ $6\frac{2}{5}$ $1\frac{1}{2}$
3. $2\frac{1}{7}$ $\frac{1}{2}$ 6 $\frac{3}{7}$
4. 15 24 $\frac{4}{5}$ $\frac{1}{3}$

Making Connections: Estimating with Fractions p. 117

Estimates will vary. Here are the *exact* answers. Are your estimates close?

1. $\frac{1}{20}$ 3. $\frac{3}{5}$
2. $\frac{1}{14}$ 4. $\frac{5}{42}$

Dividing with Mixed Numbers pp. 118–119

Part A

1. $1\frac{1}{2}$ $\frac{13}{16}$ $4\frac{1}{5}$ $3\frac{11}{15}$
2. $9\frac{3}{8}$ $\frac{1}{16}$ $2\frac{3}{4}$ 6
3. $\frac{1}{9}$ $\frac{5}{32}$ $2\frac{1}{10}$ $4\frac{4}{5}$
4. $\frac{1}{18}$ $1\frac{1}{6}$ 4 2
5. 12 $\frac{1}{16}$ 1 $\frac{1}{20}$

Part B

6. **6 pieces**   9. **4 stops**

   $5\frac{1}{4} \div \frac{7}{8} = 6$ $5\frac{1}{3} \div 1\frac{1}{3} = 4$

7. **80 boards**   10. **10 vests**

   $120 \div 1\frac{1}{2} = 80$ $11\frac{1}{4} \div 1\frac{1}{8} = 10$

8. **7 segments**   11. **2 batches**

   $10\frac{1}{2} \div 1\frac{1}{2} = 7$ $4\frac{1}{2} \div 2\frac{1}{4} = 2$

Making Connections: Estimating with Mixed Numbers p. 119

Estimates will vary, but should be close to those below.

1. Method 1: $4 \times 1 = 4$

   Method 2: $4 \times 1\frac{1}{4} = (4 \times 1) + (4 \times \frac{1}{4})$
   $= 4 + 1 = 5$

---

2. Method 1: $10 \times 2 = 20$

   Method 2: $10 \times 2\frac{1}{4} = (10 \times 2) + (10 \times \frac{1}{4})$
   $= 20 + 2\frac{1}{2} = 22\frac{1}{2}$

3. Method 1: $15 \times 5 = 75$

   Method 2: $15 \times 5\frac{1}{4} = (15 \times 5) + (15 \times \frac{1}{4})$
   $= 75 + 3\frac{3}{4}$
   $= 78\frac{3}{4}$

4. Method 1: $6 \times 4 = 24$

   Method 2: $6 \times 3\frac{1}{2} = (6 \times 3) + (6 \times \frac{1}{2})$
   $= 18 + 3 = 21$

5. Method 1: $7 \times 2 = 14$

   Method 2: $7 \times 1\frac{1}{2} = (7 \times 1) + (7 \times \frac{1}{2})$
   $= 7 + 3\frac{1}{2} = 10\frac{1}{2}$

6. Method 1: $3 \times 4 = 12$

   Method 2: $2\frac{3}{4} \times 4 = (2 \times 4) + (\frac{3}{4} \times 4)$
   $= 8 + 3 = 11$

Multiply or Divide? pp. 120–121

1. **(2) $880**

   $\frac{2}{5} \times \frac{\$2,200}{1} = \$880$

2. **(1) 375**

   $\frac{1}{2} \times \frac{750}{1} = 375$

3. **(3) 23**

   $11\frac{1}{2} \div \frac{1}{2} = \frac{23}{2} \times \frac{2}{1} = 23$

4. **(1) $\frac{1}{4}$ cup**

   $\frac{1}{3} \times \frac{3}{4} = \frac{1}{4}$

5. **(3) 5**

   $3\frac{3}{4} \div \frac{3}{4} = \frac{15}{4} \times \frac{4}{3} = 5$

6.
South Grange	Jack's House	Valley's Edge
81 miles	81 miles	

   162 miles

Multiplication and Division Equations pp. 122–123

Part A

1. (3) $p \div 3 = 3\frac{1}{2}$ 3. (3) $\$150 \div 60 = c$
2. (2) $\frac{1}{4} \times 185,000 = r$ 4. (4) $250 \div 4\frac{1}{2} = m$

Part B

You may have written any of the equations given for each problem.

5. Let x = daughter's weight

   $3\frac{1}{2} \times x = 175$
   $x \times 3\frac{1}{2} = 175$
   $175 \times x = 3\frac{1}{2}$
   $175 \times 3\frac{1}{2} = x$

6. Let x = height of 1 drum

$$3 \times x = 12\frac{3}{4}$$
$$x \times 3 = 12\frac{3}{4}$$
$$12\frac{3}{4} \div 3 = x$$
$$12\frac{3}{4} \div x = 3$$

7. Let x = original price of dress

$$\frac{1}{2} \times x = \$43.80$$
$$x \times \frac{1}{2} = \$43.80$$
$$x \div 2 = \$43.80$$
$$\$43.80 \times 2 = x$$
$$2 \times \$43.80 = x$$

8. Let x = number of film clips

$$x \times 3\frac{1}{2} = 21$$
$$3\frac{1}{2} \times x = 21$$
$$21 \div 3\frac{1}{2} = x$$
$$21 \div x = 3\frac{1}{2}$$

Solving Multiplication and Division Equations
pp. 124–125

Part A

1. $y \times \frac{1}{2} = 4$

   $y \times \frac{1}{2} \div \frac{1}{2} = 4 \div \frac{1}{2}$

   $y = 8$

2. $\frac{9}{10} \times t = 90$

   $\frac{9}{10} \times t \div \frac{9}{10} = 90 \div \frac{9}{10}$

   $t = 100$

3. $p \div \frac{3}{4} = 20$

   $p \div \frac{3}{4} \times \frac{3}{4} = 20 \times \frac{3}{4}$

   $p = 15$

4. $q \div 5 = \frac{8}{15}$

   $q \div 5 \times 5 = \frac{8}{15} \times 5$

   $q = \frac{8}{3} = 2\frac{2}{3}$

5. $3\frac{1}{2} \div \frac{1}{2} = b$

   $7 = b$

6. $y \times 12 = 6$

   $y \times 12 \div 12 = 6 \div 12$

   $y = \frac{1}{2}$

7. $5 \times t = 1,100$

   $5 \times t \div 5 = 1,100 \div 5$

   $t = 220$

8. $p \div \frac{2}{3} = 30$

   $p \div \frac{2}{3} \times \frac{2}{3} = 30 \times \frac{2}{3}$

   $p = 20$

9. $q \div \frac{1}{2} = \frac{1}{4}$

   $q \div \frac{1}{2} \times \frac{1}{2} = \frac{1}{4} \times \frac{1}{2}$

   $q = \frac{1}{8}$

10. $5 \div \frac{1}{2} = b$

    $10 = b$

Part B

You may have written any of the equations given for each problem.

11. Let s = number of children

$$\$1.03 \times s = \$4.12$$
$$s \times \$1.03 = \$4.12$$
$$\$4.12 \div s = \$1.03$$
$$\$4.12 \div \$1.03 = s$$
$$s = 4$$

12. Let s = total miles of trip

$$s \div 4 = 40$$
$$s \div 40 = 4$$
$$40 \times 4 = s$$
$$4 \times 40 = s$$
$$s = 160$$

13. Let s = son's age

$$s \times 3 = 30$$
$$3 \times s = 30$$
$$30 \div 3 = s$$
$$30 \div s = 3$$
$$s = 10$$

14. Let s = total number of women in group

$$\frac{1}{3} \times s = 13$$
$$s \times \frac{1}{3} = 13$$
$$13 \times 3 = s$$
$$s \div 13 = 3$$
$$s \div 3 = 13$$
$$s = 39$$

Fractions and Your Calculator pp. 126–127

Part A

1. 15.75   1.025   18.75

2. 6.2   .44

Part B

3. **8.05 pounds**

   $2.75 + 3.8 + 1.5 = 8.05$

4. **1,133.33 square feet**

   $\frac{1}{3} = 0.3333333$

   $0.3333333 \times 3,400 = 1,133.33$

5. **6.45 inches**

   $2.6 + 2.6 + .625 + .625 = 6.45$

6. **5 rings**

   $6 \div 1.125 = 5.33$

7. **12.25 square centimeters**

   $3.5 \times 3.5 = 12.25$

8. **5 times**

   $30 \div 5.33 = 5.6$

9. Discussions will vary. Wanda will earn $68.85 in overtime pay.

   $46.75 - 40 = 6.75$ hours

   $\$4.70 + \$5.50 = \$10.20$

   $6.75 \times \$10.20 = \$68.85$

Fractions and Money pp. 128–129

Part A

1. $2.325 rounds up to **$2.33**
2. $2.75
3. $15
4. $3.89375 rounds to **$3.89**
5. $1.05
6. $.05
7. $.42
8. $7.50

Part B

Thompson: 25.75 × $5.91 = $152.18

Alvarez: 30.5 × $9.45 = $288.23

Rico: 38.25 × $5.50 = $210.38

Kim: 39.5 × $6.75 = $266.63

Delgado: 35.75 × $5.25 = $187.69

Total Wages: $1,105.11

Part C

Mangoes: $.75 × $1.39 = $1.04

Papaya: .875 × $1.89 = $1.65

Breadfruit: 1.5 × $1.99 = $2.99

Jackfruit: .5 × $2.59 = $1.30

Kiwi: .25 × $2.19 = $.55

Kumquat: 1.333 × $2.29 = $3.05

Total Amount Spent: $10.58

Gridding in Fraction Answers pp. 130–131

1.  $\frac{11}{4}$

   Subtract: $12\frac{1}{2} - 9\frac{3}{4} = 2\frac{3}{4}$ miles

   Change to an improper fraction: $2\frac{3}{4} = \frac{11}{4}$

2.  $\frac{35}{8}$

   Divide: $17\frac{1}{2} \div 4 = 4\frac{3}{8}$ feet

   Change to an improper fraction: $4\frac{3}{8} = \frac{35}{8}$

3. $\frac{16}{3}$

   Multiply: $1\frac{1}{3} \times 4 = 5\frac{1}{3}$ cups

   Change to an improper fraction: $5\frac{1}{3} = \frac{16}{3}$

4. **36**

   Multiply: $96 \times \frac{3}{8} = 36$ employees

Unit 3 Review pp. 132–133

Part A

1. 1 $1\frac{1}{2}$ $1\frac{5}{8}$ $\frac{7}{20}$
2. $\frac{1}{2}$ $\frac{1}{2}$ $\frac{1}{12}$ $\frac{8}{21}$
3. $\frac{1}{6}$ $\frac{3}{10}$ $\frac{1}{80}$ $\frac{3}{5}$
4. 2   6 $1\frac{1}{2}$ $\frac{1}{2}$

Part B

5. 8 $3\frac{7}{8}$ $8\frac{1}{10}$ $4\frac{1}{3}$
6. $5\frac{7}{10}$ $\frac{2}{3}$ $2\frac{7}{8}$ $5\frac{13}{20}$
7. $\frac{5}{6}$ $5\frac{5}{6}$ $12\frac{3}{8}$ $3\frac{3}{10}$
8. 15 $\frac{3}{4}$ $1\frac{7}{10}$ $4\frac{2}{15}$

Part C

9. **(3) 4**

   $6 \div 1\frac{1}{2} = 6 \times \frac{2}{3} = 4$

10. **(1) 5**

    $4\frac{1}{2} + 3\frac{3}{4} + 6\frac{3}{4} = 15$ miles

    $15 \div 3 = 5$

11. **(2) 7**

    $8 \times \frac{7}{8} = 7$

12. **(3) Not enough information is given.**

    You do not know the length of the pieces that were cut off.

Part D

13. **5 inches**

    $2 + 1\frac{1}{2} + 1\frac{1}{2} = 5$

14. $\frac{5}{8}$ **inch**

    $1\frac{7}{8} \div 3 = \frac{5}{8}$

15. $\frac{3}{4}$ **inch**

    $2\frac{1}{4} \div 3 = \frac{3}{4}$

16. $\frac{1}{4}$ **inch**

    $2\frac{1}{4} - 2 = \frac{1}{4}$

217

Part E

17. 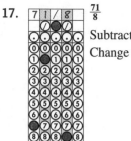 $\frac{71}{8}$

Subtract: $11\frac{1}{4} - 2\frac{3}{8} = 8\frac{7}{8}$ feet

Change to an improper fraction: $8\frac{7}{8} = \frac{71}{8}$

18. **32**

Divide: $24 \div \frac{3}{4} = 32$ sheets.

Working Together

Largest sum: $\frac{3}{4} + \frac{7}{8} = 1\frac{5}{8}$

Smallest sum: $\frac{1}{2} + \frac{2}{3} = 1\frac{1}{6}$

Largest difference: $\frac{7}{8} - \frac{1}{2} = \frac{3}{8}$

Smallest difference: $\frac{3}{4} - \frac{2}{3} = \frac{1}{12}$

New questions will vary.

Unit 4

Fractions and Ratios pp. 136–137

Part A

You may have used any of the three forms below.

1. 2:3 $\frac{2}{3}$ 2 to 3
2. 3:5 $\frac{3}{5}$ 3 to 5
3. 5:2 $\frac{5}{2}$ 5 to 2
4. 4:3 $\frac{4}{3}$ 4 to 3
5. 2:3 $\frac{2}{3}$ 2 to 3
6. 3:2 $\frac{3}{2}$ 3 to 2

Part B

Answers will vary. Here are some sample answers:

7. 1 shaded triangle: 4 dollar signs
8. 4 unshaded triangles: 1 shaded triangle
9. 4 dollar signs: 5 flowers
10. 1 unshaded circle: 5 shaded circles
11. 1 shaded triangle: 5 flowers
12. 4 unshaded triangles: 4 dollar signs

Making Connections: Simplifying Ratios p. 137

Answers will vary. This answer is based on the samples given above.

12. $\frac{4}{4}$ simplifies to 1:1

Writing a Ratio pp. 138–139

Part A

You may have used different forms.

1. $\frac{14}{4} = \frac{7}{2}$ 3. $\frac{18}{14} = \frac{9}{7}$ 5. $\frac{6}{9} = \frac{2}{3}$
2. $\frac{4}{18} = \frac{2}{9}$ 4. $\frac{9}{12} = \frac{3}{4}$ 6. $\frac{6}{12} = \frac{1}{2}$

Part B

You may have used different forms.

7. $\frac{35}{5} = \frac{7}{1}$ 9. $\frac{35}{92}$
8. $\frac{5}{20} = \frac{1}{4}$ 10. Answers will vary.

Ratios and Patterns pp. 140–141

Part A

1.

Pounds	1	2	3	4	5
Pieces	16	32	48	64	80

2.

$ Spent	$100	$200	$300	$400	$500
$ Donated	$4	$8	$12	$16	$20

3.

Dollars	1	2	3	4	5
Dimes	10	20	30	40	50
Nickels	20	40	60	80	100

4.

# Hours	1	2	3	4	5
Total Take-home Pay	$27.75	$55.50	$83.25	$111.00	$138.75
Mr. Chandler	$13.50	$27.00	$40.50	$54.00	$67.50
Mrs. Chandler	$14.25	$28.50	$42.75	$57.00	$71.25

Part B

Answers will vary. Here are some sample answers.

5. Chart 1. As the pounds increase by 1, the pieces increase by 16.
6. Chart 2. As the dollars spent increase by 100, the dollars donated increase by 4.
7. Chart 3. As dollars increase by 1, dimes increase by 10 and nickels increase by 20.
8. Chart 4. As hours increase by 1, total take-home pay increases by $27.75.

Unit Rates pp. 142–143

Part A

1. 2 times per hour   **3.** 3 walls per gallon

2. 70 times per minute   **4.** \$13.50 per ticket

                           5. 80 mufflers per day

Part B

6. $\frac{220 \text{ miles}}{4 \text{ hours}} \div \frac{4}{4} = \frac{55}{1}$ or **55 miles per hour**

7. $\frac{12 \text{ cups}}{3 \text{ quarts}} \div \frac{3}{3} = \frac{4}{1}$ or **4 cups per quart**

8. $\frac{80 \text{ miles}}{2.5 \text{ hours}} \div \frac{2.5}{2.5} = \frac{32}{1}$ or **32 miles per hour**

9. $\frac{54 \text{ ounces}}{3 \text{ boxes}} \div \frac{3}{3} = \frac{18}{1}$ or **18 ounces per box**

Part C

10. **\$11.96 for 4 pounds of ground sirloin**

$\frac{\$2.99}{1 \text{ pound}} = \frac{?}{4 \text{ pounds}}$

$\$2.99 \times 4 = \$11.96$

11. **\$.70 per pound of potatoes**

$\frac{\$2.10}{3 \text{ pounds}} = \frac{?}{1 \text{ pound}}$

$\$2.10 \div 3 = \$.70$

12. **\$3.99 per pound**

$\frac{\$7.98}{2} \div \frac{2}{2} = \frac{\$3.99}{1}$

13. a. **\$5.76**

    $\$.59 \times 3 = \$1.77$ for 3 pounds of onions

    $\$1.77 + 3.99 = \$5.76$

    b. **\$4.24**

        $\$10 - \$5.76 = \$4.24$

Understanding Proportion pp. 144–145

Part A

1. $24 = 24$; yes $2 \neq 72$; no $45 \neq 120$; no

    $36 = 36$; yes

2. $8 \neq 20$; no $60 = 60$; yes $90 \neq 84$; no

    $48 = 48$; yes

3. $42 = 42$; yes $200 = 200$; yes $21 \neq 98$; no

    $112 = 112$; yes

Part B

4. a. $1 \times 40 = 5 \times r$

    $40 = 5 \times r$

    $40 \div 5 = r$

    $8 = r$

    b. $7 \times 40 = 8 \times a$

        $280 = 8 \times a$

        $280 \div 8 = a$

        $35 = a$

c. $4 \times 15 = 12 \times q$

    $60 = 12 \times q$

    $60 \div 12 = q$

    $5 = q$

d. $3 \times 12 = 18 \times x$

    $36 = 18 \times x$

    $36 \div 18 = x$

    $2 = x$

5. a. $6 \times 30 = 36 \times w$

    $180 = 36 \times w$

    $180 \div 36 = w$

    $5 = w$

    b. $5 \times 27 = 9 \times s$

        $135 = 9 \times s$

        $135 \div 9 = s$

        $15 = s$

    c. $8 \times 12 = 16 \times d$

        $96 = 16 \times d$

        $96 \div 16 = d$

        $6 = d$

    d. $9 \times 8 = 2 \times x$

        $72 = 2 \times x$

        $72 \div 2 = x$

        $36 = x$

6. a. $2 \times 20 = 5 \times r$

    $40 = 5 \times r$

    $40 \div 5 = r$

    $8 = r$

    b. $1 \times 200 = 8 \times a$

        $200 = 8 \times a$

        $200 \div 8 = a$

        $25 = a$

    c. $6 \times 15 = 30 \times q$

        $90 = 30 \times q$

        $90 \div 30 = q$

        $3 = q$

    d. $7 \times 12 = 21 \times x$

        $84 = 21 \times x$

        $84 \div 21 = x$

        $4 = x$

7. a. $10 \times 40 = 100 \times w$

    $400 = 100 \times w$

    $400 \div 100 = w$

    $4 = w$

b. $2 \times 45 = 9 \times s$

$90 = 9 \times s$

$90 \div 9 = s$

$10 = s$

c. $6 \times 12 = 18 \times d$

$72 = 18 \times d$

$72 \div 18 = d$

$4 = d$

d. $8 \times 35 = 7 \times x$

$280 = 7 \times x$

$280 \div 7 = x$

$40 = x$

8. a. $5 \times 60 = 100 \times r$

$300 = 100 \times r$

$300 \div 100 = r$

$3 = r$

b. $3 \times 49 = 7 \times s$

$147 = 7 \times s$

$147 \div 7 = s$

$21 = s$

c. $5 \times 18 = 90 \times s$

$90 = 90 \times s$

$90 \div 90 = s$

$1 = s$

d. $10 \times 45 = 9 \times x$

$450 = 9 \times x$

$450 \div 9 = x$

$50 = x$

Making a Table pp. 146–147

Part A

1. **400 miles**

Miles	320	m
Hours	8	10

2. **5 gallons**

Walls	6	12
Gallons	2.5	g

3. **40 inches**

Centimeters	2.54	101.6
Inches	1	i

4. **90 inches**

Yards	1	$2\frac{1}{2}$
Inches	36	i

Part B

5. **No, you cannot use a proportion.**

   Subtract instead: $18 - 2.5 = \mathbf{15.5\ acres}$

6. **Yes, you can use a proportion.**

   $\dfrac{dollars}{pounds}$ $\dfrac{11}{4} = \dfrac{d}{3}$

   $\$11 \times 3 = 4 \times d$

   $\$33 = 4 \times d$

   $\$33 \div 4 = d$

   $\mathbf{\$8.25 = d}$

7. **Yes, you can use a proportion.**

   $\dfrac{newspapers}{defects}$ $\dfrac{1,000}{12} = \dfrac{40,000}{d}$

   $12 \times 40,000 = 1,000 \times d$

   $480,000 = 1,000 \times d$

   $480,000 \div 1,000 = d$

   $\mathbf{480 = d}$

8. **Yes, you can use a proportion.**

   $\dfrac{sides}{inches}$ $\dfrac{1}{3\frac{1}{2}} = \dfrac{4}{x}$

   $3\frac{1}{2} \times 4 = 1 \times x$

   $\mathbf{14\ inches = x}$

   You can also add or multiply:

   $3\frac{1}{2} + 3\frac{1}{2} + 3\frac{1}{2} + 3\frac{1}{2} = \mathbf{14\ inches}$

   or $3\frac{1}{2} \times 4 = \mathbf{14\ inches}$

9. **No, you cannot use a proportion.**

   Add instead:

   $\$4.35 + \$.75 = \mathbf{\$5.10}$

10. **Yes, you can use a proportion.**

    $\dfrac{scores}{attempts}$ $\dfrac{3}{4} = \dfrac{15}{a}$

    $4 \times 15 = 3 \times a$

    $60 = 3 \times a$

    $60 \div 3 = a$

    $\mathbf{20 = a}$

Solving Problems with Proportions pp. 148–149

Part A

You could have chosen any two of the proportions given below.

1. **(1), (3), (4)**   3. **(2), (3)**

2. **(1), (2), (3)**   4. **(1), (2), (3)**

Part B

5. **12 gallons**

$$\frac{250}{10} = \frac{300}{g}$$

$300 \times 10 = 250 \times g$

$3{,}000 = 250 \times g$

$3{,}000 \div 250 = g$

$12 = g$

6. **\$1.25**

$$\frac{8}{\$10.00} = \frac{1}{q}$$

$\$10.00 \times 1 = 8 \times q$

$\$10.00 = 8 \times q$

$\$10.00 \div 8 = q$

$\$1.25 = q$

7. **$2\frac{1}{4}$ cups of sugar**

$$\frac{1.5}{24} = \frac{s}{36}$$

$1.5 \times 36 = 24 \times s$

$54 = 24 \times s$

$54 \div 24 = s$

$2.25 = s$

$2\frac{1}{4} = s$

8. **4,860 people**

$$\frac{2}{3} = \frac{3{,}240}{s}$$

$3{,}240 \times 3 = 2 \times s$

$9{,}720 = 2 \times s$

$9{,}720 \div 2 = s$

$4{,}860 = s$

9. **40 square feet**

$$\frac{2.5}{10} = \frac{10}{p}$$

$10 \times 10 = 2.5 \times p$

$100 = 2.5 \times p$

$100 \div 2.5 = p$

$40 = p$

10. **\$37.50**

Possible proportions include the following:

$$\frac{\$15}{12} = \frac{c}{30} \qquad \frac{12}{\$15} = \frac{30}{c}$$

(There are 12 in a dozen.)

$$\frac{\$15.00}{12} = \frac{c}{30}$$

$\$15.00 \times 30 = 12 \times c$

$\$450 = 12 \times c$

$\$450 \div 12 = c$

$\$37.50 = c$

Gridding in Ratio and Proportion Answers
pp. 150–151

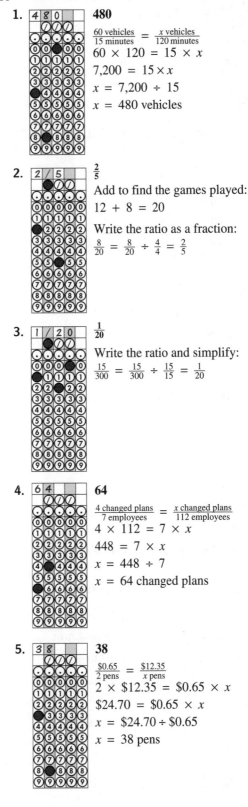

1. **480**

$$\frac{60 \text{ vehicles}}{15 \text{ minutes}} = \frac{x \text{ vehicles}}{120 \text{ minutes}}$$

$60 \times 120 = 15 \times x$

$7{,}200 = 15 \times x$

$x = 7{,}200 \div 15$

$x = 480$ vehicles

2. **$\frac{2}{5}$**

Add to find the games played:

$12 + 8 = 20$

Write the ratio as a fraction:

$$\frac{8}{20} = \frac{8}{20} \div \frac{4}{4} = \frac{2}{5}$$

3. **$\frac{1}{20}$**

Write the ratio and simplify:

$$\frac{15}{300} = \frac{15}{300} \div \frac{15}{15} = \frac{1}{20}$$

4. **64**

$$\frac{4 \text{ changed plans}}{7 \text{ employees}} = \frac{x \text{ changed plans}}{112 \text{ employees}}$$

$4 \times 112 = 7 \times x$

$448 = 7 \times x$

$x = 448 \div 7$

$x = 64$ changed plans

5. **38**

$$\frac{\$0.65}{2 \text{ pens}} = \frac{\$12.35}{x \text{ pens}}$$

$2 \times \$12.35 = \$0.65 \times x$

$\$24.70 = \$0.65 \times x$

$x = \$24.70 \div \$0.65$

$x = 38$ pens

6.

$\frac{7}{3}$

Subtract to find the non-pitchers:

$40 - 12 = 28$

Write and simplify the ratio:

$\frac{28}{12} = \frac{28}{12} \div \frac{4}{4} = \frac{7}{3}$

Calculators and Proportion Problems pp. 152–153

Part A

1.	2	6	3	28
2.	80	50	15	3
3.	8	18	1	48
4.	3	14	2	55

Part B

5. 8 pints

$(2 \times 12) \div 3 = 8$

6. 36.9 minutes

$(12.3 \times 6) \div 2 = 36.9$

7. $26.25

$(3 \times \$35) \div 4 = \$26.25$

8. 8 skirts

$(2 \times 19) \div 4.75 = 8$

9. 295 miles

$(236 \times 5) \div 4 = 295$

10. 120 pie shells

$(6 \times 20) \div 1 = 120$

Making Connections: Changing Recipe Quantities p. 153

1. $\frac{8}{9}$ cup flour

$\frac{1\frac{1}{3}}{30} = \frac{?}{20}$

$\frac{4}{3} \times 20 = 30 \times x$

$\frac{80}{3} \div 30 = \frac{8}{9}$

2. 2 eggs

$\frac{3}{30} = \frac{?}{20}$

$3 \times 20 = 30 \times x$

$60 \div 30 = 2$

3. $\frac{1}{2}$ cup walnuts

$\frac{\frac{3}{4}}{30} = \frac{?}{20}$

$\frac{3}{4} \times 20 = 30 \times x$

$15 \div 30 = \frac{1}{2}$

4. 1 cup minichips

$\frac{1\frac{1}{2}}{30} = \frac{?}{20}$

$\frac{3}{2} \times 20 = 30 \times x$

$30 \div 30 = 1$

Scale Drawings and Maps pp. 154–155

Part A

1. 3 feet

$\frac{\frac{1}{2}\,\text{inch}}{3\,\text{feet}}$

2. 6 feet

$\frac{\frac{1}{2}\,\text{inch}}{3\,\text{feet}} = \frac{1\,\text{inch}}{f}$

$3 \times 1 = \frac{1}{2} \times f$

$3 \div \frac{1}{2} = f$

$6 = f$

3. 21 feet

$\frac{\frac{1}{2}\,\text{inch}}{3\,\text{feet}} = \frac{3\frac{1}{2}\,\text{inches}}{f}$

$10\frac{1}{2} = \frac{1}{2} \times f$

$10\frac{1}{2} \div \frac{1}{2} = f$

$21 = f$

4. 81 square feet

Length and Width:

$\frac{\frac{1}{2}\,\text{inch}}{3\,\text{feet}} = \frac{1\frac{1}{2}\,\text{inches}}{f}$

$4\frac{1}{2} = \frac{1}{2} \times f$

$4\frac{1}{2} \div \frac{1}{2} = f$

$9 = f$

9 feet $\times$ 9 feet = 81 square feet in area

Part B

5. 500 miles

$\frac{1\,\text{inch}}{200\,\text{miles}} = \frac{2\frac{1}{2}\,\text{inches}}{m}$

$1 \times m = 200 \times 2\frac{1}{2}$

$m = 500$

6. 200 miles

$\frac{1\,\text{inch}}{200\,\text{miles}} = \frac{1\,\text{inch}}{m}$

$1 \times m = 200 \times 1$

$m = 200$

7. 150 miles

$\frac{1\,\text{inch}}{200\,\text{miles}} = \frac{\frac{3}{4}\,\text{inch}}{m}$

$1 \times m = 200 \times \frac{3}{4}$

$m = 150$

Unit 4 Review pp. 156–157

Part A

You may have used different forms.

1. 5:4	4. 5:14
2. 2:5	5. 3:1
3. 3:2	6. 3:2

Part B

7. **(4)** 15:29

8. **(3)** 11:12

9. **(1)** 1:23

10. **(4)** 1:3

Part C

Answers will vary.

Part D

13. 5	45	1	56
14. 3	35	2	50

Part E

15. **$2\frac{1}{4}$ pounds of beef**

$$\frac{1.5}{4} = \frac{p}{6}$$

16. **70 cans**

$$\frac{\$.05}{2} = \frac{\$1.75}{c}$$

17. **4 hours**

$$\frac{57}{1} = \frac{228}{h}$$

18. **105 females**

$$\frac{25}{15} = \frac{175}{f}$$

Part F

19. $\frac{18}{25}$

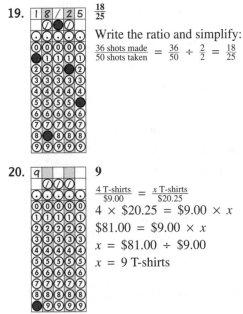

Write the ratio and simplify:

$$\frac{36 \text{ shots made}}{50 \text{ shots taken}} = \frac{36}{50} \div \frac{2}{2} = \frac{18}{25}$$

20. **9**

$$\frac{4 \text{ T-shirts}}{\$9.00} = \frac{x \text{ T-shirts}}{\$20.25}$$

$$4 \times \$20.25 = \$9.00 \times x$$

$$\$81.00 = \$9.00 \times x$$

$$x = \$81.00 \div \$9.00$$

$$x = 9 \text{ T-shirts}$$

Working Together

Ratios will vary.

Unit 5

Understanding Percents pp. 160–161

Part A

Part of Whole	Percent	Fraction	Decimal
23 out of 100	23%	$\frac{23}{100}$	.23
7 out of 100	7%	$\frac{7}{100}$	.07
93 out of 100	93%	$\frac{93}{100}$	.93
39 out of 100	39%	$\frac{39}{100}$	.39
33 out of 100	33%	$\frac{33}{100}$	.33
9 out of 100	9%	$\frac{9}{100}$	.09

Part B

1. $\frac{47}{50}$

$$\frac{100}{100} - \frac{6}{100} = \frac{94}{100}$$
$$\frac{94}{100} \quad \frac{2}{2} = \frac{47}{50}$$

2. **.25**

3. **65%**

$$100\% - 35\% = 65\%$$

4. **.40 or .4**

$$1.00 - .60 = .40 \; or \; .4$$

(You can drop the last 0.)

5. **60%**

6. $\frac{67}{100}$

7. **85%**

$$100\% - 15\% = 85\%$$

8. $\frac{7}{10}$

$$\frac{100}{100} - \frac{30}{100} = \frac{70}{100} = \frac{7}{10}$$

9. $\frac{3}{5}$

10.

Estimating the Size of Percents pp. 162–163

1. **(4)** a small part

2. **(2)** a large part

3. **(1)** more than 1 whole

4. (3) close to $\frac{1}{2}$

5. (4) a small part

Changing Decimals and Percents pp. 164–165

Part A

1. .07

2. .25

3. .099

4. .8

5. 1.65

6. .125

7. 5

8. .05

9. .5

10. .005

Part B

11. 50%

12. 50%

13. 550%

14. 5%

15. 500%

16. 12,000%

17. 1,090%

18. 65%

19. 20%

20. 2%

Making Connections: Moving the Decimal Point p. 165

1. incorrect   correct   correct   incorrect

   7% = .07   3.3 = 330%

2. correct   incorrect   incorrect   correct

          .2 = 20%   13% = .13

Changing Fractions and Percents pp. 166–167

Part A

1. $\frac{3}{10}$ $\frac{13}{100}$ $1\frac{1}{4}$ $\frac{9}{100}$ $\frac{9}{10}$

2. 1 $\frac{1}{2}$ $\frac{1}{5}$ 3 $\frac{13}{20}$

Part B

3. 20%   3%   62.5%   12.5%   50%

4. 60%   10%   35%   90%   15%

Part C

5. 80%

   4 ÷ 5 = .8 = 80%

6. $\frac{1}{3}$

   Memorize: $\frac{1}{3} = 33\frac{1}{3}\%$

7. a. 90%

   9 ÷ 10 = .9 = 90%

  b. 10%

   100% − 90% = 10%

8. $66\frac{2}{3}\%$

   Memorize: $\frac{2}{3} = 66\frac{2}{3}\%$

9. $\frac{1}{20}$

   $\frac{5}{100} = \frac{1}{20}$

10. a. 60%

   6 ÷ 10 = .6 = 60%

  b. 40%

   100% − 60% = 40%

Making Connections: Commonly Used Fractions, Decimals, and Percents p. 167

Decimal	Fraction	Percent
.1	$\frac{1}{10}$	10%
.2	$\frac{2}{10} = \frac{1}{5}$	20%
.25	$\frac{25}{100} = \frac{1}{4}$	25%
.3	$\frac{3}{10}$	30%
.333 or $.33\frac{1}{3}$	$\frac{1}{3}$	$33\frac{1}{3}\%$
.4	$\frac{4}{10} = \frac{2}{5}$	40%
.5	$\frac{5}{10} = \frac{1}{2}$	50%

Decimal	Fraction	Percent
.6	$\frac{6}{10} = \frac{3}{5}$	60%
.666 or $.66\frac{2}{3}$	$\frac{2}{3}$	$66\frac{2}{3}\%$
.7	$\frac{7}{10}$	70%
.75	$\frac{75}{100} = \frac{3}{4}$	75%
.8	$\frac{8}{10} = \frac{4}{5}$	80%
.9	$\frac{9}{10}$	90%
1.0	$\frac{10}{10}$	100%

The Percent Statement pp. 168–169

Part A

1. 40% of 15 is equal to 6.

2. 70% of 10 is equal to 7.

3. 7% of $22,000 is equal to $1,540.

4. 5% of $30 is equal to $1.50.

5. 25% of 60 is equal to 15.

Part B

6. Percent   **9.** Whole

7. Whole   **10.** Whole

8. Part   **11.** Part

Does the Answer Make Sense? pp. 170–171

Part A

1. (1) multiplication: 900

2. (2) subtraction: $298

3. (1) addition: $895

4. (2) division: 60 feet

5. (1) multiplication: 112 square feet

6. (2) subtraction: 44

Part B

7. **(2)** whole: $2,000

8. **(2)** percent: 80%

9. **(1)** part: 420,000

10. **(2)** percent: 25%

11. **(1)** part: 4.5

12. **(2)** whole: $2,300

The Percent Equation pp. 172–173

Part A

1. $.80 \times w = 6,800$

2. $n\% \times 125 = 12.5$

3. $.06 \times \$140 = p$

4. $n\% \times 2,345 = 908$

5. $.55 \times w = 15$

6. $1 \times 1,237 = p$

7. $.78 \times w = 45$

8. $n\% \times 54 = 52$

Part B

9. 30% of w is equal to $216.

$.30 \times w = \$216$

10. $n\%$ of $27 is equal to $1.35.

$n\% \times \$27 = \$1.35$

11. 90% of 280,000,000 is equal to p.

$.90 \times 280,000,000 = p$

12. 25% of 325 is equal to p.

$.25 \times 325 = p$

13. 50% of 325 is equal to p.

$.50 \times 325 = p$

Making Connections: Circle Graphs p. 173

1. 20% of $740 is $148.

Equation: $.20 \times \$740 = \$148$

2. 5% of $740 is $37.

Equation: $.05 \times \$740 = \$37$

3. 10% of $740 is $74.

Equation: $.10 \times \$740 = \$74$

4. 22% of $740 is $162.80.

Equation: $.22 \times \$740 = \$162.80$

Solving a Percent Equation pp. 174–175

Part A

1. $.30 \times w = 2,700$

$w = 2,700 \div .30$

$w = \mathbf{9,000}$

2. $n \times 20 = 15$

$n = 15 \div 20$

$n = .75$ or **75%**

3. $.95 \times 150 = p$

$\mathbf{142.5} = p$

4. $.65 \times 1,800 = p$

$\mathbf{1,170} = p$

5. $n \times 48 = 96$

$n = 96 \div 48$

$n = 2$ or **200%**

6. $n \times 350 = 84$

$n = 84 \div 350$

$n = .24$ or **24%**

7. $.10 \times w = 200$

$w = 200 \div .10$

$w = \mathbf{2,000}$

8. $.08 \times 160 = p$

$\mathbf{12.8} = p$

9. $.27 \times 13 = p$

$\mathbf{3.51} = p$

10. $.35 \times w = 140$

$w = 140 \div .35$

$w = \mathbf{400}$

Part B

11. **$12,000**

$.20 \times w = \$2,400$

$w = \$2,400 \div .20$

$w = \$12,000$

12. **6.5%**

$n \times \$240 = \$15.60$

$n = \$15.60 \div \$240$

$n = .065$ or 6.5%

13. **1,400 square feet**

$.70 \times 2,000 = p$

$1,400 = p$

14. **60 hours**

$.20 \times w = 12$

$w = 12 \div .20$

$w = 60$

15. **$5,600 in sales**

$.15 \times w = \$840$

$w = \$840 \div .15$

$w = \$5,600$

16. 50%

$n \times 34 = 17$

$n = 17 \div 34$

$n = .5 \text{ or } 50\%$

17. 2.5%

$n \times 12{,}000 = 300$

$n = 300 \div 12{,}000$

$n = .025 \text{ or } 2.5\%$

18. 62.5%

$n \times 80 = 50$

$n = 50 \div 80$

$n = .625 \text{ or } 62.5\%$

19. 1,620

$54\% \times 3{,}000 = x$

$.54 \times 3{,}000 = x$

$1{,}620 = x$

20. Wording may vary, but paragraphs should contain the following information:

The circle graph shows that of all of the people surveyed, 54% say the president is doing a good job. 35% of those surveyed say the president is not doing a good job, while 11% have no opinion.

Gridding in Percent Answers pp. 176–177

1. 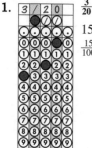 $\frac{3}{20}$

$15\% = \frac{15}{100}$

$\frac{15}{100} \div \frac{5}{5} = \frac{3}{20}$

2. 392

Find 12% of $350.

$0.12 \times \$350 = \$42$

Add: $350 + $42 = $392.

3. 40

80% of w is 32

$0.8 \times w = 32$

$32 \div 0.8 = 40$

4. 65

% of 200 is 130

$\% \times 200 = 130$

$130 \div 200 = .65 \text{ or } 65\%$

Note: The question asks, "What percent?" Fill in the number 65 only. There is no percent symbol on the grid.

5. 325

Since the sale price is 20% less than the original price, the sale price is actually 80% of the original price.

Find 80% of w is $260.

$0.8 \times w = \$260$

$\$260 \div .8 = \$325$

6. 2,584

76% of 3,400 is p

$0.76 \times 3{,}400 = p$

$2{,}584 = p$

Note: Do not grid the comma.

Statistics and Percents pp. 178–179

1. 7.5% vote for Matherson

$n \times 20{,}000 = 1{,}500$

$n = 1{,}500 \div 20{,}000$

$n = .075 \text{ or } 7.5\%$

2. 62% of contestants finish race in under 4 hours

$n \times 850 = 527$

$n = 527 \div 850$

$n = .62 \text{ or } 62\%$

3. 40% of Gray County 3- and 4-year-olds enrolled

in school

$n \times 750 = 300$

$n = 300 \div 750$

$n = .40$ or 40%

4. **90% of women surveyed prefer female doctor, study shows**

$n \times 4,200 = 3,780$

$n = 3,780 \div 4,200$

$n = .90$ or 90%

Making Connections: Draw a Circle Graph p. 179

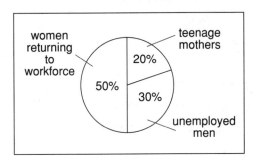

Mixed Review pp. 180–181

Part A

1. D	A	B	F
2. F	D	B	G
3. E	G	H	A

Part B

4. $\frac{2}{5}$	$\frac{1}{3}$	$\frac{7}{50}$	$\frac{9}{10}$
5. 1	$\frac{11}{20}$	$\frac{2}{25}$	$\frac{13}{20}$

Part C

6. .25	.1	.95	.04
7. .01	.015	.15	.099

Part D

8. $66\frac{2}{3}\%$	75%	62.5%	40%
9. 80%	30%	9%	12.5%

Part E

10. 8%	80%	18%	45%
11. 130%	9%	50%	10%

Part F

12. 15% of $4,400 is equal to $660.

13. 70% of 50 is equal to 35.

Part G

14. 175

15. 12%

16. 2,000

17. 25%

18. 27.2

19. 30

Part H

20. **(2) 9**

$.60 \times 15 = p$

$9 = p$

21. **(2) 26 miles**

$.50 \times w = 13$

$w = 13 \div .50$

$w = 26$

22. **(1) 16%**

$n \times 750 = 120$

$n = 120 \div 750$

$n = .16 = 16\%$

23. **(1) $4.42**

$.065 \times \$68 = p$

$\$4.42 = p$

Part I

24. **21**

75% of 28 is c

$0.75 \times 28 = c$

$21 = c$

25. **240**

45% of p is 108

$0.45 \times p = 108$

$108 \div 0.45 = p$

$240 = p$

Using a Calculator with Percents pp. 182–183

1. 72

2. 12.5%

3. 200

4. **$7.20**

$.15 \times \$48 = p$

$\$7.20 = p$

5. **18.5%**

$n \times \$360 = \$66.60$

$n = \$66.60 \div \$360$

$n = .185 = 18.5\%$

6. **50 trees**

$.90 \times w = 45$

$w = 45 \div .90$

$w = 50$

7. **17% tip**

$n = 8 \div 47$

$n = 17\%$

8. **$2,000**

$p = \$5,000 \times .40$

$p = \$2,000$

9. 3.3

10. 5%

11. 43.75

12. $10

13. **$20.70**

$.06 \times \$345 = p$

$\$20.70 = p$

14. **$198.40**

$.0625 \times w = \$12.40$

$w = \$12.40 \div .0625$

$w = \$198.40$

Two-Step Percent Problems pp. 184–185

Part A

1. **$16.72**

Step 1: $.045 \times \$16 = p$

$\$.72 = p$

Step 2: $\$16 + \$.72 = \$16.72$

2. **$9,920**

Step 1: $.20 \times \$12,400 = p$

$\$2,480 = p$

Step 2: $\$12,400 - \$2,480 = \$9,920$

3. **$32,500**

Step 1: $.08 \times w = \$50$

$w = \$50 \div .08$

$w = \$625$

Step 2: $\$625 \times 52 = \$32,500$

4. **3 calls**

Step 1: $.70 \times 30 = p$

$21 = p$

Step 2: $21 \div 7 = 3$

5. **$800**

Step 1: $.50 \times \$890 = p$

$\$445 = p$

Step 2: $\$1,245 - \$445 = \$800$

Part B

6. **$18.20**

$\$17.50 + (.04 \times \$17.50)$

$\$17.50 + \$.70 = \$18.20$

7. **$44.10**

$\$42 + (.05 \times \$42)$

$\$42 + \$2.10 = \$44.10$

8. **$397.50**

$\$375 + (.06 \times \$375)$

$\$375 + \$22.50 = \$397.50$

9. **$26,125**

$\$25,000 + (.045 \times \$25,000)$

$\$25,000 + \$1,125 = \$26,125$

10. **$16,974**

$\$16,400 + (.035 \times \$16,400)$

$\$16,400 + \$574 = \$16,974$

11. **$4.26**

$\$4 + (.065 \times \$4)$

$\$4 + \$.26 = \$4.26$

Discounts pp. 186–187

SHOPPING LIST

Item	Original Price	Discounted Pretax Price
1 potted geranium	$4.60	$ 3.91
2 boxes envelopes	$3.28 each	$ 3.28
1 tropical fish	$5.20	$ 4.68
20 pounds fertilizer	$10.80 each bag	$ 16.20
	Total Pretax Cost:	$ 28.07

Percent of Increase/Decrease pp. 188–189

Part A

1. **10%**

Change in value: $.58

Original amount: $5.80

Equation: $n\% \times \$5.80 = \$.58$

2. **28%**

Change in value: $1,400

Original amount: $5,000

Equation: $n\% \times \$5,000 = \$1,400$

3. **10%**

Change in value: $5

Original amount: $50

Equation: $n\% \times \$50 = \$5$

4. **$33\frac{1}{3}\%$**

Change in value: $.30

Original amount: $.90

Equation: $n\% \times \$.90 = \$.30$

Part B

5. **70%**

$n\% \times 350 = 245$

$n\% = 245 \div 350$

$n = 70\%$

6. **5%**

Change in value: 26

Original amount: 520

Equation: $n\% \times 520 = 26$

7. **100%**

Change in value: 10

Original amount: 10

Equation: $n\% \times 10 = 10$

8. **25%**

$n\% \times \$2,000 = \$500$

$n\% = \$500 \div \$2,000$

$n = 25\%$

9. Monthly rental prices in Dixon County rose 10% from Year X to Year Y.

Unit 5 Review pp. 190–191

Part A

1.	.3	6%	80%
2.	.67	150%	.09

Part B

3.	20%	$\frac{6}{25}$	$\frac{9}{50}$
4.	$33\frac{1}{3}\%$	$\frac{2}{3}$	37.5% or $37\frac{1}{2}\%$
5.	80%	$\frac{9}{10}$	25%

Part C

6. 20%

7. 600

8. 427.5

9. 32%

10. 1,680

11. 224

Part D

12. **8,996**

4% of 8,650 is p

$0.04 \times 8,650 = p$

$346 = p$

Add: $8,650 + 346 = 8,996$

13. **25.2**

If 30% is spent on painting, then $100\% - 30\% = 70\%$ is spent on reparation and cleanup.

70% of 36 is t

$0.7 \times 36 = t$

$25.2 = t$

Part E

14. **85%**

$n \times 20 = 17$

$n = 17 \div 20$

$n = .85$ or 85%

15. **20%**

$n \times \$18 = \$3.60$

$n = \$3.60 \div \$18$

$n = .20$ or 20%

16. **25%**

$3.50 − $2.80 = $.70 (change)

$2.80 = original amount

$n \times $2.80 = $.70$

$n = $.70 ÷ 2.80

$n = .25$ or 25%

17. **$51.90**

$.07 \times $48.50 = p$

$3.40 = p$

$48.50 + $3.40 = $51.90

18. **$165**

$.25 \times $220 = p$

$55 = p$

$220 − $55 = $165

Part F

19. CompuData of New Hampshire:

$.10 \times $1,300 = p$

$130 = p$

$1,300 − $130 = **$1,170**

New England Best Computer:

$.08 \times $1,200 = p$

$96 = p$

$1,200 − $96 = $1,104

$.05 \times $1,104 = p$

$55.20 = p$

$ 1,104 + $55.20 = **$1,159.20 (Best Buy)**

New York Wholesale Computers:

$.05 \times $1,250 = p$

$62.50 = p$

$1,250 − $62.50 = $1,187.50

$.07 \times $1,187.50 = $83.13

$1,187.50 + $83.13 = **$1,270.63**

Working Together

Shopping lists will vary.

Glossary

average the "middle value" of a group of numbers. To find an average, add a group of numbers, then divide this total by the number of values in the group (p. 71).

5 + 7 + 6 + 6 = 24
24 ÷ 4 = 6 ←——— average
  ↑
4 numbers
that were
added

balance the total value after a number has been added or subtracted. To find the balance of a checking account, subtract withdrawals and add deposits (p. 62).

circle graph a graph that shows a whole (the circle) and its parts (each wedge) (p. 173)

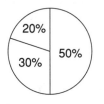

compare to decide whether a number is greater than, less than, or equal to another (p. 20)

comparison symbols math symbols used to show how number values compare (p. 21)

1.5 < 2	1.5 is less than 2.
4.1 > 3.25	4.1 is greater than 3.25.
$\frac{2}{4} = \frac{1}{2}$	$\frac{2}{4}$ is equal to $\frac{1}{2}$.

compatible numbers pairs of numbers that are easy to work with (p. 76)

250 and 50   14 and 280
(250 ÷ 5 = 50)   (14 × 20 = 280)

converting changing from one unit of measurement to another (p. 74)

12 inches = 1 foot
6 feet = 2 yards

cross product the product of the numerator of one fraction and the denominator of another fraction (p. 144)

$\frac{3}{5} \times \frac{18}{30}$ ←——— 5 × 18 is a cross product.
       ←——— 3 × 30 is a cross product.

decimal a number written with a decimal point. Decimal values smaller than 1 are written to the right of the decimal point (p. 12).

0.22
decimal value

decimal point a point that separates whole numbers from decimals and dollars from cents (p. 14)

195.001 $35.07
  ↑   ↑
  └ decimal points ─┘

denominator the bottom number of a fraction; indicates total number of parts (p. 30)

$\frac{4}{5}$ ←——— denominator (5 total parts)

digit a symbol for a number. The digits are 0, 1, 2, 3, 4, 5, 6, 7, 8, and 9 (p. 14).

digital measurement a measuring system that uses whole numbers and decimals to show values (p. 22)

digital scale a scale that shows weight as a whole number and a decimal (p. 23)

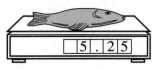

digital thermometer a thermometer that displays temperature as a whole number and a decimal (p. 23)

discount the amount by which a price has been reduced (p. 186)

A pillow priced at $20.00 is on sale for 25% off. The discount is 25% of $20, or $5. The sale price is

$20	–	$5	=	$15
original price		discount		sale price

dividend in a division problem, the number being divided (p. 72)

$$125\overline{)900} \quad 7.2 \longleftarrow \text{dividend}$$

divisor in a division problem, the number that an amount is being divided by (p. 72)

$$\text{divisor} \longrightarrow 125\overline{)900} \quad 7.2$$

equation a mathematical sentence that contains an equal sign (p. 58)

$$10 + 12 = 22 \qquad 185.5 - x = 179$$

equivalent fractions fractions that are equal in value (p. 36)

$\frac{1}{3}$ and $\frac{3}{9}$ are equivalent fractions.

estimate to find an approximate answer by using rounded or friendly numbers (p. 28)

$$\begin{array}{r} 612 \approx 600 \\ \times\,51 \approx \times\,50 \\ \hline 30{,}000 \end{array}$$

≈ means "is approximately equal to."

30,000 ← This is an approximate answer.

expression the use of mathematical symbols to represent a relationship between numbers (p. 26)

Mac had 140 dollars. Expression
He spent 62 dollars on groceries. $140 – $62

fraction a number that is written as the part over the whole. A fraction bar separates the part from the whole (p. 12).

$\frac{1}{5}$ $\frac{3}{2}$ ——— fraction bar

proper fraction   improper fraction

friendly numbers approximated numbers that are easy to work with (p. 76)

$9.5 \approx 10$ 10 is easy to work with.

≈ means "is approximately equal to."

function keys the keys on a calculator that indicate addition, subtraction, multiplication, and division (p. 24)

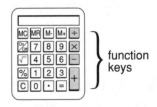

} function keys

improper fraction a fraction in which the numerator is the same size or greater than the denominator (p. 90)

$\frac{4}{3}$ is an improper fraction because $4 > 3$.

inverse operations operations that undo each other. When solving equations, these operations allow you to get the variable alone on one side of the equal sign (p. 60).

- Addition and subtraction are inverse operations.
- Multiplication and division are inverse operations.

leading zero a zero that is the only digit before a decimal point. The leading zero can be dropped without changing the value of a number (p. 16).

0.8

leading zero ⌐

like fractions fractions that have the same denominator (p. 90)

$\frac{3}{7}$ and $\frac{5}{7}$ are like fractions.

lowest terms not able to be reduced. A fraction is in lowest terms when the numerator and denominator cannot be reduced further (p. 36).

$\frac{3}{9}$ $\frac{1}{3}$

not in lowest terms   lowest terms

meter the standard unit of length in the metric system. A meter is about 39 inches (p. 74).

metric system a system of measurement based on the decimal system (p. 74).
Basic units of measurement in this system are

for length: meter
for weight: gram
for volume: liter

mileage number of miles traveled (p. 22)

miles per gallon the number of miles a vehicle can travel on one gallon of gas (p. 82).
The formula to determine miles per gallon is

$$\frac{\text{total miles driven}}{\text{number of gallons used}} = \text{MPG}$$

mixed number a number that contains both a whole number *and* a fractional amount (p. 34)

$13\frac{1}{4}$ is a mixed number.

multistep problem a problem that requires more than one computation step to solve (p. 44)

numerator the top number in a fraction. The numerator indicates the number of parts (p. 30).

$\frac{3}{10}$ ⟵ numerator (3 parts)

odometer a digital meter that measures distance traveled (p. 22)

5 5 4 7 6 8

order of operations the acceptable order in which to do computation in a multistep problem:

1. any operation in parentheses
2. multiplication and/or division, from left to right
3. addition and/or subtraction, from left to right

(p. 78)

percent a part of a whole that is divided into 100 equal parts. The symbol % means percent (p. 12).

- 25 percent is 25 parts out of 100 parts.
- 25% means 25 percent.

percent of decrease the percent by which a value has gone down (p. 188)

A price drops from \$30 to \$25. The percent of decrease is

$n\%$ $\times$ 30   =   5

percent of   original   change in
decrease   price   value

$n\% = .1666$ or $16\frac{2}{3}\%$

percent of increase the percent by which a value has gone up (p. 188)

A price is raised from \$25 to \$30. The percent of increase is $n\%$ $\times$ 25   =   5

percent of   original   change in
decrease   price   value

$n\% = .20$ or **20%**

233

percent statement a statement that can help you solve a percent problem:

A percent of a whole is equal to the part. (p. 168)

place value the position a digit holds in a number (p. 14)

proper fraction a fraction in which the numerator is smaller than the denominator (p. 120)

$\frac{13}{20}$ is a proper fraction because 13 < 20.

proportion two equal ratios or fractions (p. 134)

rate a type of ratio that compares one unit of measurement with another. *Miles per hour* is a rate; *price per pound* is a rate (p. 142).

ratio a comparison of one number to another (p. 134)

ratios: 3 to 4 $\frac{3}{4}$ 3:4

repeating decimal the decimal that results from a division problem that does not come out even (p. 80)

$$.333333333 \longleftarrow \text{repeating decimal}$$
$$3\overline{)1}$$

rounding changing the value of a number slightly to make it easier to work with (p. 50)

35.75 can be rounded to 35.8 or 36.

scale drawing a drawing that uses proportions to represent actual measurements (p. 154)

similar figures figures that are proportional in size (p. 145)

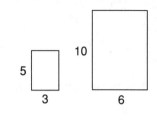

statistics groups of numbers, or data, that have been collected and organized to present information (p. 178)

table a chart that shows numbers in columns and rows in order to make them easier to read (p. 146)

XXX	XX	XXX	XXX
1	XX	XX	X
2	XX	XX	X
3	XX	XX	XX
4	X	XX	XX

row → ... column

unit price the price of one unit of something— for example, *one pound of apples* or *one gallon of gas* (p. 143)

unknown see *variable* (p. 26)

unlike fractions fractions that do not have the same denominator (p. 90)

$\frac{2}{3}$ and $\frac{2}{5}$ are unlike fractions.

variable a letter used to replace an unknown number value in an expression or an equation (p. 26)

variable

$\$550 \times p = \$2,200$

whole number a number equal to or greater than 1 that *precedes* a decimal point (p. 14)

3.5

whole number ⌐⌐ decimal

Tool Kit

The Five-Step Problem-Solving Plan

1

Understand the question.

What are you being asked to find?
Put the question in your own words.

2

Decide what information is needed to solve the problem.

Word problems may give you *more* numbers than you need or *not enough* numbers to solve the problem.

3

Think about how you might solve the problem.

- To combine, add.
- To find a difference, subtract.
- To find a total of equal parts, multiply.
- To find equal parts of a total, divide.

4

Estimate an answer.

About how large or small should the answer be? Round the numbers to make them easy to estimate with.

5

Solve the problem. Check your answer.

Do the computation.
Does your answer make sense?
Is it close to your estimate?
Is it a reasonable solution to the question?

Tool Kit

Fraction Chart

As the denominator of a fraction gets larger, the size of the fraction gets smaller.

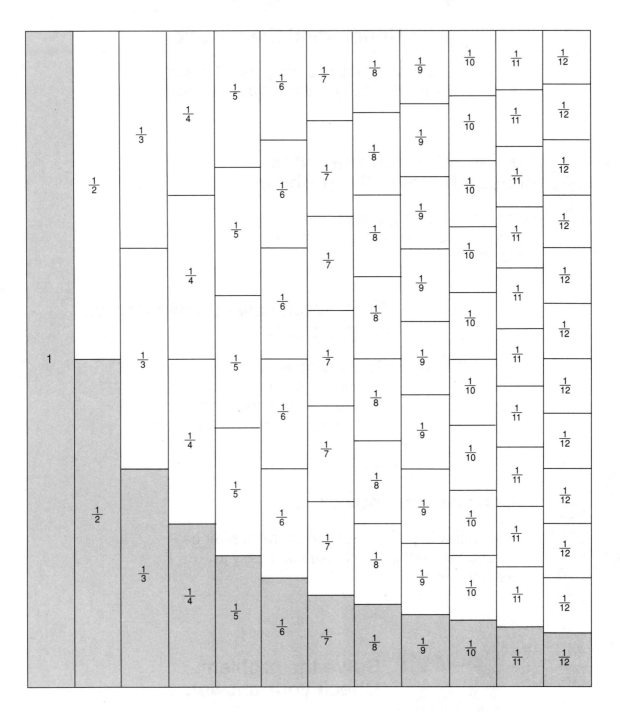

Tool Kit

Decimal, Fraction, and Percent Equivalencies

Decimal	Fraction	Percent
.1	$\frac{1}{10}$	10%
.2	$\frac{1}{5}$	20%
.25	$\frac{1}{4}$	25%
.3	$\frac{3}{10}$	30%
.333 or .33$\frac{1}{3}$	$\frac{1}{3}$	33$\frac{1}{3}$%
.4	$\frac{2}{5}$	40%
.5	$\frac{1}{2}$	50%
.6	$\frac{3}{5}$	60%
.666 or .66$\frac{2}{3}$	$\frac{2}{3}$	66$\frac{2}{3}$%
.7	$\frac{7}{10}$	70%
.75	$\frac{3}{4}$	75%
.8	$\frac{4}{5}$	80%
.9	$\frac{9}{10}$	90%
1.0	$\frac{10}{10}$	100%

Tool Kit

Measurement Tools

A **measuring cup** is used to measure liquid. Measuring cups usually have either English measurements (cups and ounces) or metric measurements (milliliters). The measuring cup on the left measures cups and ounces.

Scales are used to measure weight. Scales usually use either English measurements (ounces or pounds) or metric measurements (grams or kilograms). The scale on the right measures pounds.

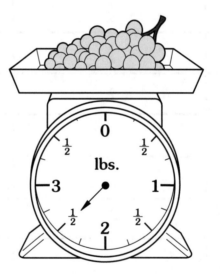

A **ruler** is used to measure length. An English ruler measures in inches. A metric ruler measures in centimeters (cm) and millimeters (mm). The ruler on the right shows both English and metric measurements.

Tool Kit

Calculator Basics

Some tests allow you to use a scientific calculator for part of the test. A scientific calculator has many functions. You will use only the basic functions for your work in this text. Study the diagram to find the keys you will need. If you are using a different scientific calculator, the keys may be located in a different place, but they will have the same purpose.

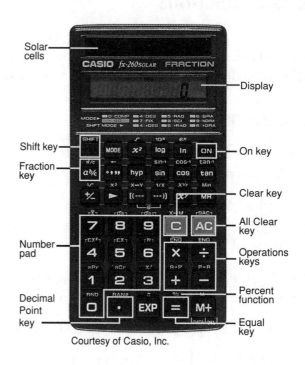

Courtesy of Casio, Inc.

Special Keys

ON Resets the calculator.

AC The All Clear key erases all numbers and operations from the current calculation.

C The Clear key erases only the last number or operation entered. Use this key to correct a mistake.

a%c Used to enter fractions and mixed numbers. Press a second time to change fractions to decimals.

SHIFT Used to access the second function of a key.

d/c The change fraction function is a second function, in yellow, above the fraction key **a%c** . Press **SHIFT** and then **a%c** to change mixed numbers to improper fractions and back.

% The percent function is a second function, in yellow, above the equal sign. Press **SHIFT** and then **=** to find percents.

Tool Kit

Basic Functions

A scientific calculator works much like the basic calculator on pages 24 and 25. Before beginning a calculation, you should make sure the display reads 0. The letters DEG should also appear in the display window. You can reset the display by pressing $\boxed{\text{ON}}$.

Fractions

You can enter a fraction on some scientific calculators. The display shows the parts of the fraction separated by the $\lrcorner$ symbol. For example, $1\frac{2}{3}$ will be displayed as | $1\lrcorner2\lrcorner3.$ |

To enter a fraction, use the fraction key $\boxed{a\frac{b}{c}}$ to separate the parts of a fraction. Then press $\boxed{=}$ to display the fraction in lowest terms. Press $\boxed{a\frac{b}{c}}$ again to change the fraction to a decimal.

Use $\boxed{\text{SHIFT}}$, $\boxed{a\frac{b}{c}}$, or *d/c* to change a mixed number to an improper fraction. Use this function when you need to enter a mixed number on a five-column grid.

Example 1: Reduce $\frac{6}{8}$ to lowest terms. Then change to a decimal.

Press: $\boxed{6}$ $\boxed{a\frac{b}{c}}$ $\boxed{8}$ $\boxed{=}$ Your display reads: | $3\lrcorner4.$ | which means $\frac{3}{4}$.

Press: $\boxed{a\frac{b}{c}}$ Your display reads: | 0.75 |

Example 2: Add $2\frac{1}{5}$ and $1\frac{7}{15}$. Write the answer as an improper fraction in lowest terms.

Press: $\boxed{2}$ $\boxed{a\frac{b}{c}}$ $\boxed{1}$ $\boxed{a\frac{b}{c}}$ $\boxed{5}$ $\boxed{+}$ $\boxed{1}$ $\boxed{a\frac{b}{c}}$ $\boxed{7}$ $\boxed{a\frac{b}{c}}$ $\boxed{1}$ $\boxed{5}$ $\boxed{=}$

The display reads: | $3\lrcorner2\lrcorner3.$ | , which means $3\frac{2}{3}$.

Change to an improper fraction. Press: $\boxed{\text{SHIFT}}$ $\boxed{a\frac{b}{c}}$

The display reads: | $11\lrcorner3.$ | , which means $\frac{11}{3}$.

Percents

Example 1: Find 40% of 55.

Press: $\boxed{5}$ $\boxed{5}$ $\boxed{\times}$ $\boxed{4}$ $\boxed{0}$ $\boxed{\text{SHIFT}}$ $\boxed{=}$ Your display reads: | $22.$ |

Example 2: 12 is 10% of what number?

Press: $\boxed{1}$ $\boxed{2}$ $\boxed{\div}$ $\boxed{1}$ $\boxed{0}$ $\boxed{\text{SHIFT}}$ $\boxed{=}$ Your display reads: | $120.$ |